GENEROUS DIVINE LOVE

Kenneth J. Collins

Generous Divine Love

The Grace and Power
of Methodist Theology

Nashville

GENEROUS DIVINE LOVE

Copyright © 2025 Kenneth J. Collins

All rights reserved.

No part of this work may be reproduced or transmitted in any form or by any means, electronic or mechanical, including photocopying and recording, or by any information storage or retrieval system, except as may be expressly permitted by the 1976 Copyright Act, the 1998 Digital Millennium Copyright Act, or in writing from the publisher. Requests for permission should be addressed to Permissions, Abingdon Press, 810 12th Avenue South, Nashville, TN 37203-4704, or emailed to permissions@abingdonpress.com.

ISBN: 9781791039592

Library of Congress Control Number has been requested.

Scripture quotations unless noted otherwise are from the Common English Bible. Copyright © 2011 by the Common English Bible. All rights reserved. Used by permission. www.CommonEnglishBible.com.

Scripture quotations marked (NIV) are taken from the Holy Bible, New International Version ®, NIV®. Copyright © 1973, 1978, 1984, 2011 by Biblica, Inc.™ Used by permission of Zondervan. All rights reserved worldwide. www.zondervan.com. The "NIV" and "New International Version" are trademarks registered in the United States Patent and Trademark Office by Biblica, Inc.™

Scripture quotations noted (NRSV) are taken from the New Revised Standard Version of the Bible, copyright 1989, Division of Christian Education of the National Council of the Churches of Christ in the United States of America. Used by permission. All rights reserved.

Scripture quotations marked (GNT) are from the Good News Translation in Today's English Version—Second Edition © 1992 by American Bible Society. Used by Permission.

Book cover of "Generous Divine Love: The Grace and Power of Methodist Theology" by Kenneth J. Collins. The cover shows a glowing white cross with rays of light in yellow, orange, blue, and purple radiating from it, set against a dark background.

MANUFACTURED IN THE UNITED STATES OF AMERICA

Contents

Acknowledgments – vii

Introduction – ix

1. God Is Holy Love – 1
    God Loves All People – 13

2. Humanity: All People Are Created in the Glorious Image and Likeness of God – 17
    All Human Beings Were Created Very Good – 19
    All Human Beings Were Created Beautiful and Glorious – 23

3. Humanity: All People Are Fallen – 29
    All Are Fallen: Original Sin, Death and Corruption – 33
    All Are Utterly Fallen: Total Depravity – 40
    All Are Utterly Dependent Upon God for Any Good – 43

4. The Holy Spirit Works in All People: Prevenient Grace – 44
    Prevenient Grace Is Given to All People – 46
    Wesleyan Theology Can Acknowledge Every Good Wherever It Is Found – 50

5. Christ Identifies with All People – 53
    Christ Identifies with All People – 55

6. Christ Died for All People – 66
    Christ Bore the Punishment for All People – 67
    Christ Died for All People – 72

7. The Church Is For All People – 77
    The Church Is For All People – 90

8. God Has Forgiven All People of Everything – 98
    All Can Be Saved (The Gospel as a Universal Offer) – 99
    All Can Be Forgiven of Everything – 101
    All Can Know That They Are Saved and Forgiven
        (Assurance) – 111

9. All People Can and Must Be Born Again – 118
    All Must Be Born Again – 121
    All Can Be Born Again – 124
    All Can Be Set Free
        (From the Power and Dominion of Sin) – 126
    All Can Be Set Free (To Love God and Neighbor) – 129
    All Can Know That They Are Born Again (Assurance) – 132

10. Entire Sanctification: What It Is and Is Not – 138

11. All the Children of God Can Receive Entire Sanctification – 151
    All Can Be Saved to the Uttermost – 153
    All Can Know That They Are Saved to the Uttermost – 163

12, Death and the Greater Powers of Grace – 165

13. The Emblems of a Very Generous Theology – 178
    All Can Die Well – 190

Epilogue: John Wesley Died Well – 193
    All Can Live *Forevermore!* – 196

Notes – 199

Acknowledgments

I am grateful for the ongoing conversations that I have had in Methodist studies, broadly conceived, with all of the following people: Russell Richey, Ted Campbell, Jason Vickers, Kevin Watson, Chris Johnson, Luther Oconer, Ryan Danker, Kathy Armistead, Bill Kostlevy, Doug Matthews, Jerry Walls, Steve and Sharon Bussey, Steve Martyn, Mike Voigts, Amy Pritchard Sheffield, and Bill Walker. Special thanks go to Jonathan Powers to whom I turned after the manuscript had been completed. Though I had included several hymns within the narrative by that point, I knew that I needed his expertise in order that the rich Methodist voice, which of course includes that of Charles as well, might be heard even more clearly, and in another very important form. I am in his debt. And finally to all those students who have welcomed me in my travels especially those in Sao Paulo, Brazil; Tallinn, Estonia; Seoul, Korea; and Tokyo, Japan, I say thank you. You have given me so much! All the rest is gratitude.

Kenneth J. Collins
Ash Wednesday, 2025

Introduction

Many secularizing forces are in play globally, driven by technology and advances in artificial intelligence. For the first time in human history, humanity itself may soon be displaced. Much earlier, at the end of the nineteenth century, few cultural leaders in Europe and elsewhere were especially worried when Nietzsche proclaimed that God is dead. That lack of concern was due, in large part, to the intellectual failure—especially in Western civilization—to realize that the death of God always *entails* the death of humanity. In other words, theology does affect anthropology after all. Remove the heavens, and earth itself is changed. Cast off eternity and time itself is different. Wipe away the horizon and human hopes are limited, even flatfooted. Eliminate God from the picture and a humanity that had been created in the blessed image and likeness of God is no longer properly recognized and is therefore already in a real sense dead. Nietzsche had made preparations for only one funeral. He should have prepared for two.

On a much happier note, John and Charles Wesley always considered humanity in light of its proper source. That is, *all people* have been created by a God of holy love who is radiantly beautiful, and that beauty is best understood in terms of an inexhaustible fountain of sheer and uncanny *goodness* best expressed in holiness. For the Methodists, then, theology and anthropology are always connected. A theological exploration will not only reveal who God is but who humanity is as well. And though John Wesley's theology repeatedly considers the divine and human relation, his theology is not just another theology. It is remarkably distinct in some important and enduring ways. For one thing, it is a theology that is marked by recurring, even triumphant, freedom and, as a consequence, characterized by great and abounding joy. And though Wesley took great care to communicate the genius of the Christian faith through such instruments as penny tracts and sermons as a literary device and teaching tool, in the end his theology is perhaps best

Introduction

sung, rather than read or recited. Charles Wesley gave voice to all of this and more in his carefully crafted hymns that have resounded from age to age. The engaged, worshipful community that was early Methodism, called forth by a God of holy love, lost itself in adoration and praise, glorifying a generous and holy God who had given an abundance of gifts along the way—the chief gift of course the gift of the Father's Son, Jesus Christ, himself.

In the early twentieth century W. B. Fitzgerald (1856–1931), a British Methodist, hinted at the generous nature of Wesleyan theology in his four pity statements as follows:

> All need to be saved.
> All can be saved.
> All can know they are saved.
> All can be saved to the uttermost.[1]

Today we are in a different place in Methodism in general and in Wesley studies in particular. Due to the wonderful advance of resources through the careful labors of Albert Outler, Frank Baker and others, we can explore the generous nature of John Wesley's theology by lifting up not simply four statements, highlighting the outgoing, redemptive love of God, but so many more. Indeed, this larger vision will take the form of a journey that will explore the welcoming, generous nature of John Wesley's practical theology, and as expressed so ably in the hymns of his brother, Charles. This labor will demonstrate key differences between Wesleyan Methodist theology and that of some other theological traditions.

Moreover, in order to give readers a guide of sort along the way, key sections of the text will be marked with *italics* when they showcase the generosity of God in significant ways, and therefore of John Wesley's theology as well. Beyond this feature, the flow of the chapters will follow the divine and human relationship by beginning with God, and then proceeding to the very good creation of humanity that has been marred by a subsequent fall. The journey will then continue as God is revealed to humanity in new awe-evoking ways, not simply as a Creator, but also as a humble, sacrificial Redeemer. This journey proceeds such that by the end of life's journey, the redeemed—who are no longer alienated from a God of holy love, but are forgiven and renewed—will be marked by heart-felt praise. John Wesley himself expressed such praise as he lay dying on his own bed:

> I'll praise my Maker while I've breath,
> And when my voice is lost in death
> Praise shall employ my nobler powers.
> My days of praise shall ne'er be past,
> While life, and thought, and being last,
> Or immortality endures.[2]

The generous nature of Methodist theology is especially evident in the universal provision that has been made for the forgiveness of sins, as affirmed by both John and Charles, and for a renewal of nature in that Christ died *for all people*. In other words, the offer of salvation is extended to everyone, none are excluded from this embrace, but that offer which is remarkably broad and wide, and in which there is no lack, must in turn be *received*. Indeed, the reception of the gracious offer of redemption, which has so many practical consequences in human life, takes place in what John Wesley, himself, called *repentance*, and he identified it as the porch of religion as revealed in his following observation: "Our main doctrines, which include all the rest, are three, that of repentance, of faith, and of holiness. The first of these we account as it were, the *porch of religion*; the next, the door; the third, religion itself."[3]

In fact, so important was repentance to John Wesley and the eighteenth century Methodists that it became the very substance of the *General Rules of the United Societies* in the threefold form of "doing no harm,"[4] joined to "doing good,"[5] and also expressed in "attending upon all the ordinances of God."[6]

What all of this means then is that repentance is at the very heart of what it means to be a Methodist then as now. John Wesley expressed this same basic truth of the Christian faith *liturgically* in his *Sunday Service* prepared for the American Methodists, as humble sinners, open to transformation in being, approached the Lord's Table seeking both forgiveness and renewal: "Ye that do truly and earnestly repent of your sins, and are in love and charity with your neighbours, and intend to lead a new life, following the commandments of God, and walking from henceforth in his holy ways; Draw near with faith, and take this holy Sacrament to your comfort; and make your humble confession to Almighty God, meekly kneeling upon your knees."[7] Simply put, the God of holy love who is merciful enough to accept us as we are is good enough not to leave us as we are. Accordingly, an exciting and grace-filled journey awaits. The grace of God ever calls us forward. To be sure,

Introduction

the flow of salvation, marked by so much generosity and love along the way, is an invitation to become beautiful as Christ is beautiful, and that beauty is ever resplendent in holiness or as John Wesley, himself, had so often put it, in "holy love,"[8] a grace that in the end marks the lives of the saints. In so many ways, then, the reception of such a transforming gift is and remains nothing less than exciting. Let the journey begin!

1. God Is Holy Love

"God is love, and those who remain in love remain in God and God remains in them."
(1 John 4:16b).

Though the claim is often made, even in the twenty-first century, that all monotheistic faiths such as Judaism, Christianity and Islam, are essentially teaching the same thing, the basic beliefs of each of these major world religions actually suggest otherwise. It is only the Christian faith, for example, that revisions ethics in very surprising ways and therefore counsels its followers: "If anyone slaps you on the right cheek, turn to them the other cheek also" (Matt. 5:39), and "If anyone forces you to go one mile, go with them two miles" (Matt. 5:41). Indeed, the Christian faith is remarkably different from others in that it insists that the "normal way" of thinking about so many things in life will in the end be turned upside down in its claim that "the last will be first and the first will be last" (Matt. 20:16). And if all of these pithy counsels were not a significant enough challenge to usual ways of thinking, even religious thinking, the Christian faith then urges its followers to love, yes love, their enemies. What's going on here? In one word, Jesus.

God as revealed in Jesus Christ by the power of the Holy Spirit is the proper starting point for any discussion of the divine in Christian circles, and it naturally was for John Wesley as well. Such a teaching does indeed make a difference. In fact, it's a game changer. If this doctrinal journey were not to begin here, if it instead started out with some abstract notion of God, a basic level of theism, then a highly impersonal and removed notion of the deity would likely emerge. Such a god would in effect be a monad, a self-referential unit, off by itself, an isolated god, one separated from believers in a string of unreachable superlatives, one so utterly transcendent as hardly to be related to humanity at all. Wisely John Wesley, along with his brother, Charles, did not start with Hellenistic abstractions, hailing from Plato and Aristotle, in their own practical theologies. Such an approach in the end could only ignore how God has been revealed to humanity in Jesus Christ.

> "Jesus, the name to sinners dear,
> The name to sinners given!
> It scatters all their guilty fear,
> It turns their hell to heaven."[1]

The Personal Attributes of God

God Is Triune

In preparing the *Sunday Service* for the American Methodists in 1784, John Wesley included a number of helpful resources to assist the newly-grounded church that was no longer under the authority of the Church of England. To guide and strengthen the doctrinal convictions of this fledgling American church, now set at full liberty, Wesley included his revision of the Anglican Thirty-Nine Articles that were now reduced to the Methodist twenty-four. The very first article witnesses to what difference the revelation of God in Jesus Christ by the power of the Holy Spirit actually makes, that is, Christology readily leads to deep theological considerations, and so the first article is a triune witness to the glory of God as revealed in the following:

> There is but one living and true God, everlasting, without body, parts, or passions; of infinite power, wisdom and goodness; the Maker and Preserver of all things both visible and invisible. And in unity of this Godhead there are three Persons of one substance, power, and eternity; the Father, the Son and the Holy Ghost.[2]

Wesley's preferred way of referring to the Christian Godhead was to employ the traditional language of the Anglican Bishop John Pearson (1613-1686) in his *An Exposition of the Creed* as Albert Outler has pointed out.[3] As a competent practical theologian, Wesley also weaved the language of the Three-One in several of his works. In fact, the phrase, "There are three that bear record in heaven, the Father, the Word, and the Holy Ghost: And these three are one,"[4] though found only in his King James translation, appeared more than a dozen times in his writings.[5]

In citing such language, Wesley believed that he was keeping close to a biblical idiom by letting the words "Three" and "One," as found in other New Testament texts, do most of the heavy lifting here, so to speak. In other words, Wesley did not insist upon using the exact words "Trinity" or even "person" for that matter since they are not found in the biblical text.[6] However, he immediately added, to clarify his point: "I use them myself without scruple, because I know of none better."[7] Indeed, Wesley believed that the language of the Three-One was necessary in terms of the outworking of practical Christian discipleship. Thus, for example, in his sermon, "On the Trinity," he observed, "But the thing which I here particularly mean is this: The knowledge of the Three-One God is interwoven with all true Christian faith; with all vital religion."[8] No doubt for emphasis Wesley then added: "Therefore, I do not see how it is possible for any to have vital religion who denies that these Three are One."[9] Now that is emphatic! Accordingly, a stanza, drawn from a hymn from Charles Wesley, of which his brother John approved, displays this basic and necessary teaching of the Christian faith:

> Hail, Father, Son, and Spirit, great
> Before the birth of time,
> Enthroned in everlasting state,
> Jehovah, Elohim!
>
> A mystical plurality
> We in the Godhead own,
> Adoring One in Persons Three,
> And Three in nature One.[10]

By employing this language which affirms that there are "Persons Three" whose nature is "One," both John and Charles Wesley took very seriously the matter of how God has been revealed to humanity in Jesus Christ along with its attending consequences for just how the divine is now understood. Once such revelation occurs there can be no turning back. For one thing, "relationality," so difficult to picture or envision, is at the heart of *who God essentially is*. In other words, even before the creation of the world, in which creatures would eventually rise, "relation" already had very much to do with the divine being. In fact, in the Christian understanding of the Godhead, there is a community of relations, Father, Son and Holy Spirit, at the very heart of who God is, who the Most High has been revealed to be. As the Wesley brothers would have learned from their own Anglican tradition, the Father loves the Son; the Son loves the Father and the Holy Spirit proceeds from the Father and from the Son.[11]

God Is Love

With the relational essence of the Godhead in place, John Wesley affirmed that God is love. Notice that he did not state that God is loving, though the Divine Being surely is that, but that God *is love.* In his *NT Notes* on 1 John 4:8, Wesley explained: "God is often styled holy, righteous, wise; but not holiness, righteousness, or wisdom in the abstract, as he is said to be love; intimating that this is his darling, reigning attribute, the attribute that sheds an amiable glory on all his other perfections."[12] Moreover, at the end of his sermon, "Free Grace," in which Wesley distinguished his theology from the Calvinist notions of George Whitefield, he appended to this sermon a hymn, though he was not likely its author,[13] one of whose stanzas celebrates this basic Christian truth which is at the very heart of the faith:

> Thy darling attribute I praise
> Which all alike may prove
> The glory of thy boundless grace,
> Thy universal love.[14]

This love of God, the Almighty's "darling attribute," never had a beginning, and it will never have an end. Being the very essence, the substance, of who God is, this attribute is eternal. "Love existed from eternity, in God, the great ocean of love,"[15] Wesley declared.

God Is Holy Love

In order to ensure that the Methodists were rightly focused on the love of God as revealed in Jesus Christ, a love distinct and uncanny in its power and beauty, Wesley would often not let the word love stand alone, lest it be misunderstood. Rather it must be accompanied by one little adjective that made a world of difference, namely, "holy." Three examples should suffice to demonstrate this truth.

First of all, John Wesley employed the language of holy love not only in terms of the Almighty but also with respect to believers, created in the divine image, as they offered themselves up, consecrated their hearts to God, actions that have been associated with the process of sanctification. For example, in his sermon, "The Circumcision of the Heart," drafted in 1733, Wesley wrote: "Other sacrifices from us he would not; but the living sacrifice of the heart he hath chosen. Let it be continually offered up to God through Christ, in flames of holy love."[16]

Second, so integral was holy love to Wesley's overall theology, especially in his understanding of who God is, that he made a number of important connections (creation and the imago Dei, for example) with this distinct terminology. Thus, in his sermon, "The Law Established Through Faith, Discourse Two," written in 1750, Wesley maintained: "Faith, then, was originally designed of God to re-establish the law of love. . . . It is the grand means of restoring that holy love wherein man was originally created."[17]

Third, Wesley did something in an early sermon that some Protestant theologians and pastors, then as now, were loathe to do, that is, he connected love, that is holy love, the very essence of who God is, and the moral law, itself. This strong connection between holy love, the divine essence, and the moral law all point to the purity, the distinctiveness and the utter goodness of God, that the Most High is good beyond imagination without any admixture of evil at all. To illustrate, in his sermon, "The Original, Nature and Properties and Use of the Law," written in 1750, Wesley describes this life-affirming and ennobling law, which expresses the moral goodness of God, in terms of the following characteristics:

- "an incorruptible picture of the high and holy One that inhabiteth eternity"
- "the face of God unveiled"
- "the heart of God"
- "divine virtue and wisdom assuming a visible form"
- "the original ideas of truth and good"
- "a copy of the eternal mind"[18]

Moreover, when Wesley considered just what difference the holiness of God made in terms of its uncanny moral power, he noted that the Almighty is "infinitely distant from every touch of evil. 'He is light and in him is no darkness at all.'"[19] Publishing the following stanza from Charles to convey his meaning, Wesley affirmed:

> Holy as thee, O Lord, is none!
> Thy holiness is all thy own;
> A drop of that unbounded sea
> Is ours, a drop derived from thee.
>
> And when thy purity we share,
> Thy only glory we declare;
> And humbled into nothing, own
> Holy and pure is God alone.[20]

Accordingly, the moral dimension of holy love and the divine being, a window on the utter goodness of God, will be an enduring theme in the theology of both John and Charles. Indeed, it will be necessary to track this moral dimension in order to understand John Wesley's sophisticated articulation of the magnificent and remarkably generous grace of God.

In a similar fashion, during the twentieth century, Emil Brunner, a Swiss Protestant theologian, stressed that "Holiness is the Nature of God, that which distinguishes Him from everything else."[21] In other words, holiness is "not a quality which God possesses in common with other beings."[22] It is a characteristic or trait that sets the Holy One apart. In short, holiness, on the one hand, creates distance but love, on the other hand, seeks communion. It looks like these two words then are heading in extraordinarily different directions. How can the holiness of God be understood as love, and the love of God be understood as holiness especially when John Wesley affirmed the simplicity, the unity, of the Divine Being?[23] The answer lies, Brunner maintained in his own day, in the recognition that "the truth of the Holiness of God is completed in the knowledge of His love."[24] In other words, "the Holiness of God is the basis of the self-communication which is fulfilled in love."[25] Again, though holiness renders the divine love distinct, uncanny, numinous and even awe-evoking, it can, after all, be communicated to humanity. In the end when the radiant energy of holiness seeking communion in love will be fulfilled, it will constitute nothing less than the sanctification and bliss of humanity. This is, of course, a consequence of the presence of God in human life.

In light of such a reflection, Wesley was obviously not wrong then to connect these two seemingly opposite words of both love and holiness. They do indeed belong together. In fact, there is no proper appreciation for the Christian understanding of God without them. It is, after all, how God has been revealed in Jesus Christ especially in the darkest of places, at Golgotha, where the holy love of God overcame all the distance of separation in a love that is and remains both radiantly beautiful and inviting.

The Essential Attributes of God

As the essential attributes of God are considered, which display the nature of the Most High, it must be borne in mind that they are the attributes of the triune God who, according to Wesley, has been revealed in Jesus Christ by the power of the Holy Spirit. In other words, in terms of the Christian Godhead, it is the community of persons, Father, Son and Holy Spirit that is eternal, omnipresent, omniscient and omnipotent, etc. To fail to keep that perspective in mind runs the risk not only of wallowing in abstractions, not discerning the proper relations, but also of forgetting that even these additional attributes are nothing apart from the holy love that ever informs them.

Eternity

In exploring the eternity of God, Wesley made an important distinction that will not only lay out the kind of being that God is, but it will also illuminate the temporal dimensions of existence and display in what way the Most High is immanently within them as well as transcendently above them. This very helpful distinction is none other than *a parte ante* (duration without beginning) and *a parte post* (duration without end), and it is fairly easy to understand.

By the first phrase, *a parte ante*, Wesley affirmed that eternity in the sense of duration without beginning is a divine-making characteristic. In other words, only God is eternal in this way. There cannot be "two Gods or two Eternals."[26] Matter and energy, for example, are not and cannot be eternal in this manner. Simply put, God's essence is to exist whereas matter and energy came into being with time/space itself in a dependent and contingent way. Again, there never was a time when God was not. Indeed, the Almighty transcends time itself. Commenting on Exodus 3: 14 ("God said to Moses, 'I AM WHO I AM. This is what you are to say to the Israelites: 'I AM has sent me to you'"), Wesley pointed out: "This explains his name Jehovah, and signifies, 1st, That he is self-existent; he has his being of himself, and has no dependence upon any other. And being self-existent he cannot but be self-sufficient, and therefore all-sufficient, and the inexhaustible fountain of being and bliss."[27]

Since God is both self-existent and self-sufficient according to Wesley, then the Most High cannot be reduced to a thing-in-the-world as so often happens even in twenty-first questioning such as "Who made God?" That very question, entailing cause and effect, is proof positive that the questioner, unlike Wesley, has not understood the God class. In other words, that question fails to appreciate the kind of being that God is. Again, God is not a thing, an object, with temporal limitations, caught up in cause/effect relations. Remember God's essence is to exist. Or to put it in another, even more pungent way, God cannot not exist. Wesley understood that clearly; he neither confused the Creator with the creature nor with the things that have been made.

By the second phrase, *a parte post,* Wesley maintained that eternity in the sense of duration without end is "not an incommunicable attribute of the great Creator; but he has been graciously pleased to make innumerable multitudes of his creatures partakers of it."[28] More specifically, the Holy One "has imparted this not only to angels, and archangels, and all the companies of heaven, . . . but also to the inhabitants of the earth who dwell in houses of clay."[29] In terms of human beings, then, a point to be developed in a later chapter, there is yet a rich sense in which they have been fashioned for eternity, properly understood, that is, to know, love and enjoy God forever.

> O God, thou bottomless abyss,
> Thee to perfection who can know?
> O height immense, what words suffice
> Unfathomable depths thou art!
> O plunge me in thy mercy's sea;
> With love embrace and cover me![30]

1. God Is Holy Love

Omnipresence and Omniscience

Eternity without a beginning (*a parte ante*) has demonstrated how God transcends the created order and cannot be limited by time. The omnipresence of God reveals how the Almighty cannot be limited by space, restricted to any corner of the universe, but is everywhere throughout the whole creation underscoring a rich divine immanence. Put another way, holy love is everywhere; God's glory is everywhere; we are ever surrounded by it if we have the eyes to see it. Wesley explained: "there is no point of space whether within or without the bounds of creation, where God is not."[31] Beyond this, Wesley considered what are some of the practical consequences of the omnipresence of God for human behavior as revealed in the following:

> Yea, suppose one of your mortal fellow-servants, suppose only a holy man stood by you, would not you be extremely cautious how you conducted yourself, both in word and action? How much more cautious ought you to be when you know that not a holy man, not an angel of God, but God himself, the Holy One 'that inhabiteth eternity', is inspecting your heart, your tongue, your hand every moment! And that he himself will surely bring you into judgment for all you think, and speak, and act under the sun![32]

The omniscience or all-knowing attribute of a God of holy love, ever personal and relational, is "a clear and necessary consequence of his omnipresence."[33] The two attributes are strongly related. Wesley reasoned in the following manner: "If he [God] is present in every part of the universe, he cannot but know whatever is, or is done there."[34] In other words, the Holy One knows "all the connections, dependencies, and relations, and all the ways wherein one of them can affect another."[35] Nothing then escapes the divine vision which sees all things in a moment, in an eternal now. Moreover, just as Wesley drew out the practical implications of omnipresence so too did he do likewise in terms of divine omniscience: "How are ye affected to the omniscience and omnipresence of God? Men naturally would rather have a blind idol, than an all-seeing God; and therefore do what they can, as Adam did, to 'hide themselves from the presence of the Lord.'"[36] These last two attributes, then, taken together highlight not only the truth of divine knowledge, its extent and reach, but also the significance of human responsibility in light of an ever-present and all-knowing God who remains in all places and at all times, the same yesterday, today and forever, and nothing less than a God of holy love.

> Present alike in every place,
> Thy Godhead we adore;
> Beyond the bounds of time and space
> Thou dwell'st for evermore.
>
> In wisdom infinite thou art,
> Thine eye doth all things see,
> And every thought of every heart
> Is fully known to thee.[37]

Omnipotence

When theologians ancient or modern consider the omnipotence of God they usually begin with a litany of qualifications in order to show what omnipotence does *not* entail. To illustrate, the omnipotence of God does not mean that the Holy One can create a square circle or can make an object so heavy that it could not be divinely lifted or any other inherently contradictory thing. However, Wesley did not begin here. Instead he got straight to the matter at hand and explored the omnipotence of God in two key and very practical ways. First of all, divine omnipotence is yet another way of underscoring divine independence on the one hand and human dependence on the other. In other words, the Almighty is "the only agent in the material world, all matter being essentially dull and inactive, and moving only as it is moved by the finger of God."[38] Again, the Holy One is "the spring of action in every creature, visible and invisible, which could neither act nor exist without the continued influx and agency of his almighty power."[39] Simply put, humanity has no life or agency apart from God, the One who is always prior and all powerful. Commenting on Acts 17:28 ("For in him we live and move and have our being"), Wesley showed how divine omnipotence plays out in a very basic way in human life. He explained: "This denotes his necessary, intimate, and most efficacious presence. No words can better express the continual and necessary dependence of all created beings, in their existence and all their operations, on the first and almighty cause, which the truest philosophy as well as divinity teaches."[40]

Second, Wesley considered the omnipotence of God not simply in terms of nature, that is, living and moving in God, but also in terms of grace, in other words, that great supernatural change in being that can only be brought about by divine omnipotent power. In a letter to a supposed John Smith, Wesley elaborated: "That 'the conversion of sinners to this holiness is no miracle at all,' is new doctrine indeed! So new to me, that I never heard it before, either among Protestants or Papists. I think a miracle is a work of omnipotence, wrought by the supernatural power of God. Now, if the conversion of sinners to holiness is not such a work, I cannot tell what is."[41] Furthermore, to the question, "Why then have not all men this faith?"[42] Wesley replied: "'It is the gift of God.' No man is able to work it in himself. It is a work of *omnipotence*. It requires no less power thus to quicken a dead soul, than to raise a body that lies in the grave. It is a new creation; and none can create a soul anew, but He who at first created the heavens and the earth."[43]

> Thou, my God, art good and wise,
> And infinite in power:
> Thee let all in earth and skies
> Continually adore!
> Give me thy converting grace
> That I may obedient prove,
> Serve me Maker all my days,
> And my Redeemer love.[44]

The Relational Attributes of God

It is clear by now that God has many attributes. The first set, the essential attributes, concern the very nature and being of the Holy One or to put it another way, what God essentially is apart from all other considerations, that is, separate from any relation to an "other." The relational attributes of God, however, are not like that. Instead, they focus on how the eternal One relates precisely to the "other," as both the Creator of all beings that have ever existed and as their rightful Governor.

Creator

God freely choose to bring into being the universe, the earth, and everything else along with it. Out of the glorious, outreaching love of God, the world (with its many kinds of beings) was created. All of this was done not out of any need on God's part. To be sure, the Divine Being has always been complete and perfect, not lacking anything. The Holy One, the One who called Adam and Eve into being, did not need to be fulfilled by creating the "other," the one *over against*. Again, God is self-sufficient having no lack. Nevertheless out of a vast, unfathomable love, enormous freedom, and generosity, God has chosen to create: "God began creation at what time seemed good; . . . set the times for every nation to come into being; . . . the place and the circumstances for the birth of each individual. . . ."[45] Creation, then, for John Wesley is a *sovereign* act. It is a species of free grace. It underscores the work of God alone, and it is done in utter liberty. God was free to create or not. Wesley explained, "As a Creator, he has acted, in all things, according to his own sovereign will."[46] The consequence of such divine freedom is that all beings receive their lives as the sheer gifts that they are bespeaking of the goodness, the beneficence, and the power of the Lord.

Governor

Once God creates, however, the Most High has taken on a self-imposed limitation of freedom. Theologians have expressed this difference in terms of a technical distinction. This distinction is actually not difficult to understand. In terms of creation, for example, God has absolute freedom and can choose to create or not, a condition that underscores the divine sovereignty as just noted above. With the creation of human beings, however, the Holy One, is of course not responsible *to* these beings but now *for* these beings. Given the very goodness of the divine nature, God will therefore act ever in accordance to what justice and mercy require for all human beings. Such activities then constitute none other than the divine role of Governor, and this is the second major relational attribute of God. It is another way of how the Creator relates to creatures. Wesley explained: "On the contrary, we have the fullest evidence that the eternal, omnipresent, almighty, all-wise Spirit, as he created all things, so he continually superintends whatever he has created. He governs all, not only to the bounds of creation, but through the utmost extent of space; and not only through the short time that is measured by the earth and sun, but from everlasting to everlasting." [47]

Accordingly, when God acts as a Governor, "he no longer acts as a mere Sovereign, by his own will and pleasure but as an impartial Judge, guided in all things by invariable justice."[48] Given the differences between the relational attributes of God as both a Creator and as a Governor, it is important then that these two roles never be confused or mixed. For example, if the freedom entailed in the sovereign act of creation was somehow or other applied to God's role as Governor, then the danger would arise of a neglect or even of an outright denial of the moral and legal order that lies at the heart of divine justice, which itself is a reflection of the divine goodness. Wesley therefore was to the point on this score: "Let then these two ideas of God the Creator, the sovereign Creator, and God the Governor, the just Governor, be always kept apart."[49] Consequently, to ask for a God that is not just is to ask for less, much less. God's justice may be tempered by mercy but justice and the good that in holds in place can never be lost in either the theology of John or Charles.

> Thou Judge of quick and dead,
> Before whose bar severe,
> With holy joy, or guilty dread,
> We all shall soon appear;
> Our cautioned souls prepare
> For that tremendous day,
> And fill us now with watchful care,
> And stir us up to pray.[50]

God Loves All People

The moral power of holy love, the sheer goodness of God, with the relations of love at the heart of who God is, all of this means not only that the Most High loves all people who will ever be created, but also that the Almighty cannot do otherwise. Put another way, precisely because God is good, with no evil at all, then it is in accordance with the divine nature to love all people without exception and to seek for them the highest good which is none other than the knowledge and love of God. Though this last statement may come as a surprise to some Christians who have been taught otherwise, it nevertheless is a basic scriptural truth that is a consequence of the very nature of God. Put another way, the sheer goodness of the Almighty, as well as a reflection on the glory of the gospel in its blessed universality, underscores the gracious reality that all really does mean all. In confronting the mistaken notion that God does not really love all people in seeking their highest good but instead brings some of them into being precisely in order to damn them in an eternity of torment, and that somehow or other this celebrates the "glory" of

God, Wesley responded strongly to this aberrant teaching as is evident in the following excerpt drawn from his 1739 sermon, "Free Grace":

> Now, what can possibly be a more flat contradiction than this, not only to the whole scope and tenor of Scripture, but also to all those particular texts which expressly declare, "God is love?" Again: They infer from that text, "I will have mercy on whom I will have mercy," (Rom. ix. 15,) that God is love only to some men, viz., the elect, and that he hath mercy for those only; flatly contrary to which is the whole tenor of Scripture, as is that express declaration in particular, "The Lord is loving unto every man; and his mercy is over all his works." (Psalm cxlv. 9.)[51]

Moreover, Wesley was so emphatic on this last point that he took up this matter once more several years later in his treatise *Predestination Calmly Considered*, published in 1752, in which he exclaimed:

> But it is written, "God is love," love in the abstract, without bounds; and "there is no end of his goodness." His love extends even to those who neither love nor fear him. He is good, even to the evil and the unthankful; yea, without any exception or limitation, to all the children of men. For "the Lord is loving" (or good) "to every man, and his mercy is over all his works."[52]

Precisely because of who God is the Most High cannot do otherwise. Simply put, God is not free to act in a way contrary to the divine nature itself. An attribute of sovereignty then can never clash with or worse yet overrule holy love. Divine freedom would not and could never do that. To think otherwise constitutes not theological sophistication, as is so often claimed, but the error of an unrestrained theological imagination and logic that fails to get the very foundations of theology, its basic elements, right. Consider this: sovereignty is not and has never been an essential attribute of God but a relational one. To be sure, God was Father before the Most High was ever sovereign.[53] The internal relations of the three persons of the Christian Godhead describe *who God is* in terms of essential being, namely holy love. Such a love will not only be creative, bringing into being creatures who were not, but it will also will the highest good for all as Charles knew so well.

> Come, sinners, to the gospel feast;
> Let every soul be Jesus guest;

> Ye need not one be left behind,
> For God hath bidden all mankind
>
> Sent by my Lord, on you I call;
> The invitation is to all:
> Come all the world; come, sinner, thou!
> All things in Christ are ready now.[54]

Observe in the table below that sovereignty relates only to God's role as Creator. Once humanity is created the Most High takes on a self-imposed limitation. Accordingly, divine sovereignty is necessarily limited in terms of God's role as Governor, in which justice is the key, and in terms of redemption, itself, in which the freedom of those who are created as *persons* in nothing less than the *image and likeness of God* has to be taken into account as well. In other words, the divine freedom is after all restricted, at least in some sense, in light of *the kinds of creatures* that have been created, even those bearing the very image and likeness of God. The Most High, then, would not and could not coerce, force or determine such created beings. They are persons reflective of the very image of God, even in a sinful condition. They are not stones. Moreover, God's role as Redeemer reveals how both the divine relational and essential attributes are in play with respect to the plight of humanity through the work of the God/human, Jesus Christ, the Mediator, a subject to be developed in a subsequent chapter. Let it be sufficient at this point simply to indicate that God's role of Redeemer is not informed so much by the relational attribute of sovereignty as by the essential attribute of holy love, in other words by who God is, and this of course makes the theology of John Wesley and the Methodists remarkably generous in properly reflecting the Most High.

Creator	**Governor**	**Redeemer**
Relational Attribute	Relational Attribute	Relational Attribute
In Utter Freedom	In Justice and Mercy	In Holy Love
Sovereign	Governor	Redeemer/Mediator
		The Essential Attribute of Holy Love Re-emerges through the work of the Mediator: Just *and* Loving

Wesley's profound insight that God is "holy love" rather than merely "loving" transforms our understanding of the divine character and the human relationship with the Almighty. This is not semantic precision for its own sake, but theological clarity that shapes pastoral practice and Christian discipleship. When we grasp that holiness and love are not competing divine attributes but unified expressions of God's essential nature, we discover a God who is both transcendently pure and intimately present, both righteously just and graciously merciful.

The practical implications are enormous. A God of holy love cannot act capriciously or show favoritism, yet neither can such a God remain distant from creation's suffering. This understanding liberates us from false dilemmas that have plagued Christian theology—we need not choose between God's justice and mercy, between divine sovereignty and human freedom, between particular election and universal love. In Wesley's vision, these apparent tensions resolve in the magnificent coherence of holy love that creates freely, governs justly, and redeems graciously.

As we turn to examine humanity's condition and God's response in subsequent chapters, we carry with us this foundational truth: the God revealed in Jesus Christ is neither a remote deity of philosophical abstraction nor a sentimental figure who winks at sin, but the Holy One whose very essence is love—love powerful enough to create worlds, pure enough to demand righteousness, and generous enough to offer redemption to all.

2. Humanity: All People Are Created in the Glorious Image and Likeness of God

> *"So God created humankind in his image, in the image of God he created them; male and female he created them." Genesis 1:27 (NRSV)*

From eternity God, who is both good and holy, determined to share the divine life with a creation that would be brought into being out of utter freedom by a sovereign and ever-powerful will. For John Wesley God was free to create or not as the last chapter has already pointed out. In other words, there was not anything lacking in the divine nature such that creation would somehow or other complete it. Rather, in creating both time and space, as well as all the creatures within it, the Almighty acted "according to his own good pleasure."[1] Such a free and sovereign will, outgoingly manifested in holy love, established Wesley noted, "the number of the stars, of all the component parts of the universe, and the magnitude of every atom, of every fixed star, every planet, and every comet."[2] He then added: "As Sovereign, [God] created the earth, with all the furniture of it, whether animate or inanimate; and gave to each such a nature, with such properties."[3]

In reflecting on the early verses of Genesis, Wesley pointed out that the Hebrew word "Elohim," employed therein, is in the plural form and is therefore suggestive of "The plurality of persons in the Godhead, Father, Son, and Holy Ghost."[4] As a careful exegete, Wesley maintained that the "doctrine of the Trinity, which, tho' but darkly intimated in the Old Testament, is clearly revealed in the New."[5] So then, in order for the full deposit of Scripture to emerge on this important topic, Wesley drew from the contributions of both the Old Testament and the New, in particular from both Genesis and Colossians. In doing so, he was not only able to affirm the role of the Holy Spirit "hovering over the waters," (Genesis 1:2) but he was also able to declare the very strong role of the Son of God in bringing about the created order as expressed by the Apostle Paul in Colossians 1:16-17. Beyond this, the roles of Father, Son and Holy Spirit in creation were displayed poetically by Charles Wesley in a hymn composed in 1767, one that his brother John clearly embraced as well:

> The Lord, and the eternal Word
> We our Creator see,
> The Spirit of his mouth concur'd
> And gave the worlds to be:
> The Father, Son, and Holy Ghost,
> God in Three Persons One,
> Created that celestial host,
> And made our earth alone.[6]

The Creation of Humanity

When John Wesley turned his attention to the creation of humanity in particular, he once again stressed both the divine sovereignty and freedom. Though some theologies make little room for the work of God alone in their reflections, in which everything is understood in terms of divine and human cooperation, that approach will simply not work here. In fact, in describing the bringing into being of humanity, Wesley underscored the work of God *alone*, what Augustine had called operant grace, as displayed in his celebration of the wonders of free grace in his sermon, "Salvation by Faith," preached at Oxford in June 1738. Wesley exclaimed:

> ALL the blessings which God hath bestowed upon man, are of his mere grace, bounty, or favour; his free, undeserved favour; favour altogether undeserved; man having no claim to the least of his mercies. It was free grace that "formed man of the dust of the ground, and breathed into him a living soul," and stamped on that soul the image of God, and "put all things under his feet."[7]

Following the account laid out in the first chapter of Genesis, Wesley pointed out that humanity "was made last of all the creatures."[8] In this way, the man and the woman would be able to see "the whole visible creation"[9] before them, from the canopy of stars displayed in the heavens to the animals grazing in the fields. This was both an "honor and favor."[10] In reflecting upon this distinct flow of human creation Wesley observed, it was "*an honor*, for the creation was to advance from that which was less perfect, to that which was more so and *a favor*, for it was not fit he should be lodged in the palace designed for him, till it was completely fitted and furnished for his reception."[11] This advance and sequencing, indicative of a *created order*, reveals that human life was intentionally (designed) and purposively (directed towards an end) brought into being by the Most High, demonstrating that human beings were not the product of "either blind chance or inexorable necessity,"[12] Wesley warned, but that their being, their very existence, was flush with meaning. God clearly had something in mind for the last of the creatures. It was to know, love and enjoy God both in the present and throughout eternity.

> Maker, Saviour of mankind,
> Who hast on me bestowed
> An immortal soul, designed
> To be the house of God,
> Come, and now reside in me,
> Never, never to remove;
> Make me just, and good, like thee,
> And full of power and love![13]

All Human Beings Were Created Very Good

The opening chapter of Genesis, which describes the days of creation, is literarily distinct in that the device of repetition is an important part of the structure that holds the narrative together. To illustrate, the phrase "was good" is placed after a description of the work of the Creator in six key places, at the end of all the following verses: 4, 10, 12, 18, 21, and 25. Picking up on this structure in his own *OT Notes*, John Wesley explored many of the ways in which creation is good as is evident in his following observations:

- Good, for it is all agreeable to the mind of the creator.
- Good, for it answers the end of its creation.
- Good, for it is serviceable to man, whom God had appointed lord of the visible creation.
- Good, for it is all for God's glory; there is that in the whole visible creation which is a demonstration of God's being and

perfections, and which tends to beget in the soul of man a religious regard to him.[14]

Beyond this, the first chapter of Genesis is not only made up of recurring elements but also all of these same elements are caught up in an even larger structure that culminates in a climax. That is, after the six phrases "was good" are all carefully laid out, the last phrase, which occurs after the creation of human beings, comes with something of a twist. All is now described as "*very good.*" Wesley explained this difference in his own commentary on these verses in the following way: "Of each day's work (except the second) it was said that it was good, but now it is very good. For, now man was made, who was the chief of the ways of God, the visible image of the Creator's glory."[15] The very goodness of humanity, created in innocence, is undoubtedly then a reflection of the goodness of the Creator. In other words, as God is the source, the origin, of everything that is good, so then those who have been brought into being, indicative of their origin as "the visible image of the Creator's glory,"[16] will be good as well.

In a similar way, just as the goodness of God is indicative of the moral dimension of the Divine Being, a dimension that can be expressed in the form of moral law (a point developed in the previous chapter), so too does humanity participate in this goodness and in a moral dimension as well that together can be expressed in the form of moral law. Along these lines, in his sermon, "The Original, Nature, Properties and Use of the Law," drafted in 1750, Wesley employed two key phrases, "supreme unchangeable reason," and "the everlasting fitness of things," that together illustrate, at least in some sense, the distinct content of human nature.[17] In other words, human nature as created by God is expressive of a distinct and well-chosen *created order* that itself is expressive of the good and holy will of the Most High. The moral law, then, in this setting represents the illumination of such goodness and holiness in the form of law, now viewed as a gift, a resource, into which humanity can look in order to understand both the will of God as well as their own created nature.

Humanity as Complex Beings

In one sense men, women and children are like God; in another sense, however, they are not. It is helpful at this point to begin with the differences. First of all, human beings are unlike God in that they have bodies. God, however, is "spirit, and those who worship him must worship in spirit and truth" (John 4:24b). Though the eternal Word, as Scripture clearly reveals, can and did take on flesh, as in the incarnation, God the Father has never done so. Second, the very nature or essence of God, unlike that of human beings, is simple; it is neither complex nor compounded. In other words, it is not composed of parts, that is, of flesh and spirit, of body and soul. It simply *is* in all of its divine simplicity and perfection. Human beings, however, are not like that. They are composite beings, that is, they are made up of both body and soul.

The Body

As John Wesley considered the human body in particular, he underscored its smallness in the larger scheme of things. He exclaimed "so diminutive a creature"[18] is man or woman especially when we consider the size of their bodies or the length of their lives. In terms of the former, Wesley posed the question in the following manner: "What is man with regard to his magnitude?"[19] He then rephrased the question and replied: "what is any one individual compared to all the inhabitants of Great Britain? He shrinks into nothing in the comparison. How inconceivably little is one compared to eight or ten millions of people? Is he not, 'Lost like a drop in the unbounded main'?"[20] And in terms of the latter, the temporal dimensions of human life, Wesley emphasized "the littleness of man the inexpressible shortness of his duration,"[21] by making the pungent observation, "it is any wonder that a man of reflection should sometimes feel a kind of fear, lest the great, eternal, infinite Governor of the universe should disregard so diminutive a creature as man—a creature so every way inconsiderable, when compared either with immensity or eternity!"[22] But human beings are not simply bodies; they are souls as well.

> Jesus, all-atoning Lamb,
> Thine, and only thine I am;
> Take my body, spirit, soul,
> Only thou possess the whole![23]

Soul and Spirit

Dependent in some sense upon the prior reflections of Rene Descartes, Wesley observed in his own writings that "I find something in me that thinks,"[24] what the seventeenth-century French philosopher had referred to earlier as the *res cogitans*. The various powers of this "something in me that thinks" is expressed by Wesley in terms of perception, the formation of ideas, judgment in terms of them, as well as in reflections upon the mind's own operations.[25]

Moreover, the use of language, especially in the form of an internal dialog in which the self can become an object of its own deliberations, is suggestive of a spirit that can be distinguished from the body. Put another way, what the self is cannot be exhausted in a simple description of the body or even in terms of the brain itself that three-pound hunk of grey matter. Indeed, the reality of consciousness was not well understood in the eighteenth century; it is still not understood well today. There are, after all, dimensions of human experience, as expressed in the recursive nature of language ("I'm thinking of your thinking of my thinking of you!"), for example, that apparently transcend the body and are not exhaustively explained through physiology. At times Wesley referred to this elusive reality as spirit, a reality that is not capable of being either empirically discerned or utterly reduced to matter, and at other times he referred to it simply as soul. And though some will distinguish soul and spirit in a tripartite anthropology of body, soul and spirit, John Wesley apparently considered the specific terms soul and spirit to be equivalent as, for example, in his notes on Genesis in which he exclaimed: "The soul is a spirit, an intelligent, immortal spirit, an active spirit, herein resembling God, the Father of spirits, and the soul of the world."[26] Thus, when the spirit is "lodged in an earthly tabernacle,"[27] it is then that the language of soul is most appropriate. Simply put, a soul is an embodied spirit.[28]

Since God is spirit then human beings are in some sense like the Most High in that humanity has its life, its very form of existence, in terms of spirit as well. Wesley wrote: "God did not make him mere matter, a piece of senseless, unintelligent clay, but a spirit like himself (although clothed with a material vehicle)."[29] What distinguishes spirit from matter in Wesley's estimation is that the former entails "an innate principle of self-motion,"[30] but the latter does not.[31] Beyond this, Wesley taught that the spirit given to humanity, housed in a tabernacle of clay, is an immortal spirit, one that cannot die and is therefore very precious. To illustrate, in his sermon "What is Man," written in 1787, Wesley not only affirmed the ongoing reality of human spirit, its immortal nature, but he also expressed a number of value judgments in terms of its worth as is evident in the following:

> . . . the body is not the man; that man is not only a house of clay, but an immortal spirit; a spirit made in the image of God, an incorruptible picture of the God of glory; a spirit that is of infinitely more value than the whole earth; of more value than the sun, moon, and stars put together; yea, than the whole material creation. Consider, that the spirit of man is not only of a higher order, of a more excellent nature than any part of the visible world, but also more durable, not liable either to dissolution or decay.³²

Though humanity in terms of its body is sharply limited with respect to both time and space, as noted earlier, when it is considered in terms of the spirit that God has given it, and which in some sense reflects both the divine glory and eternity, it is then that a proper estimation of these embodied spirits, these souls, can begin to emerge. For Wesley, then, a human spirit, an embodied soul, is of "more value than the whole earth . . . than the whole material creation."³³ The authority behind such as statement, of course, is not John Wesley but Jesus Christ, himself, as revealed in the following familiar words drawn from the pages of the Gospels: "What good is it for someone to gain the whole world, yet forfeit their soul?" (Mark 8:36). This statement is often glossed over quickly especially today, and when that happens its truly radical nature will likely be missed. What Jesus had declared in the first century, and what Wesley maintained in his own age, was that a human soul, given both its origin and its nature, was of more value than all matter, of more worth than all the *things of the world*. Put another way, a single human soul in its life was of more value than an entire galaxy of stuff without life. In short, persons, living souls, were and are ever more important than matter or things. That's an important and unavoidable consequence of the kind of beings God choose to create in humanity.

All Human Beings Were Created Beautiful and Glorious

The Image and Likeness of God

In creating human beings, the man and the woman, God invested their being with some of the glory and beauty of the divine character, itself, in fashioning them in nothing less than the image and likeness of God. Wesley cited the relevant text in his *Notes on the Old Testament:*

> Then God said, "Let us make mankind in our image, in our likeness, so that they may rule over the fish in the sea and the birds in the sky, over the livestock and all the wild animals, and over all the creatures that move along the ground." So God created mankind in his own image, in the image of God he created them; male and female he created them (Genesis 1:26-27).

Being well acquainted with the nature of the Hebrew language, Wesley recognized in a way that some other Christian traditions did not, that the phrase "the image and likeness" does not point to two different things, that is, the image being one thing and the likeness yet another. Instead, it was a rhetorical way, a Hebraism, of referring to the very same reality but now with added emphasis. More important, this honor and glory was not given to any other creature but only to humanity, to males and females, created in the beauty and glory of the Most High. So understood, Wesley recognized that the dignity of human beings does not consist in what they *do or do not do or in what they have or do not have but in what they are*, in their essential being, in their very nature, a being and nature that they have received as a sheer gift from a God of holy love. Put another way, human dignity is not a function of the vagaries of the approval of others or of a social order that typecasts whole classes of people. Instead it is conferred as a gift to all human beings by a good and gracious Creator. And such a gift renders them both beautiful and glorious. God has been most generous.

The Natural Image

So important is the image of God, the *imago Dei*, in understanding a human being properly, that John Wesley explored this glorious image along three major lines: the natural, political and moral images. To illustrate this important anthropological truth, Wesley considered the natural image, first of all, in terms of humanity being created as *spiritual* beings (what we might call *homo spiritualis*) in that they are endowed with understanding, will and liberty and are therefore capable of transcendence, that is, of participating in something greater than themselves.

The last mark of the natural image, liberty, readily flows out of a consideration of the second, that is, the created human will and its relation to

2. Humanity: All People Are Created in the Glorious Image and Likeness of God

divine love. In what may be the most utterly free human action of all, love can only arise in a context of *liberty* in which human beings first of all receive the divine favor and then respond freely in love. In his sermon, "On Predestination," Wesley explained why such a liberty is so crucial to the very nature of the image of God:

> Indeed if man were not free he could not be accountable either for his thoughts, words, or actions. If he were not free, he would not be capable either of reward or punishment. He would be incapable either of virtue or vice, of being either morally good or bad. If he had no more freedom than the sun, the moon, or the stars, he would be no more accountable than they.[34]

So then not only does the characteristic of liberty highlight the moral dimensions of the image of God in that human beings are capable of both vice and virtue in a way that *things are not*, but it also illuminates the larger trajectory of human life, that it has a proper direction and orientation, toward God, of course, who is the fulfillment, the goal, the perfection of their being. And that life in God is richly manifested in the freedom of holy love.

The Political Image

The image of God can be explored in a second major way in terms of what Wesley called "the political image." That is, there must be ongoing governance in terms of the created order with the goal of preserving the good gifts given by a generous Creator. To this end, humanity was given the great honor of ruling with God in terms of the things that have been made, specifically in terms of the lower creation. In his sermon, "The General Deliverance," for example, Wesley explained: "So that man was God's vicegerent upon earth, the prince and governor of this lower world; and all the blessings of God flowed through him to the inferior creatures. Man was the channel of conveyance between his Creator and the whole brute creation."[35]

Observe in the words of Wesley just cited that the viceregency of humanity has to do with "this lower world"[36] and with respect to "the inferior creatures."[37] Again, men and women are the channel of conveyance to those under them, to "the whole brute creation."[38] In this context, that is, in terms of the political image, Wesley wrote nothing about some human beings being the viceregents of God whereby they then rule over other human beings.

The Moral Image

If one pays attention to Wesley's rhetoric in the sense of how he uses language, getting down to his particular word choices, it will be readily apparent that when he explored the moral image of God in which humanity was created, the words "righteousness" and "true holiness" were invariably in the mix. By such language Wesley wanted to underscore that the tempers or dispositions[39] of the heart of human beings were all rightly directed towards God as their highest end at their creation in which the state of human existence could suitably be described in terms of both innocence and "rectitude."[40]

In other words, the moral image is a description, a mark, a characteristic of how the goods of the *imago Dei* are held in relation to a God of holy love who is the goal, the high end, of all human existence. Simply put, humanity enters into the life of God, of righteousness and true holiness, by participating in what God is, namely, the relations of holy love.

Indeed, so important was the moral image in Wesley's estimation of the *imago Dei* that he wrote the following: "This universal righteousness, which is the moral image of God, is far the noblest part of that image in which Moses represents man to have been originally created."[41] Righteousness and true holiness expressive of a proper relation to God is the most important of all. Charles expressed this true poetically in the following verse:

> That blessed law of thine,
> Jesu, to me impart:
> Thy Spirit's law of life divine,
> O write it in my heart!
> Implant it deep within,
> Whence it may ne'er remove,
> The law of liberty from sin,
> The perfect law of love.[42]

The Purpose of Humanity

With the rise of science in the seventeenth century, as reflected in the works of Galileo Galilei (1564-1642) and Johannes Kepler (1571-1630), the older Aristotelian way of thinking about things was transformed in that formal causes (what's the design of something?) as well as final causes (what's the purpose of something?) simply dropped out. They were displaced by an

2. Humanity: All People Are Created in the Glorious Image and Likeness of God

unswerving focus on material (what a thing is) and instrumental (how it came to be) causation. Accordingly, by the time of the eighteenth century few of the leading thinkers in England, such as John Locke (1632-1704) and later David Hume (1771-1786) were asking the question, "What is the purpose of a human being"? In this shifting intellectual and methodological environment it was a question that no longer made much sense. Nevertheless, John Wesley as a practical theologian, who affirmed both reason and revelation, was still reckoning with the significance of being created in the image and likeness of God, suggestive of both design and purpose, and so he continued to ask precisely this kind of question.

Interestingly enough, John Wesley took up the whole matter of purpose, that is, to what end was humanity created?, in an indirect way, by considering what was the difference between humanity, on the one hand, and the rest of the animal realm, on the other. Though Aristotle in the *De Anima* had distinguished the rational soul from the vegetative and sensate souls, Wesley, however, immediately conceded that the major difference between human beings and all other animals was not reason. In his sermon, "The General Deliverance," for instance, he explained: "What then makes the barrier between men and brutes? The line which they cannot pass? It was not reason. Set aside that ambiguous term: exchange it for the plain word, understanding, and who can deny that brutes have this?"[43]

So then, the chief characteristic of human beings, indicative in some sense of the purpose for which they have been made, was none other than, "man is capable of God, the inferior creatures are not. . . . This is the specific difference between man and brute—the great gulf which they cannot pass over."[44] It will be recalled that the natural image of God, made up of understanding, will and liberty, underscored that humanity was created a spiritual being. It is therefore the conjunction of this image along with the moral one, manifested in righteousness and true holiness, and the political one, in vicegerency, that displays the distinguishing mark of human beings, what sets them apart from all other creatures. In other words, the *imago Dei* expressed in the worship and adoration of God in holy love gets at the very heart of what a human being is, and to what end it has been created. Such a posture is indicative of the very nature of humanity, what it is, along with the purpose, the goal, of its being. Charles Wesley expressed this abundant and enduring truth in the following lines from his hymn:

> Hail, Father, Son and Spirit, great
> Before the birth of time,
> Enthroned in everlasting state,
> Jehovah, Elohim!
>
> A mystical plurality
> We in the Godhead own,
> Adoring One in Persons Three,
> And Three in nature One.
>
> From thee our being we receive,
> The creatures of thy grace;
> And raised out of the earth, we live
> To sing our Maker's praise.[45]

"To sing our Maker's praise,"[46] then is a very human thing to do. In fact, humanity has been created in order to do this very thing both now and forevermore. The worship and adoration of God is always the way forward in any age. No intellectual or cultural developments could ever displace it.

3. Humanity: All People Are Fallen

"So when the woman saw that the tree was good for food, and that it was a delight to the eyes, and that the tree was to be desired to make one wise, she took of its fruit and ate; and she also gave some to her husband, who was with her, and he ate. Then the eyes of both were opened, and they knew that they were naked; and they sewed fig leaves together and made loincloths for themselves." (Genesis 3:6-7)

Though men and women were created in the magnificent image and likeness of God, and though their lives in terms of thoughts, words and deeds all evidenced the beauty and glory of God who was the source of every good gift, nevertheless they did not remain in this blessed state. Adam and Eve were created good and innocent, to be sure, yet their condition was mutable. Things could change.

The Fall

John Wesley chronicled the loss of innocence, the descent into sin and evil of Adam and Eve, by making some observations on Genesis, Chapter Three, in his *Notes on the Old Testament* as well as in several other places in his published writings. In his assessment of the essence of sin, Wesley departed from a well-grounded Augustinian tradition, at least in some sense, that would identify the heart of sin with self-curving pride. Such a Latin tradition was reflected in the judgment of the *Rule of Saint Benedict* as well as in the much later work, *The Imitation of Christ* which Wesley read and cherished. Remarkably enough, Wesley's estimation of sin was more radical in the sense of getting to the root of the problem. In his judgment, behind sinful pride was the deeper problem of unbelief. Thus, in his focus on the sin of Adam and Eve, as attested in Genesis 3:6, Wesley pointed out "Here sin began, namely, unbelief. 'The woman was deceived,' says the Apostle [in 1 Timothy 2:14)]. She believed a lie: she gave more credit to the word of the devil than to the word of God."[1] Elsewhere, in his commentary on Hebrews 3:12, Wesley observed: "Unbelief is the *parent* of all evil, and the very essence of unbelief lies in departing from God, as the living God—the fountain of all our life, holiness, happiness."[2] Simply put, unbelief is "the confluence of all sins."[3]

This identification of unbelief as the root of all subsequent evils, as its parent, underscores that sin must preeminently be understood as a perverted *relation*. In other words, out of alienation from a God of holy love, pride, self-will and all subsequent evils invariably flow. Out of unbelief and alienation every other evil disposition of the heart arises. Accordingly, the problem of sin is compounded for sinners, from those estranged from the very source of being and love, in that the darkness of sin, in its depths of alienation, prevents those so stricken from realizing the importance of the invisible, in this case of *relation*, even if it is perverted one. Charles Wesley understood these dynamics so well as is evidenced by the following lines of a hymn he composed:

> Shut up in unbelief I groan,
> And blindly serve a God unknown
> Till thou the veil remove;
> The gift unspeakable impart,
> And write thy name upon my heart,
> And manifest thy love.[4]

The way forward then will entail both illumination and trust: "As Satan began his work in Eve by tainting her with unbelief, so the Son of God begins his work in man by enabling us to believe in him."[5]

The Consequences of the Fall

Death

The fall of Adam and Eve into sin, the disruption of the relation between God and humanity, resulted first of all in death. John Wesley apparently viewed the appropriate passage of the fall, Genesis 3:1-19, through the lens of Romans 5:14 so that he would clearly understand all that was entailed in this Old Testament passage. The Apostle Paul had written in the first century, "Nevertheless, death reigned from the time of Adam to the time of Moses, even over those who did not sin by breaking a command, as did Adam, who is a pattern of the one to come."

Though death can be understood in a threefold way in terms of temporal, spiritual and eternal death, it is principally temporal and spiritual death, that is, the death of the body and soul, that both the Apostle Paul and Wesley had in mind in this setting. The body became "corruptible and mortal,"[6] Wesley wrote. It now languished and died. Moreover, the extent of death involved not simply Adam and Eve but it was vast and universal, a reign that no human being could ever avoid with the exception of Jesus Christ. Wesley referred to it therefore as a veritable kingdom as in the following passage: "*Death reigned*—And how vast is his kingdom! Scarce can we find any king, who has as many subjects, as are the kings whom he hath conquered!"[7] And he added underscoring its extent: "Even over infants who had never sinned, as Adam did, in their own persons; and over others [it reigned], who had not, like him, sinned against an express law."[8]

> And am I only born to die?
> And must I suddenly comply
> With nature's stern decree?
> What after death for me remains?
> Celestial joys or hellish pains
> To all eternity.[9]

Beyond this, the theme of spiritual death is also a part of the Genesis narrative as Wesley clearly recognized: "For the moment he [Adam] tasted that fruit he died. His soul died, was separated from God; separate from whom the soul has no more life than the body has when separate from the soul."[10] Again, "the sentence of death passed on that body, which before was impassive and immortal. And this immortal having put on mortality, the next stroke fell on its companion: the soul felt a like change through all her powers, except only that she could not die."[11]

If, however, as Wesley clearly taught, the soul is immortal then what could the death of the soul possibly mean? How does a soul die and yet live? Wesley had considered this very issue in an early sermon he had drafted, "The Image of God," in which he explained, as just pointed out above: ""the soul felt a like change through all her powers, except only that she could not die."[12] So then, Wesley maintained not only that the soul became mortal through sin, but also that it will ever continue to exist—an apparent contradiction.

However, elsewhere in his writings, in his sermon, "Justification by Faith," Wesley considered the death of the soul not in a literal way but in a metaphorical one, that is, the soul is dead in the sense that it is alienated from the life of God; nevertheless, it continues to exist.[13] "Their bodies indeed are 'crushed before the moth,'" he reasoned, "but their souls will never die. God made them, as an ancient writer speaks, to be 'pictures of his own eternity.'"[14]

Corruption

The second major consequence of the fall of Adam and Eve was the loss of the favor of God as well as the corruption of their natures especially in terms of the harm done to the blessed image of God in which they were created. This consequence, once again, must be relationally understood. In terms of the *natural image of God,* the understanding of Adam was shaken; it was confused and often in error. "It mistook falsehood for truth, Wesley pointed out, "and truth for falsehood. Error succeeded and increased ignorance."[15] In short, the understanding no longer perceived the things of God clearly. Likewise, the human *will* was now corrupted. It was overrun with the sinful passions of "anger, hatred, fear and shame,"[16] and it suffered enormous loss "when its guide [the understanding] was thus blinded."[17] Though disrupted in terms of the proper end towards which it should be ever directed, the will, as with the understanding, yet remained in place. The last aspect of the natural image to be despoiled was *liberty*. In his sermon, "The Image of God, Wesley explored the nature of this significant loss: "Liberty went away with virtue; instead of an indulgent master it was under a merciless tyrant. The subject of virtue became the slave of vice."[18] For his part, Charles Wesley expressed a similar truth in the following way:

> Fain would I know my utmost ill,
> And groan my nature's weight to feel;
> To feel the clouds that round me roll,
> The night that hangs upon my soul:
> The darkness of my carnal mind,
> My will perverse, my passions blind,
> Scattered o'er all the earth abroad,
> Immeasurably far from God.[19]

In a similar fashion, the *political image* was greatly debased though it too still remained in place. Men and women were originally meant to be the "great channel of communication between the Creator and the whole brute creation,"[20] such that the blessings of the Most High would be showered upon the lower creation through humanity. With the descent into sin, however, those blessings were necessarily cut off.[21] Now men and women became not a blessing but a curse to those creatures below them. "By his apostasy from God," John Wesley noted, "he [Adam] threw not only himself, but likewise the whole creation, which was intimately connected with him, into disorder, misery, death."[22]

Though the natural and political images of God yet remained, even though they were greatly corrupted, the *moral image of God*, marked by righteousness and holiness, was utterly effaced. Overrun with brutal passions and shameful appetites, Adam's relationship to God was disrupted. Put another way, the tempers and dispositions of his heart were no longer marked by the simplicity of holiness and the beauty of righteousness. That is, relational change resulted in a change of heart, a dispositional change. Adam was now cut off, in alienation and fear, from the source of all holiness and righteousness, that is, the holy love of God. The *imago diaboli*, in some sense, now replaced the *imago Dei* with devasting consequences for the rest of humanity. With this loss of holiness came the loss of happiness as well. The unholy tempers of the heart, such things as jealousy, envy and a revengeful spirit, would never lead to happiness nor even to the peace, the serenity of heart, in which humanity had been created. This transformation in *being* was nothing less than horrific.

All Are Fallen: Original Sin, Death and Corruption

Original Sin

Through the careful reflections of Augustine (354-430) during the debate with Pelagius, the Western church conceived of original sin as the inheritance of Adam and Eve communicated to the rest of humanity. This all-too-human legacy consisted chiefly in the universality of death and a corrupted nature. So important was the doctrine of original sin to John Wesley's overall practical theology that he referred to it as one of three "fundamental doctrines" of the Christian faith. Wesley remarked: "Have a constant eye to the analogy of faith, the connection and harmony there is between those grand, fundamental doctrines, original sin, justification by faith, the new birth, inward and outward holiness."[23]

Wesley found this traditional teaching on original sin in the documents of his own Anglican heritage, that is, in the Thirty-Nine Articles in particular. However, when Wesley reproduced the specific Anglican article (Article IX) that pertained to original sin for the American church in 1784 in his *Sunday Service*, he greatly edited this Article that had hailed from the time of the English Reformation such that what remained now became Article VII of the *Methodist Articles*. The italicized material (with the addition of a bracketed excerpt) is all that was left after Wesley's careful editing:

> *Original sin standeth not in the following of Adam, (as the Pelagians do vainly talk;) but it is the* fault and *corruption of the Nature of every man, that naturally is engendered of the offspring of Adam; whereby man is very far gone from original righteousness, and is of his own nature inclined to evil,* [*and that continually.*] so that the flesh lusteth always contrary to the Spirit; and therefore in every person born into this world, it deserveth God's wrath and damnation. And this infection of nature doth remain, yea in them that are regenerated; whereby the lust of the flesh, called in Greek, φρονημα σαρκος, (which some do expound the wisdom, some sensuality, some the affection, some the desire, of the flesh), is not subject to the Law of God. And although there is no condemnation for them that believe and are baptized; yet the Apostle doth confess, that concupiscence and lust hath of itself the nature of sin.[24]

Observe in the Anglican Article above not only has Wesley removed the words "fault and" in the American rendering of the opening sentence but he has also omitted everything else after his insertion of the phrase, "and that continually." This editorial move was likely done to insure that the guilt of Adam's sin, as it might have pertained to the rest of humanity in a very practical manner, has already been cleansed away through the atoning blood of Jesus Christ for all of Adam's heirs. Naturally, then, the language of "deserveth God's wrath and damnation," was likewise taken away. In other words, if any are lost, it will be due not to Adam's fault but due to their own participation in sin.

Beyond this, the purpose of this shift from the one Article to the other can be illustrated in terms of the condition of infants born after the fall. To illustrate, in a letter drafted in 1776, Wesley explained: "Therefore no infant ever was or ever will be 'sent to hell for the guilt of Adam's sin, 'seeing it is cancelled by the righteousness of Christ as soon as they are sent into the world."[25] In particular, Wesley associated this liberty with the cleansing waters of baptism: "What are the benefits we receive by baptism, is the next point to be considered. And the first of these is, the washing away the guilt of original sin, by the application of the merits of Christ's death."[26]

Death Again

Adam was created immortal and yet mutable. What gifts he enjoyed could be lost with the result that all of humanity would be effected. Romans 5:12 lays out just how this occurred: "Therefore, just as sin entered the world through one man, and death through sin, and in this way death came to all people, because all sinned" (Rom. 5:12). In other words, as a result of the fall of Adam, the very nature of humanity has been transformed such that all are now mortal. And though the guilt of original sin is washed away in the waters of baptism for infants and adults, predicated on the atoning work of Jesus Christ, no human being escapes this negative inheritance from Adam in terms of death, a consequence that implies both guilt, on some level, and even punishment, because as the Apostle Paul wrote, "all sinned." Wesley explained: "God does not look upon infants as innocent, but as involved in the guilt of Adam's sin: otherwise death, the punishment denounced against that sin, could not be inflicted upon them."[27] Again in his treatise on original sin, Wesley reasoned:

> Their sufferings, therefore, yea, and those of all mankind, which are entailed upon them by the sin of Adam, are not the result of mere mercy, but of justice also. In other words, they have in them the nature of punishments, even on us and on our children. Therefore, children themselves are not innocent before God. They suffer; therefore, they deserve to suffer.[28]

The trajectory that both Scripture and John Wesley lay out can be expressed in the following schema:

$$\text{Sin} \rightarrow \text{Punishment} \rightarrow \text{Death}$$

Death Again

If death is a punishment which is applied to all of humanity in the wake of Adam's sin (Genesis 3:16-19), then all are yet in some sense implicated in both the sin and the guilt of Adam, even infants, as the preceding material indicates. In other words, the issue of guilt now has to understood in a twofold way. Yes, the atoning blood of Jesus Christ covers the guilt of Adam's sin so that no child (or adult for that matter) is ever held accountable for such guilt in a legal, juridical way, as noted earlier, one that would warrant condemnation. Nevertheless, the issue of guilt does indeed emerge once more for both infants and adults, but this time in the context of the universality of human mortality. In other words, death is viewed by both the author of Genesis and Wesley as a punishment that from another corner raises the specter of guilt once more, though in a different manner.

Moreover, it is precisely in this context of sin, punishment, and death that the question of Adam being a federal head or representative of humanity is best understood. This is not to deny, however, that Adam's federal headship will *also* relate to the whole matter of corruption. It will. At any rate, John Wesley explored the basic logic here in his following observation: "With him [Adam] all fell in his first transgression. That they are all born liable to the legal punishment of sin proves him the federal as well as natural head of mankind; whose sin is so far imputed to all men, that they are born 'children of wrath,' and liable to death."[29]

Though Wesley obviously employed the language of a "federal head" in his writings, nevertheless he did not insist on its usage. "But as neither representative, nor federal head, are scripture words, it is not worthwhile to contend for them," Wesley observed. What he did contend for, however, was that "The state of all mankind did so far depend on Adam, that, by his fall, they all fell into sorrow, and pain, and death, spiritual and temporal."[30] In a similar vein, Charles Wesley wrote as follows:

> While dead in trespasses I lie,
> Thy quick'ning Spirit give:
> Call me, thou Son of God, that I
> May hear thy voice and live.
>
> While full of anguish and disease,
> My weak, distempered soul
> Thy love compassionately sees—
> O let it make me whole.[31]

3. *Humanity: All People Are Fallen*

A Question of Frameworks

The scriptural exploration of sin, punishment, and death as reflected in the account of Genesis Chapter Three is best understood in terms of a moral (the holy law of love) and legal (the moral law) framework as offering a clue as to why punishment rightly occurs. Such a framework continues throughout the Wesleyan order of salvation especially when the ministrations of the moral law, which are ongoing, are clearly in view. However, this moral and legal framework appears to be in tension with another that John Wesley employed as well. To illustrate, in his sermon on "Original Sin," Wesley considered redemption to be the healing of a diseased soul, not the meting out of punishments. "It is therapeia psyches, God's method of healing a soul which is thus diseased, Wesley wrote, "Hereby the great Physician of souls applies medicines to heal this sickness; to restore human nature. . . ."[32]

In light of the preceding evidence, it appears that a tension has emerged between two of the principal frameworks that Wesley employed to think through the process of redemption, broadly speaking. To illustrate this problem, the therapeutic scaffolding seems to be bumping up against a legal, juridical one, with so many questions left unanswered: Are the sick responsible for their disease? Are the ailing accountable? And who punishes the ill, anyway? Such questions seem to make no sense at all in this current context; they appear to be by and large inappropriate. Perhaps the therapeutic model of redemption then is incapable of expressing adequately the active rebellion, the disobedience, and the faithlessness, as well as the propensity to depart from the living God that are all involved in sin. Again, why should the diseased be punished at all? Why are death and punishment the lot of sinners when they are only ill? Should they not rather be pitied as the victims of something that was done to them? This problem of suitable frameworks raised by the specter of sin, punishment, and death is not going away. It will break out a second time when *the extent* of original sin is considered below.

Corruption Again

In 1740 Dr. John Taylor, who was a Dissenting minister in Norwich and budding Hebrew scholar, published a book on original sin that not only disturbed John Wesley but also Jonathan Edwards who claimed that the work, "did so much towards rooting out the underlying ideas of the Westminster Confession."[33] For his part, Wesley thought that Dr. Taylor had soft-pedalled the inheritance of a corrupted nature from Adam, and that the Hebrew scholar was therefore content to wallow in the trite moralism so expressive of a moderate and enlightened age. Beyond this, in accordance with the Council of Carthage (A.D. 418) and the Second Council of Orange (A.D. 529), Wesley wanted to make it clear that he and the Methodists rejected any Pelagian notions that the substance of original sin consists not in *corruption* but in *imitation*. "I verily believe no single person since Mahomet has given such a wound to Christianity as Dr. Taylor,"[34] Wesley wrote. Though the contents of this work deeply disturbed Wesley, he did not take up his pen in opposition until 1757 when he produced his largest theological treatise ever, *The Doctrine of Original Sin: According to Scripture, Reason, and Experience*. Because Wesley knew that many would not wade through this lengthy composition, a couple of years later he reduced the substance of his treatise to a more manageable sermon form.

It is important to recognize at the outset that in the context of the doctrine of original sin and its consequences, when Wesley employed the language of the "natural state" or the "natural man," this language is not to be confused with the term the "natural man," in the typology of natural, legal and evangelical as found in the sermon, "The Spirit of Bondage and Of Adoption."[35] Wesley explained what he meant by such language as it plays out in the context of original sin in his following observation: "From all these we learn concerning man in his natural state, *unassisted by the grace of God*, that 'all the imaginations of the thoughts of his heart' are still 'evil, only evil', and that continually."[36] In other words, here is a corrupted inheritance unmitigated by the grace of God.

So understood, the corruption of original sin entails *atheism* in that now by *nature* God is not in the thoughts of humanity. "By none of these [natural faculties]," Wesley wrote, "could we attain the knowledge of God. We could no more perceive him by our natural understanding than we could see him with our eyes."[37] As a consequence, "having no knowledge," Wesley reasoned, "we can have no love of God, [for] we cannot love him we know not."[38] Again, no doubt for emphasis, Wesley pointed out: "No man loves God by nature, no more than he does a stone, or the earth he treads upon. What we love, we delight in: but no man has naturally any delight in God. In our natural state we cannot conceive how anyone should delight in him."[39]

Since humanity is alienated from God, and marked by unbelief, it is not surprising that pride in the form of self-curvature is the immediate consequence of this distorted relationship. "We have set up idols in our heart," Wesley warned. "We worship ourselves when we pay that honor to ourselves which is due to God only. Therefore all pride is idolatry; it is ascribing to ourselves what is due to God alone."[40] Observe in this context that Wesley was not describing a moral foible in this corruption of pride as if it were simply a form of braggadocio or self-assertion. Rather, he was exploring a far more basic, systemic, existential and spiritual problem that makes the self, whether manifested in low or high self-esteem, the center of all valuation, an orbit of enslaving self-curvature from which it cannot by nature escape. "Whithersoever they move, Wesley pointed out, they cannot move beyond the circle of self."[41] Charles noted as well:

> Pity, and heal my sin-sick soul;
> 'Tis thou alone canst make me whole,
> Fall'n, till in me thine image shine,
> And cursed I am, till thou art mine.[42]

Strongly associated with pride is self-will, in other words, that will whose circumference is remarkably small due to the ongoing drag of self-absorbed pride. Wesley explained: "Ask the man, 'Why did you do this? He answers because I had a mind to it. What is this but, 'Because it was my will;' that is, in effect, because the devil and I agreed; because Satan and I govern our actions by one and the same principle."[43] What is Wesley's judgment in light of this turn of affairs? "The will of God meantime is not in his thoughts,"[44] he reasoned. Accordingly, self-will represents not only a limitation; it also suggests bondage, an encasing of the self, an alienation from God.

So caught up in pride and self-will, the heirs of Adamic corruption then go beyond even the evil that had marked Satan in his infamous fall. "We run into an idolatry whereof he is not guilty, Wesley wrote, "I mean *love of the world*."[45] But just what does it mean to love the world? Taking 1 John 2:16 as he guide, Wesley answered this question along the familiar gateways to temptation noted by the Apostle: "the desire of the flesh," in the form of the "sensual appetites,"[46] "the desire of the eye," in "the pleasures of imagination,"[47] and "the pride of life," in regarding what other people think, "the love of applause,"[48] a posture that can easily result in slavery and that of a very abject form. So then atheism, a heart of unbelief, has issued in the troika of pride, self-will and love of the world. This is the unenviable inheritance that has been bequeathed to all of humanity, with none excluded but Jesus Christ.

Furthermore, Wesley drew a strong and interesting connection between original sin, the nature of the problem, and the new birth, the nature of the cure. He reasoned: "Know your disease! Know your cure! Ye were born in sin; therefore 'ye must be born again', 'born of God'. By nature ye are wholly corrupted; by grace ye shall be wholly renewed. 'In Adam ye all died'; in the second Adam, 'in Christ, ye all are made alive.'"[49] Wesley likely made this theological move to demonstrate that the problem of original sin would be impervious to moral reform projects, educational cures, or any other *natural* human effort, period. In other words, such corruption could not be cured by nature but only by *divine supernatural grace*. Put another way, humanity cannot resolve the problem of the corruption of original sin simply because humanity itself is the problem.

All Are Utterly Fallen: Total Depravity

Total Depravity

It is clear by now that original sin in the form of the corruption that has been passed onto humanity is so contrary to the will of the God who had created Adam and Eve beautiful and glorious, an emblem of the divine Being. At this point, then, it is appropriate to ask the question: "what is the nature and extent of such corruption, that is, the carnal nature or inbred sin, that mars the souls of humanity"? Wesley's answer to this query will once again demonstrate a strong Western Augustinian view, well-embraced by the English Reformation of the sixteenth century, an answer that will distinguish his view in some important respects from that of other theological traditions, Eastern Orthodoxy in particular.

In exploring the nature and extent depravity, Wesley offered two key passages in his sermon, "Original Sin," published in 1759. The first passage is as follows: "Hence we may . . . learn that all who deny this—call it 'original sin' or by any other title—are but heathens still in the fundamental point which differences heathenism from Christianity."[50] In other words, in this context, Wesley is claiming that if anyone denies that humanity has received a negative inheritance of corruption, thereby wallowing in the mistaken notion that by nature people are basically good, then such a view will result in a departure from the Christian faith itself. Though this statement is admittedly strong, given Wesley's understanding of the natural state, that is, apart from all grace, his second observation, which focuses more clearly on the extent of depravity, is even stronger as is evident in the following:

> Here is the shibboleth. Is man by nature filled with all manner of evil? Is he void of all good? Is he wholly fallen? Is his soul totally corrupted? Or, to come back to the text, is 'every imagination of the thoughts of his heart evil continually'? Allow this, and you are so far a Christian. Deny it, and you are but a heathen still.[51]

So then, though these two passages appear to be claiming the same thing, upon closer examination, it is evident that their claims are actually different. To illustrate, the first passage relegates those to the status of heathenism who simply deny in a general way the doctrine of original sin, itself, as Wesley and some important Christian traditions had defined it. However, the second passage claims so much more, and this has often been missed in the interpretation of Wesley's practical theology. Observe that this second passage relegates those to the status of a heathen who deny the *extent* of original sin, in other words, that it results in being "wholly fallen"[52] and "totally corrupted."[53] This teaching itself is the shibboleth as Wesley clearly stated in this second passage above. Beyond this, the text just cited is not idiosyncratic, and oddity, but is in line with the similar language of negative superlatives that Wesley employed throughout his writings in describing the extent of original sin as demonstrated in the following evidence:

- "thou are corrupted in every power, in every faculty of thy soul, that thou art totally corrupted in every one of these, all the foundations being out of course."[54]
- "every imagination of the thought of man's heart is evil, only evil, and that continually."[55]
- "an inexhaustible fund of ungodliness and unrighteousness, [so] deeply and strongly rooted in the soul that nothing less than almighty grace can cure it."[56]
- "only evil continually,"[57]
- "entire depravity and corruption."[58]
- "dead in trespasses and sins"[59]

A Question of Frameworks Once More

In light of such evidence, Albert Outler pointed out that Wesley "sought to compound the Latin tradition of total depravity with the Eastern Orthodox view of sin as disease . . . and of salvation as *therapeia psyches*,"[60] not realizing that this compound was essentially unworkable. To be sure, it is precisely in this setting of original sin that the puzzle of suitable frameworks breaks out once more. Earlier this was considered in the context of the juridical structure of sin, punishment, and death. Now it will be considered in terms of total depravity, a doctrine that Wesley so clearly affirmed.

One way of solving this riddle is to point out that the language of salvation as therapy, as employed by Wesley, was largely a metaphorical attempt, the taking up of a particular rhetoric, to describe salvation in a very general way. However, given the extent of depravity, Wesley also had to take up the rhetoric of a Western juridical tradition that moved in a much different direction. This observation is not to deny the usefulness of the metaphor of healing that even Jesus, himself, appealed to (Mark 2:17) when he described *the kind of people* to whom he was sent (those in need, by way of analogy). It is just that this metaphor may never have been intended to apply to the whole *compass of redemption*, and every step along the way, as alluded to earlier.

The Eastern Orthodox view on this matter is much different. After the fall, humanity is not "totally corrupted," as Wesley and the Magisterial Reformers would have it, dead in trespasses and sins, such that it is unable to cooperate with God, to respond to the Most High. Rather, even after the fall, Eastern Orthodoxy insists that humanity yet remains free and obviously well enough to cooperate with God at every step along the way.

It is impossible, however, to add an Eastern therapeutic view, with its associated co-operant grace, that is, of divine and human working, on top of a Western view that argues as a result of original sin, in the natural state, humanity is *dead* in sin, totally depraved and utterly corrupted, and as such it can literally do nothing at this point to alter its condition. What is called for then in the face of these stark realities is not cooperant grace, divine and human working, a sheer impossibility here, but what Augustine called operant grace or what Wesley, himself, termed free grace, that is, the work of God alone.

All Are Utterly Dependent Upon God for Any Good

When some people both within and without the Methodist tradition encounter John Wesley's teaching on the natural state and his doctrine of original sin, especially in terms of its extent, they balk at the idea of its totality, the notion of being utterly fallen, totally corrupted. The response at times is almost unthinking, even visceral. However, this is simply to view this teaching in a negative way. However, the genius of what Wesley, as well as the Western theological tradition, taught on this score must be considered in a different way as well, in a positive one, in order to see the full import of this crucial teaching which is nothing less than a shibboleth.

Viewed in a *positive manner*, Wesley's doctrine of total depravity reveals that *humanity is utterly dependent upon God for any good that it has*. This is a basic, foundational truth that is at the heart of Wesley's theological trajectory. It is one of the more important fingerprints of his basic theological posture. It is a highway, to change the metaphor, to Wesley's artfully developed doctrine of both sin and grace. After the debacle of the fall and the corruption left in its wake in original sin, and given the totality of depravity, due to the alienation of the relationship between God and humanity, if salvation is ever to be a possibility at all, in the face of such human impotence, then the Most High must not only initiate the process of salvation but God must also, at least in this area, act *sovereignly*. This large and generous role of the Most High will be developed in the following chapter in terms of the faculties of prevenient grace which must be viewed not as a species of cooperant grace but once again of free grace. They are the handiwork of a God who is refreshingly generous and loving in the face of human sin and corruption.

4. The Holy Spirit Works in All People: Prevenient Grace

"Your word is a lamp for my feet, a light on my path" (Psalm 119:105).

"The true light that gives light to everyone was coming into the world" (John 1:9).

The last chapter on the doctrine of the fall struck a very somber chord in John Wesley's practical theology. However, one of the many reasons why Wesley is such a faithful guide to serious Christian discipleship is that he honestly and accurately portrays both the nature and the extent of human sin. Never once does he water down the substance of this Christian teaching in order to please the "moderate" clergy of his own age or those beyond the church who simply would not tolerate, in this period of enlightenment, such a dark and thoroughgoing description of human malaise. However, the human condition is not accurately described simply in terms of sin as Wesley knew full well. A complete picture of the human condition only arises after a broad consideration of grace as well. Indeed, it is the careful balance of both sin and grace that makes Wesley's practical theology remarkably realistic on the one hand and refreshingly optimistic on the other hand. Such a generous optimism emerges from and is empowered by nothing less than the rich grace of God administered by the Holy Spirit.

The Holy Spirit as the Initiator of the Process of Redemption

The Holy Spirit who is "of one substance, majesty, and glory with the Father and the Son,"[1] initiates the process of redemption such that where sin abounds, through the fall of Adam and Eve, grace will abound all the more. In other words, in the wake of the fall, grace is immediately given not only to illuminate the way back to God but also to empower and restore. The generosity of John Wesley's practical theology then is clearly evident in the vibrant and restorative activity of the Holy Spirit very early on, well before other theologies have even begun to reckon seriously with the grace of God.

Lycurgus Starkey has referred to the Holy Spirit in his own work as "the imperceptible providential presence of the divine Spirit in and about all men as the creative and sustaining ground of life itself."[2] As Scripture puts it more simply, "For in him we live and move and have our being" (Acts 17:28). In other words, not even the fall, not even the marks of total depravity, can utterly eliminate what good remains, especially in terms of the vestiges of the natural image of God, that ever point to the Creator, who is their source. This ongoing dependence of humanity upon God, even in the face of alienation, remains in the form of *being*, a grace of God mediated by the Holy Spirit (who is Life itself) through a marred natural image that has not been extinguished, not even by sin, but still remains.

Beyond this, the Holy Spirit will be the source of every good gift, every good work that will emerge in the lives humanity. In his *A Farther Appeal to Men of Reason and Religion* Wesley affirmed, "the whole work of salvation, every good thought, word, and work, is altogether by the operation of the Spirit of God."[3] Accordingly, in the face of the darkness of sin into which humanity has fallen, the work of the Holy Spirit will in part be one of an ever-expanding illumination of what things are presently corrupted and deformed and how they can be transformed in the future by grace. As Wesley put it, the Holy Spirit opens "the eyes of our understanding; bringing us out of darkness into marvelous light."[4]

This significant role of the Holy Spirit early on, in this setting of darkness and sin, points to the rich and broad pneumatological (with the Holy Spirit as Initiator and Administrator) orientation of John Wesley's practical theology. In other words, the Holy Spirit has been wonderfully active, illuminating and giving gifts, even before humanity is even aware of this. This prior activity, superintended by the Spirit of the Living God, is what Wesley often referred to as prevenient grace. In short, God is always ahead; the Most High always acts first. In terms of salvation humanity never initiates, and it *receives* well before it ever responds. Moreover, what is so very important here, an emblem of John Wesley's engaging and inviting practical theology, is that God is oriented to all, to everyone who has been created in nothing less than the image and likeness of God. That ongoing image, through the ministrations of the Holy Spirit, is an expression of the enormous good will and generosity of the Creator for every creature.

Prevenient Grace Is Given to All People

So then, one way in which Wesley's practical theology will differ in terms of the theological tradition of Augustine, Luther and Calvin is that it maintains that no one has been left in the natural state, apart from all grace, because God has *already* acted sovereignly in the administration of prevenient grace, that grace which literally goes before salvation properly speaking. In his sermon, "On Working Out Our Own Salvation," for instance, Wesley explained:

> For allowing that all souls of men are dead in sin by nature, this excuses none, seeing there is no man that is in a state of mere nature; there is no man, unless he has quenched the Spirit, that is wholly void of the grace of God. No man living is entirely destitute of what is vulgarly called "natural conscience." But this is not natural; it is more properly termed "preventing grace."[5]

Wesley's doctrine of prevenient grace grew out of a careful reflection on Scripture as well as on his own Anglican tradition. His favorite text to explore this boon that quite literally goes before, that is present even before people are aware of it, is John 1:9: "The true light that gives light to everyone was coming into the world." Observe in this passage not only does this grace entail illumination but that it is also universal, not dependent upon the vagaries of time, circumstance, geography or culture. Moreover, it is likewise not dependent in any way on human power or merit. It is freely given to all by a God of holy love. It is a sheer gift, bespeaking of the divine goodness and generosity. "Every man has a greater or less measure of this," Wesley declared, "which waiteth not for the call of man."[6]

In a similar fashion, in articulating the doctrine of prevenient grace, Wesley appealed to Article X of the Anglican Thirty-Nine Articles though he made one minor omission when he reproduced this Article for the American Methodists (which now emerged as Article VIII) in his *Sunday Service*. The text is as follows:

> The condition of man after the fall of Adam is such that he cannot turn and prepare himself by his own natural strength and works to faith, and calling upon God: Wherefore we have no power to do good works pleasant and acceptable to God, without the grace of God by Christ preventing us, that we may have a good-will, and working with us, when we have that good-will.[7]

What did Wesley leave out? Of the original Anglican wording of "by his own natural strength and good works," Wesley omitted, for whatever reason, the word "good," though the word does appear in the remainder of the Methodist Article. This may have simply been an editorial judgment to avoid redundancy.

The initial restoration entailed in prevenient grace that Almighty God brings about in the wake of human depravity is a sovereign restoration, to be sure, the work of God *alone* given the extent of human corruption. In this setting, then, prevenient grace is best understood not as a species of cooperant or responsible grace, of divine and human working, but of free grace. In other words, in this context it will be helpful to make a distinction between the four faculties that God will sovereignly restore, as an instance of free grace, and the overtures that will be made by the Holy Spirit later on through these faculties, a move that will indeed initiate the movement of cooperant grace. Both John and Charles Wesley had a rich appreciation for the sovereign grace of God given the extent of sin as revealed in the following stanzas:

> Glory to God, whose sovereign grace
> Hath animated senseless stones;
> Called us to stand before his face,
> And raised us into Abraham's sons.
>
> Thou only, Lord, the work hast done,
> And bared thine arm in all our sight,
> Hast made the reprobates thine own,
> And claimed the outcasts as thy right.[8]

Prevenient Grace as the Sovereign, Universal Restoration of Faculties

Free Will

Given the theological reality of total depravity prior to the reception of prevenient grace, the very restoration of free will through divine, sovereign action is not to be viewed as a natural faculty, one indicative of a human capacity, but as an instance of *grace*. Robert Childs has already helpfully pointed out the declension that took place in nineteenth century American Methodism in the shift from free grace to free will,[9] one that has been claimed by others to be representative of John Wesley's own view. It is not. For Wesley, however, what freedom is restored is not a thing of nature, a natural capacity, but one of grace that highlights ongoing dependence on its enabling source. In his *Predestination Calmly Considered*, drafted in 1752, Wesley elaborated:

> But I do not carry free-will so far: (I mean, not in moral things:) Natural free-will, in the present state of mankind, I do not understand: I only assert, that there is a measure of free will supernaturally restored to every man, together with that supernatural light which "enlightens every man that cometh into the world." But indeed, whether this be natural or no, as to your objection it matters not.[10]

Conscience

Many twenty-first century ethicists understand conscience as a social product, a capacity that is forged out of the fires of societal norms, prescriptions and mores. Moreover, scientists have argued that evolutionary biology as a discipline is sufficient to explain the rise of conscience as a survival mechanism of the species. Observe that in each instance, whether in terms of sociology or biology, conscience is deemed to be a natural capacity. The view of John Wesley, however, was much different than this. Once again, conscience is not a thing of nature but of *grace*. Wesley wrote:

> No man living is entirely destitute of what is vulgarly called natural conscience. But this is not natural: It is more properly termed, preventing grace. Every man has a greater or less measure of this, which waiteth not for the call of man. Everyone has, sooner or later, good desires; although the generality of men stifle them before they can strike deep root, or produce any considerable fruit. Everyone has some measure of that light, some faint glimmering ray, which, sooner or later, more or less, enlightens every man that cometh into the world.[11]

Underscoring the universality of this gift of grace that goes beyond the walls of the church, Wesley pointed out: "Something of this is found in every human heart, passing sentence concerning good and evil not only in all Christians, but in all Mahometans, all pagans, yea the vilest of savages."[12] This grace is given to everyone that bears a human face.

Moral Law

The sovereign restoration of the moral law that had been corrupted by sin is necessary, in some sense, since this law is strongly associated with the moral image of God, itself, as manifested in goodness, righteousness and true holiness. Indeed, Albert Outler maintained that "The 'original' of the Law is man's inborn moral sense—not 'natural' in the deist sense but, rather, as an aspect of the residual imago Dei."[13] So understood, the moral law, "God manifested to creatures as they are able to bear it,"[14] has an ethical dimension that makes it remarkably serious, and not therefore to be confused with sentimentality, self-will or indulgence, since it is ever focused on what is genuinely good, the highest good of all, namely, God. Wesley observed:

> But it was not long before man rebelled against God, and by breaking this glorious law well nigh effaced it out of his heart; . . . And yet God did not despise the work of his own hands; but being reconciled to man through the Son of his love, he in some measure re-inscribed the law on the heart of his dark, sinful creature.[15]

So then, with this re-inscription of the moral law, sovereignly given, a species of prevenient grace, this endowment, this gift, may suggest that all knowledge does not come through the senses, after all, for with this sovereign illumination also comes human responsibility. On even deeper manifestations of grace in terms of the moral law, Charles noted a similar dynamic:

> That blessed law of thine,
> Jesu, to me impart:
> Thy Spirit's law of life divine,
> O write it in my heart!
> Implant it deep within,
> Whence it may ne'er remove,
> The law of liberty from sin,
> The perfect law of love.[16]

Basic Attributes of God

Although Wesley grew up during the Enlightenment, during the age of John Locke and Immanuel Kant, and though his basic approach to human knowledge was largely empiricist, mediated through the senses, as Matthews has carefully argued,[17] nevertheless his view of human knowing left room for what looks like a more intuitivist approach especially in terms of the knowledge of the basic attributes of God. To illustrate, Wesley began with Paul's affirmation in Romans 1:20, "For since the creation of the world God's invisible qualities—his eternal power and divine nature—have been clearly seen, being understood from what has been made, so that people are without excuse," but then he connected this verse to his favorite one on prevenient grace, that is, John 1:9. The result of this combination is that Christ is identified as that light by which God's invisible qualities are made known to all people. In other words, such universal knowledge is not a matter of nature but once again of grace.[18] In his commentary on Romans 1:20, Wesley explained: "For what is to be known of God—Those great principles which are indispensably necessary to be known, 'is manifest in them; for God hath showed it to them' — By the light which enlightens every man that cometh into the world."[19]

> Then infuse the teaching grace,
> Spirit of truth and righteousness;
> Knowledge, love divine impart,
> Life eternal to my heart.[20]

Wesleyan Theology Can Acknowledge Every Good Wherever It Is Found

Prevenient Grace and the Power of John Wesley's Theology

The two key elements of prevenient grace explored so far that, first of all, God has already acted even before one is aware of such activity, and secondly that in the face of the debilitating effects of original sin the Most High has restored key faculties that reconstitute personhood and thereby render humanity savable, both of these benefits indicate that God is free to work both within and outside the church. In other words, prevenient grace is a universal benefit, it is the favor of God shown to all humanity regardless of social location or even religious affiliation. Charles Wesley expressed this truth so well, the encompassing dimension of grace that marks the generosity of God:

> What shall I do my God to love,
> My loving God to praise?

4. The Holy Spirit Works in All People: Prevenient Grace

> The length, and breadth, and height to prove,
> And depth of sovereign grace?
>
> Thy sovereign grace to all extends,
> Immense and unconfined:
> From age to age it never ends;
> It reaches all mankind.[21]

To be sure, it is the universality of this prevenient grace that not only empowers John Wesley's practical theology (and that of Charles as well) but also makes it remarkably generous in its operations since it is able to acknowledge the good wherever it is found. Indeed, one of the basic requisites of a sound and powerful theology is that it is able to call the good, "good," and evil, "evil." Not all theologies, however, are able to do this—surprisingly enough. Take for example the theology found in some Christian traditions that contends unless the activity, program or benefit explicitly mentions the name of Christ it is of the devil. In this way, all the good done by twelve-step programs, for example, in helping people receive the prevenient grace of God is not recognized at all. In fact these programs are called evil in this oddly drawn theological configuration. To illustrate this point, Martin and Deidre Bobgan in their book, *Twelve Steps to Destruction: Codependency/Recovery Heresies* argue along the following lines:

> Most systems of codependency and addiction recovery are based upon various psychological counseling theories and therapies and upon the religious and philosophical teaching of Alcoholics Anonymous (AA). In short, such programs are based upon the wisdom of man and the worship of false gods.[22]

Setting the good that twelve-step programs do at odds with the goodness of God's grace manifested in Jesus Christ, the authors can only categorize such programs as "one big psychoheresy."[23] Would it not have been better to view such programs as an instance of God's prevenient grace, which is after all Christologically based (John 1:9), even if such grace might not be acknowledged by its recipients? In John Wesley's understanding of divine grace and favor, which empowers his theology, God is so very good, gracious and generous that the Most High breaks bondages even when the source of such deliverance is not rightly acknowledged by its recipients. But it is certain that whenever bondages are broken, Christ has done the work, whether admitted or not, whether acknowledged or not. Such is the power and efficaciousness of prevenient grace that allows Wesley's very generous theology to recognize and affirm good *wherever it is found*, perhaps outside the institutional church, but never apart from Christ.

The Conjunctive Nature of Wesley's Practical Theology

The last two chapters on human creation and the fall as well as this current one on the prevenient action of God have demonstrated the priority of free grace in John Wesley's theology.[24] Not only was it free grace "that formed man of the dust of the ground, and breathed into him a living soul,"[25] but it was also free grace in the form of the sovereignly restored faculties of prevenient grace that displayed once again the work of God *alone* in the wake of human sin. Now two senses of divine priority can be distinguished. On the one hand, God is temporally prior to humanity in both being and action. That is, God always initiates; the Most High always makes the first move. This is the broad sense of "prevenience," and it is descriptive of John Wesley's entire theology from creation to glory.[26] On the other hand, the Almighty is soteriologically prior, and at times acts alone, and must do so, simply because human cooperation with God is not yet a possibility either in terms of creation, itself, or in terms of utter depravity, the face of original sin.

The genius of Wesley's intricate theological balance of grace, then, both of free grace and cooperant grace, means that the divine and human cooperation that eventually emerges in his theology, can only do so *after* the sovereign restorative activity of God has occurred. Consequently cooperant grace must itself be caught up into the larger conjunction of both free and cooperant grace in which the former will yet remain the lodestar, the leading motif, of Wesley's gracious and remarkably generous theology, reflective in some sense of who God is. In this setting then any divine and human acting can only be rightly understood against the larger backdrop of the divine benevolence and goodness, in generously offering humanity sheer gifts (creation and the restoration of faculties) in order that humanity might then be able to participate in and enjoy the rich life of God. And though some theologies maintain that such participation can only be rightly understood in terms of cooperant grace, it will be demonstrated in the chapters ahead that free grace, for Wesley, richly informs participatory themes as well. Indeed, Wesley's entire theology is grounded in giftedness because God as revealed in Jesus Christ is a gift giver par excellence.

5. Christ Identifies with All People

> *"The Word became flesh and made his dwelling among us. We have seen his glory, the glory of the one and only Son, who came from the Father, full of grace and truth." (John 1:14)*

Precisely because God is holy love, the Most High has already acted in the wake of human sin in giving the gifts of the four faculties of prevenient grace, administered by the Holy Spirit, to all of humanity, none excluded. Those gifts, explored in the last chapter, were predicated on the person and work of Jesus Christ. Put another way, these reestablished faculties point beyond themselves to the greatest gift of all who is none other than the *person* of Jesus Christ. Accordingly, in this current chapter the person and work of Christ will be explored as the way in which the Holy One of Israel has chosen to confront the reality of human sin head on in all its seriousness while at the same time offering the sheer gift, indeed, the treasure of Christ, the Son of God, as the way to abiding forgiveness, lasting renewal, and as a consequence human flourishing.

The Person of Jesus Christ

The revelation of God manifested in Jesus Christ by the power of the Holy Spirit was of such world-shattering significance during the first century (offering a new way to think about the Most High) that it took the Church literally centuries to reflect upon this revelation in order to express it in a clear doctrinal form. The labors of the ancient church, in terms of its doctrine of Christ, are evident in the first four ecumenical councils of Nicaea (325), Constantinople (381), Ephesus (431), and Chalcedon (451). Later on, the Church of England, during its significant and necessary reform in the sixteenth century, expressed the substance of the teaching of the ancient church in the pithy form of her Thirty-Nine Articles.

Well aware of this doctrinal heritage of the ancient church, and reaffirmed in his own Church of England tradition, John Wesley brought forth the substance of the Anglican Article pertaining to Christ in the Second Methodist Article of Religion that reads as follows:

> The Son, who is the Word of the Father, the very and eternal God, of one substance with the Father, took man's nature in the womb of the blessed Virgin; so that two whole and perfect natures, that is to say, the Godhead and Manhood, were joined together in one person, never to be divided; whereof is one Christ, very God and very Man, who truly suffered, was crucified, dead, and buried, to reconcile his Father to us, and to be a sacrifice, not only for original guilt, but also for actual sins of men.[1]

The Divine Nature

In light of the Methodist Article above, the key to the proper understanding of Jesus Christ, worked out by the ancient ecumenical church, and affirmed by the Church of England as well as by the Methodists, was the formula *one person in two natures*. In his own Christology, John Wesley took great care to affirm both the unity of the person and the distinctiveness of the natures. These are not to be confused. Thus, in terms of the latter, Wesley distinguished the divine and human natures of Christ so that each would be properly understood. For example, with respect to the divine nature, Wesley so revered Christ, recognizing him as "very God of very God,"[2] that he taught there is a categorical, not a minor, difference between Jesus Christ and all other human beings, even between the celebrated figures of all the major world religions.[3] To illustrate, in his commentary on John 1:1 Wesley pointed out that "There was no creature, in respect of which he could be styled God in a relative sense."[4] In other words, every other religious leader as a creature, from Moses to Mohammed, no matter how celebrated or extolled, was simply human. Jesus Christ, however, is also divine.

Wesley also considered the divinity of Christ in terms of the specific language employed in the Nicene-Constantinopolitan Creed from the fourth century. That is, Jesus Christ is of "one substance" with the Father. In other words, Christ is of the very same nature as the Father, a nature that is divine. This means, of course, that all the divinity-describing characteristics such as eternity, for example, that pertain to the Almighty pertain to Christ as well, to the Word who has become flesh. Indeed, in his *Notes on the New Testament* Wesley affirmed that not only is Christ the Word made flesh but he is also "supreme, eternal, [and] independent."[5] Beyond this, John Wesley included a stanza from a hymn, which his brother, Samuel, Jr. had worked with as well, in his sermon, "On Eternity," that states this truth remarkably well:

> Hail, God the Son, with glory crown'd
> When time shall cease to be;
> Throned with the Father through the round
> Of whole eternity![6]

So then, contrary to what the ancient heretic Arius had taught in the fourth century, in other words, that there was a time when the Word was not, John Wesley heartily declared the eternity of the Word that was with God, as the Gospel of John clearly states, before all things were made. Again in his sermon, "Spiritual Worship," Wesley noted that the inspired writers of the Bible gave Christ "all the titles of the most high God."[7] They ascribed to him "all the attributes and all the works of God." Simply put, Jesus Christ is truly Immanuel, God with us.

Christ Identifies with All People

The Human Nature

Though John Wesley did not employ the specific word "incarnation" often, the idea carried by this term, that the Word became flesh, was developed at length in his *Notes on the New Testament*. With respect to this theme, Wesley considered the verse Matthew 1:23: "The virgin will conceive and give birth to a son, and they will call him Immanuel" (which means 'God with us'"). Employing the variant spelling of this Hebrew word, Wesley observed in his notes on this verse that "Emmanuel; . . . was no common name of Christ, but points out his nature and office; as he is God incarnate, and dwells by his Spirit in the hearts of his people."[8] Moreover, in his reflections on this same verse, Wesley made the connection to a crucial passage from the Old Testament, to the Book of Isaiah, in particular, that reads as follows: "For to us a child is born, to us a son is given, and the government will be on his shoulders. And he will be called Wonderful Counselor, Mighty God,

The Human Nature

Everlasting Father, Prince of Peace" (Isaiah 9:6). Here, in other words, in this passage is the relation drawn between the birth of a child and being called the "Mighty God," a relation that opens up and illuminates the material from Matthew. In a similar fashion, Charles Wesley made the connection between Christ, the incarnation, and the Great I Am in the following stanza underscoring the identity of the One who became flesh:

> Glory be to God on high, and peace on earth descend
> God comes down, he bows the sky, and shows himself our friend
> God th'in visible appears, God the blest, the great I AM
> sojourns in this vale of tears, and Jesus is His name[9]

Viewed from one perspective, the incarnation entails a movement, a descent, from the glorious form of the divine (which yet breaks through at the transfiguration, Matthew 17:2) to the humble form of a servant, being a true human being, that is, a man who was open to the full range of human suffering as he walked the earth. In his commentary on Philippians 2:7, for instance, Wesley explained: "He was content to forego the glories of the Creator, and to appear in the form of a creature; nay, to be made in the likeness of the fallen creatures; and not only to share the disgrace, but to suffer the punishment, due to the meanest and vilest among them all."[10]

That the Word has become flesh and is truly human reveals that the Most High did not remain in the starry heavens, so to speak, aloof, untouched by the tragedies of life. The Word after all became flesh, and though he was innocent, he was yet subject to all the evil that would be done to him by others, by sinful human beings. Beyond this, Christ was hungry, tired, thirsty, and at times lonely. He experienced the vagaries of life as well as the broad range of human emotions. And he was spared neither grievous physical and emotional suffering (as underscored below) nor the anguish of death. In these ways, at the lowest depths of the incarnation, which Wesley repeatedly affirmed in his publications, the clear and unequivocal human nature of Christ was resoundingly affirmed especially in the midst of suffering. Jesus was a true human being in every way but for sin.

> Didst thou not in our flesh appear,
> And live and die below
> That I may now perceive thee near,
> And my Redeemer know?[11]

Wesley, however, not only distinguished the divine and human natures of Christ in a manner that clearly resonates with Scripture, but he also affirmed in a very vigorous way the *unity* of the person of Christ. In other words, though Christ is truly human, he is not merely human. This emphasis on the unity of the person of Christ, that he therefore deserves a recognition and an honor not accorded to other human beings, may lead some to conclude that Wesley did not, after all, take the human nature of Christ seriously or fully into account.[12] Indeed, some may be offended by Wesley's habit of balking at using the word "Dear," for example, or other "fondling kinds of expression,"[13] in terms of Christ because such words smacked of a familiarity that Wesley deemed inappropriate. Indeed, he called such an approach, "Knowing Christ After the Flesh," which is also the title of a sermon on this very topic. Simply put, the humanity of Christ though real is never alone. It is always in relation to the divine nature, a divinity and therefore an honor that must ever be taken into account with respect to the one person of Jesus Christ. Charles Wesley expressed this truth well in the following:

> God in this dark vale of tears
> A man of griefs was seen;
> Here for three and thirty years
> He dwelt with sinful men.
> Did they know the Deity?
> Did they own him, who he was?[14]

The Non-Mediatorial Activity of Christ

The section heading above may seem like a mouthful of words and therefore somewhat perplexing but the idea that this heading expresses is actually easily understood. Since Christ is truly divine then the working of the Son of God was something that was happening well before the foundation of the world. To illustrate, the Son of God was involved in the very creation of the world as recorded in several passages from the New Testament. In terms of John 1:3, for example, John Wesley pointed out that all things "were made by the Word."[15] And with respect to the following verse, John 1:4, Wesley added that Christ "was the foundation of life to every living thing, as well as of being to all that is."[16] Indeed, so intricately involved was the Word of God in the creation of the world that Wesley declared it was the Word that pronounced the very words "Let there be light; and there was light." as recorded in Genesis 1:3. In other words, "He is the Word whom the Father begat or spoke from eternity; by whom the Father speaking, maketh all things."[17]

The Word of God, however, does not simply create, bringing into being that which was not, but he also *sustains and preserves* that which has been made. To illustrate, in his sermon, "Spiritual Worship," drafted in 1780, Wesley lifted up Romans 11:36 and explained: "'Of him, and through him, and to him, are all things:' Of him, as the Creator, — through him, as the Sustainer and Preserver, — and to him, as the ultimate End of all."[18] In other words, as truly divine and eternal, the Word of God is "the Supporter of all the things that he hath made. He beareth, upholdeth, sustaineth, all created things by the word of his power, by the same powerful word which brought them out of nothing."[19] Indeed, so great is the role of the Word of God in terms of sustaining and preserving that every being, whether acknowledged or not, is dependent for its existence upon Christ. Wesley explained in this same sermon:

> He is now the life of everything that lives, in any kind or degree. He is the Source of the lowest species of life, that of vegetables, as being the Source of all the motion on which vegetation depends. He is the Fountain of the life of animals; the Power by which the heart beats, and the circulating juices flow. He is the Fountain of all the life which man possesses in common with other animals.
>
> And if we distinguish the rational from the animal life, he is the Source of this also;[20]

The Creator and Sustainer of all things will also become the Governor, knowing what paths will lead to holiness and happiness for those created in the image and likeness of God. Conformity to the will of God, who is utterly good, will therefore lead to bliss.

The Mediatorial Activity of Christ

The mediatorial activity of Christ is a reflection of his two natures as both truly human and truly divine. Since this twofold nature is the case *uniquely* in terms of the person of Christ, then he alone of all other human beings is the One who can mediate the despoiled relationship, the wide alienation, between God and humanity, due to sin. Moreover, such mediatorial activity must be seen broadly in terms of the active ministry of Jesus on the earth as he proclaimed the kingdom of God, healed the sick, cast out demons and raised the dead. At times Wesley referred to this labor as the "active righteousness" of Christ as in his landmark sermon, "The Lord Our Righteousness."[21] But there is more. Christ not only had a very active prophetic ministry serving others, but he also suffered grievously at the hands of evil people in what can be termed a passive ministry or what Wesley referred to as the "passive righteousness of Christ,"[22] his priestly role, that was expressed for all the world to see, in the midst of torture, mocking and shame, at Golgotha. Charles Wesley expressed this so ably in poetic form:

> Who can sound the depths unknown
> Of thy redeeming grace?
> Grace that gave thine only Son
> To save a ruined race!
> Millions of transgressors poor
> Thou hast for Jesu's sake forgiven,
> Made them of thy favour sure,
> And snatched from hell to heaven.[23]

The active ministry of Jesus while he was on the earth can be understood in two keys ways. First of all, the very coming of Christ must be recognized as the sheer gift that it is: "For God so loved the world that he gave his one and only Son, that whoever believes in him shall not perish but have eternal life" (John 3:16). In a couple of places in his writings John Wesley underscored the giftedness entailed here, in other words, that God the Father, gave the precious gift of the Son precisely because the Most High, given the divine nature, loves all human beings. "It pleased God," Wesley exclaimed, "to give his only-begotten Son to take our nature upon him, to be 'found in fashion as a man. . . .'"[24] So marvelous is this gift, given at such great cost, that Wesley paraphrased the appropriate Scripture text, drawn from the Book of Hebrews, in order to highlight this grand truth: "This is that great salvation foretold by the angel before God brought his first-begotten into the world."[25]

Second, the coming of the gift of the Son marks an illumination, an enduring light, that shines upon all people. Wesley's favorite text that illustrates these two basic truths is none other than John 1:9 that reads as follows: "The true light that gives light to everyone was coming into the world." Given the divine nature, which is utterly good, not intermingled with evil at all, the coming of Christ also naturally marks a standard in terms of moral goodness that reveals evil for what it is. Wesley explained: "In the fullness of time, when iniquity of every kind, when ungodliness and unrighteousness had spread over all nations, and covered the earth as a flood; it pleased God to lift up a standard against it, by 'bringing his first-begotten into the world.'"[26] Notice also that such an illumination is given to all people not simply to Christians or to any other theists. The gift of the Son, the coming of Christ, then changes human history forever because such an illumination cannot be denied. In other words, it cannot be pretended that such a light was never offered. What is done with that light, however, is another matter.

The Offices of Christ

For the sake of clarity and a deeper understanding, it is best to explore the ministry of Christ, especially in terms of his mediatorial activity, in terms of three roles or offices, that is, in terms of his being a prophet, priest and king. This is precisely John Wesley's approach as revealed in his *Letter to a Roman Catholic* in which he observed:

> I believe that Jesus of Nazareth was the Saviour of the world, the Messiah so long foretold; that, being anointed with the Holy Ghost, he was a Prophet, revealing to us the whole will of God; that he was a Priest, who gave himself a sacrifice for sin, and still makes intercession for transgressors; that he is a King, who has all power in heaven and in earth, and will reign till he has subdued all things to himself.[27]

Given the importance of these offices, it will be helpful to consider each one of these in turn and at length.

Prophet

As the Messiah, the Anointed One, Jesus proclaimed the Word of God to the people. In a more particular fashion, he taught the wisdom that comes from on high, a genuine gift to humanity, in his Sermon on the Mount. The substance of Christ's teaching in this setting, was none other than the moral law that Wesley specifically identified as "the way to heaven,"[28] in his sermon "Upon Our Lord's Sermon on the Mount, Discourse the First." This sermon, then, is of special importance in displaying the prophetic office of Christ, with its teaching and proclamation, because Wesley's larger purpose in producing his entire collection of *Sermons on Several Occasions* in the first place was none other than to show "the way to heaven, with a view to distinguish this way of God from all those which are the inventions of men."[29]

The love of God for all of humanity, since Jesus taught the multitudes on the mount, as the Gospel of Matthew reveals, is evident in the gift of this teaching that illuminates the path towards wisdom, the love of God, and therefore towards human thriving. Wesley exclaimed, "He [Christ] is teaching us the true way to life everlasting, the royal way which leads to the kingdom. And the only true way; for there is none besides—all other paths lead to destruction."[30] Again this law is the very substance of wisdom because it is intimately connected to the nature of Christ, his divine being, since this law was "never so fully explained, nor so thoroughly understood, till the great Author of it himself," Wesley observed, "condescended to give mankind this authentic comment on all the essential branches of it."[31] Charles Wesley sung this truth in the following way:

> Prophet, to me reveal
> Thy Father's perfect will:
> Never mortal spake like thee,
> Human prophet like divine;
> Loud and strong their voices be,
> Small, and still, and inward thine![32]

So important was the nature of this moral law proclaimed by Christ on the Sermon on the Mount, whose Old Testament expression was the Ten Commandments, that Wesley spent considerable time and effort exploring it in several sermons. This law, which is not to be confused with the ceremonial law or the Mosaic dispensation,[33] is "an incorruptible picture of the high and holy One that inhabiteth eternity."[34] Indeed, in his sermon, "The Original, Nature, Properties and Use of the Law," drafted in 1750, Wesley outlined the essence, the nature of this law as proclaimed by Christ in a prophetic way, in terms of all of the following characteristics:

- It is the face of God unveiled[35]
- It is the heart of God disclosed to man[36]
- It is . . . the express image of his person[37]

The Offices of Christ

- The law of God is all virtues in one[38]
- What is the law but divine virtue and wisdom assuming a visible form?[39]
- What is it but the original ideas of truth and good, which were lodged in the uncreated mind from eternity[40]
- it is supreme, unchangeable reason; it is unalterable rectitude[41]
- it is the everlasting fitness of all things that are or ever were created.[42]
- The law of God . . . is a copy of the eternal mind, a transcript of the divine nature[43]
- Yea, it is the fairest offspring of the everlasting Father, the brightest efflux of his essential wisdom, the visible beauty of the Most High[44]

The last characteristic of the moral law as being "the fairest offspring of the everlasting Father," caused Deschner to question, "Is Christ the only begotten of the Father?"[45] However, all of the characteristics above, including the last, demonstrate once again that there is no variance between the being of God, the divine nature, which has a Christological expression of course, and the express will of the Most High as displayed in the nature and *form* of the moral law.

Priest

The priestly office of Christ, especially in terms of mediation, making atonement and intercession, is illuminated by a consideration of the person of Christ in his twofold nature. In other words, since God and humanity are alienated from each other due to human rebellion and sin, then it is precisely the God/Human who can overcome this divide. From God's side of the relationship, divine wrath bars the way. In particular, the Almighty takes holiness, justice and the moral order, reflective of the divine being and goodness, very seriously. How could God do otherwise? Accordingly, without the mediation and atonement that must take place first, the sinner would experience God not as a comforting savior but as a consuming fire. As the Book of Hebrews states: "It is a dreadful thing to fall into the hands of the living God," (Hebrews 10:31), or what Wesley, himself, referred to as God's "avenging justice."[46] From the human-ward side of things, however, the relationship is despoiled by sin in the form of indifference, stubborn independence, anger, fear and perhaps even hatred of God. Given this painful reality, how could human beings ever love the Most High and enjoy the very presence of God's Spirit in their lives, a communion and fellowship for which they have been made? For both sides of the relationship, then, a mediator is necessary, someone who is both divine and human, in other words, one who is not a part of the problem. Indeed, it is Jesus Christ alone, as Charles Wesley clearly recognized, that can calm the fears of sinners:

> Jesus the name that charms our fears,
> That bids our sorrows cease;
> 'Tis music in the sinner's ears,
> 'Tis life, and health, and peace.[47]

A Question of Frameworks

When John Wesley considered the work of the mediator, Jesus Christ, to bring about at-one-ment between God and humanity, he employed two larger frameworks, not one, to illustrate how the mediating work of the priestly office of Christ would play out over the entire course of a redeemed life. The first framework considers the atoning work of Christ not only in terms of holiness, the moral law as well as the justice of God, as just noted briefly above, but also in light of, at least in some sense, the additional roles of Christ as both a Governor and Judge, roles that cannot be separated from who he is in the unity of his person and as the holy and incarnate Word. Accordingly, in this larger framework Wesley focused on the Godward side of things, once more, in which holiness, the moral law, and justice were preeminent. To illustrate, in describing the speaker at the Sermon on the Mount, for example, Wesley wrote:

> Let us observe, who it is that is here speaking, that we may take heed how we hear. It is the Lord of heaven and earth, the Creator of all; who, as such, has a right to dispose of all his creatures; the Lord our Governor, whose kingdom is from everlasting, and ruleth over all; the great Lawgiver, who can well enforce all his laws, being "able to save and to destroy," yea, to punish with "everlasting destruction from his presence and from the glory of his power."[48]

John Lawson in his excellent book, *The Wesley Hymns as a Guide to Scriptural Teaching*, has taken the Godward side of things into account and has argued if atonement is ever to occur, that is, if God and humanity are to be reconciled, then other considerations simply must be factored in as John Wesley himself had affirmed. Lawson explained:

> God is the moral Governor of the human race, and cannot exercise free forgiveness in such a way as to allow men and women to suppose that sin is merely condoned. It is wholly for the good of mankind that the moral law should be fully upheld by due punishment for sin, and by due submission made to God. Therefore the wrath of God must be satisfied.[49]

Viewed in another—very pungent though honest—way, sinners are in rebellion through sin and disobedience against a God of holy love who, given the very goodness of the divine nature, must call them into account.

This first large framework, as important as it is in the context of atonement, is not however enough. In fact, Wesley employed a second major framework in which human beings were viewed principally not so much as rebellious, guilty sinners (though they remained that) but as diseased, sick souls, who were therefore in need not of the ministrations of a Governor and Righteous Judge even though such roles were, in some sense, the backdrop for Christ's priestly efforts, but they were in need of a Great Physician who would heal their sin-sick souls. The classic text for this second larger framework is found in the *Preface* to Wesley's very large treatise on the doctrine of original sin:

> And who might not say, upon this supposition, 'I can't see that we have much need of Christianity.' Nay, not at all, for 'They that are whole have no need of a physician.' And the Christian Revelation speaks of nothing else but the great "Physician" of our souls; nor can Christian Philosophy, whatever be thought of the Pagan, be more properly defined than in Plato's word: It is *therapeia psuches*, "the only true method of healing a distempered soul." But what need of this, if we are in perfect health? If we are not diseased, we do not want a cure. If we are not sick, why should we seek for a medicine to heal our sickness?[50]

If Wesley had simply employed this second framework to explore the atoning work of Christ, which focuses on the human-ward side of things, that is, overcoming human resistance to the reception of God's love, then justice,

5. Christ Identifies with All People

the moral order, as well as the divine goodness, radiant in its glory, would not be sufficiently taken into account. Ever balanced in his practical theology, Wesley weaved both large frameworks, a juridical and a therapeutic one, in his overall view on the atoning work of Christ. In fact, Wesley took up the first framework of holiness, justice and an ongoing moral order, the Godward side of things, through exploring two key theories of the atonement: the satisfaction theory and the penal substitution theory. He took up the second framework of grace and favor as Christ the Great Physician addressed the human-ward side of things by offering the healing balm of salvation. This last emphasis is evident in what some have called the moral influence theory of the atonement. In light of this, it will be helpful to explore the priestly role of Christ in general, and his atoning work in particular, in terms of these three major theories of the atonement, a task that will be taken up in the following chapter.

6. Christ Died for All People

*"For God so loved the world
that he gave his one and only Son,
that whoever believes in him shall not perish
but have eternal life." (John 3:16)*

The preceding chapter left off at the exploration of the priestly work of Christ in general in reconciling both God and humanity, and in particular in terms of what three major theories of the atonement, developed throughout the rich history of the church, are helpful in illuminating much of what John Wesley had written about the reuniting work of Christ. After each one of these three theories or models is carefully considered, this current chapter will conclude in reflecting on the third major role of Jesus, namely, Christ the King, a role that in a real sense is the culmination of both the prophetic and priestly roles.

Atonement as Satisfaction

In viewing the atoning work of Christ as a satisfaction, Wesley was helped in this effort through the resources of his own Anglican Church. Drawing from Thomas Cranmer's *Homily on Salvation*, Wesley reproduced the substance of this teaching, as it related to satisfaction, and with some editing along the way, such that it surfaced in his landmark sermon, "The Lord Our Righteousness," as follows: "These things must necessarily go together in our justification: upon God's part his great mercy and grace, upon Christ's part the satisfaction of God's justice and on our part faith in the merits of [Jesus] Christ.["][1]

So important was the satisfaction of divine justice as well as upholding the integrity of the moral order that was itself a reflection of the divine goodness and being, that when Wesley composed the Articles of Religion for the American Methodists, Article XX was a verbatim quotation of the earlier

Church of England Article that reads, in part, as follows: "The Offering of Christ once made is that perfect redemption, propitiation, and satisfaction, for all the sins of the whole world, both original and actual; and there is none other satisfaction for sin, but that alone."[2]

The language of satisfaction actually goes back to the eleventh century when Anselm of Canterbury employed it in this medieval setting with respect to the satisfaction of the divine honor. This Italian, Benedictine monk developed his theory of the atonement at considerable length in his book *Cur Deus Homo* (Why God Became Human), and he made the case why a divine/human mediator was necessary in order for atonement and reconciliation to occur.

The late Harald Lindstrom affirmed the prominence of the satisfaction theory in Wesley's writings and maintained that "the legal order and the judicial system emerge as the governing principle."[3] In other words, the atoning work of Christ satisfies the justice of God. Charles Wesley expressed this truth as well in the following stanza.

> For me I now believe he died;
> He made my every crime his own;
> Fully for me he satisfied;
> Father, well-pleased behold thy Son![4]

Christ Bore the Punishment for All People

Atonement as Penal Substitution

Towards the end of 1739 a number of people who were deeply convinced of their sins approached John Wesley and asked if he might pray with them. They also wanted his advice on how to "flee the wrath to come."[5] In fact, the only requirement that Wesley, himself, held up to become a Methodist was this very desire to flee the wrath of God. Afterwards, of course, as people entered the life of Methodism they became members of a class meeting, and they were then introduced to the Rules of the United Societies. At any rate, the wrath of God as well as divine justice were two themes very prominent in the early life of Methodism, and Wesley wrote about such painful realities often. For example, in a letter drafted to William Law in 1756, Wesley understood the difficulty of factoring in the wrath of God in his overall theology but insisted upon this very thing nevertheless. He declared, "As nothing is more frequently or more expressly declared in Scripture than God's anger at sin and His punishing it both temporally and eternally. . . ."[6] In fact, Wesley was very critical of a whole group of preachers whom he called the "promise-mongers,"[7] that is, everyone who "deals in the promises only, without ever showing the terrors of the law; that slides over 'the wrath of God revealed from heaven against all ungodliness and unrighteousness,' and endeavours to heal those that never were wounded."[8] What was Wesley's judgment here? He concluded, "These promise-mongers are no Gospel Ministers."[9]

Beyond this, late in his career, in 1778, Wesley wrote to Mary Bishop, recalled the earlier conversation he had had with William Law, and counseled her in the following manner:

> Although, therefore, I do not term God, as Mr. Law supposes, 'a wrathful Being,' which conveys a wrong idea; yet I firmly believe He was angry with all mankind, and that He was reconciled to them by the death of His Son. And I know He was angry with me till I believed in the Son of His love; and yet this is no impeachment to His mercy, that He is just as well as merciful.[10]

In light of this preceding evidence, and much more could be cited, John Wesley obviously acknowledged the well-developed scriptural theme of the wrath of God, interlaced throughout a number of books of the Bible, simply because in his estimation far too much was at stake not to do so. As Lawson pointed out, "The notion of the divine wrath is that God's world is a moral order, wherein penalty for sin is inevitable."[11] Indeed, Wesley had declared to William Law that "Whoever therefore denies God to be capable of wrath or anger acts consistently in denying His justice also."[12] Not to be confused with human wrath, of course, which is likely hateful and therefore sinful, divine wrath has to be understood as God's determined, unending opposition to sin and evil precisely because the Most High is both holy and good. In short, wrath is a love word, a *holy love* word. To ask for anything else then is actually to ask for less, much less. It is to ask for a god that either tolerates the committing of sin, the arising of evil, and the breaking of the moral order or else one who doesn't think these matters are of very great importance anyway. In other words it asks for a god that in the end is neither holy nor good.

Well acquainted with Scripture, with both the Old and New Testaments, Wesley was keenly aware of the moral order displayed therein, expressive of the holiness, justice and goodness of God, as well as of the penalties executed by the Almighty as a rightful and just punishment when this order is transgressed. Recall the early chapters of Genesis in which human sin and rebellion were met with the undeniable punishment of death. Bear in mind the structure of this biblical material expressed earlier:

$$\text{Sin} \rightarrow \text{Punishment} \rightarrow \text{Death}$$

Moreover, when Isaiah considered this ongoing theme in his own work, the central problem of humanity, he highlighted the role of the Messiah as the one who was not only a sin-bearer but one who also bore the punishment "that brought us peace." Isaiah exclaimed:

> Surely he took up our pain and bore our suffering, yet we considered him punished by God, stricken by him, and afflicted. But he was pierced for our transgressions, he was crushed for our iniquities; the punishment that brought us peace was on him, and by his wounds we are healed (Isaiah 53:4-5).

Wesley's notes on this passage above are highly instructive, a key to his very balanced theology. He explained: "Those punishments by which our peace, our reconciliation to God, was to be purchased, were laid upon him by God's justice with his own consent."[13] Elsewhere in his treatise on original sin Wesley reflected upon this same passage in the following way: "Our sins were the procuring cause of all his sufferings. His sufferings were the penal effects of our sins. 'The chastisement of our peace,' the punishment necessary to procure it, 'was' laid 'on him,' freely submitting thereto. . . ."[14] In other words, Christ bore the penalties, the punishments, due to sinners because of their rebellion against a holy God and a just moral order, an order that is never cancelled but is ongoing, as is clearly evident in Christ's own Sermon on the Mount. Charles Wesley, for his part, expressed this truth in the following way:

> Is crucified for me and you,
> To bring us rebels back to God;
> Believe, believe the record true,
> Ye all are bought with Jesu's blood:
> Pardon for all flows from his side:
> My Lord, my Love is crucified.[15]

Beyond this, when John Wesley considered the truth of 1 Peter 2:24, "He himself bore our sins" in his body on the cross, so that we might die to sins and live for righteousness; by his wounds you have been healed," he understood this passage in a way that reveals once again that Christ bore the punishment due to sinners, in other words, that he stood in their place, bore their burden, and received their just penalty as a sin bearer, as the Messiah. Commenting on the particular phrase, "Who himself bore our sins" (1 Peter 2:24), Wesley wrote, "That is, the punishment due to them."[16] Simply put, the theory of the atonement expressed here is none other than penal substitution in which the penalty of sin falls upon the Redeemer who as a true human being stands in the place of sinners. The words of a hymn composed by Charles and John Wesley help to develop this theme as well:

> All ye that pass by,
> To Jesus draw nigh:
> To you is it nothing that Jesus should die?
> Your ransom and peace,
> Your surety he is:
> Come, see if there ever was sorrow like his.
>
> For what you have done
> His blood must atone:
> The Father hath punished for you his dear Son.
> The Lord, in the day
> Of his anger, did lay
> Your sins on the Lamb, and he bore them away.
>
> My pardon I claim;
> For a sinner I am,
> A sinner believing in Jesus's name.
> He purchased the grace
> Which now I embrace:
> O Father, thou know'st he hath died in my place.[17]

It may be that in recent reassessments of the atoning work of Christ (and no particular scholar is identified here), the therapeutic framework of Christ, as the Great Physician, is mistakenly applied to the entire length of the order of salvation, that is, to sinners who are steeped in their sins, animated in their rebellion, and therefore unreconciled to a God of holy love. Indeed, the therapeutic framework drives out the issue of punishment, rendering it unnecessary, even offensive. However, if these sinners are simply deemed to be sick souls in need of a physician, in other words, if this is all that is in view, then the holiness, justice and goodness of God have all, once again, been ignored as if they didn't matter! Who punishes the sick? Who rebukes or condemns those who have gotten ill? Who judges the infected? And who, by the way, kills their Great Physician during the visit?

Such a problematic approach is not only an inappropriate use of a very helpful framework, as properly applied elsewhere, but it also leaves in its wake a number of troubling questions, one of which is: why does the Great Physician have to be sacrificed at all? It makes little sense because the framework of the Great Physician, in which salvation is *therapia psyches*, relates largely, though not exclusively, to the process of healing that takes place at conversion (and afterwards) when sinners are forgiven their sins (a moral act) and become holy for the first time. So understood, the ongoing process of redemption, of becoming increasingly holy, plays out as the Great Physician applies the medicines of salvation to the faithful and willing soul—or to the sinner who has now had enough guilt and bondage in life, and therefore willingly receives by faith both Christ and his benefit.

Moreover, if sacrifice is all that matters, to the exclusion of any consideration of punishment, then why the cross at all with its torture, mocking and shame? Indeed, the passion of Christ in the form of abject pain and suffering, both physical and psychological, both emotional and spiritual, seems like such an unnecessary and unwarranted excess, a degrading, pain-filled extravagance. Why couldn't Christ, in the larger providence of God the Father, have simply been sacrificed in the manner of the Levitical sacrifices: that is, with a slitting of the throat, quickly bleeding out, and then sudden death? Again, if sacrifice is all that is necessary in the atoning work of Christ then such a quick and relatively painless approach would supposedly get the job done— or would it? It is a truism that all people suffer at least at some point in their lives. Is there a sense, however, clearly attested to in Scripture, that the suffering of Christ is *unique*, emblematic of who he is as both divine and human, as the one and only Mediator? Indeed, the sacrifice-only view of the atonement refuses to see the many ways in which Christ actually suffered, in all of its many dimensions, with punishment included. Such a view is therefore not mindful of either the depths of being treated as sin, a genuine sin bearer, or the horrors, the harrowing experience, of a judgment painfully borne. Recall the words of Isaiah cited earlier and now repeated for emphasis: "Surely he took up our pain and bore our suffering, yet we considered him punished by

God, stricken by him, and afflicted. But he was pierced for our transgressions, he was crushed for our iniquities; the punishment that brought us peace was on him, and by his wounds we are healed" (Isa. 53:4-5).

In light of the preceding, what Wesley was simply unwilling to do was to abandon the penal framework especially when the evil of both sin and of sinners themselves was clearly in view. Such an abandonment would be ill advised. It would represent the application of the therapeutic model in areas where it simply does not belong. In short, it would fail to recognize some of the deeper, more poignant, ways in which Christ actually suffered. Robbing Christ of measures of his suffering, it would also, in some sense, rob him of measures of his glory.

Christ Died for All People

Atonement as Moral Influence

Reconciliation entails the coming together of two parties not one. The atoning, mediatorial work of Christ then not only satisfies the righteous justice of God, the Godward side of things, but it also overcomes the alienation, division and separation from the human-ward side in a magnificent display of uncanny, humble, sacrificial love, the kind of love that can melt the stony hearts of rebellious sinners. Indeed, those so transformed by grace now marvel at what God the Father has done in offering the gift of his only begotten Son, Jesus Christ, at Calvary. The Almighty has been generous at every turn.

The often-quoted verse that expresses not only the resplendent love of God the Father but also that of the Son of God who died for the sins of the whole world is none other than John 3:16: "For God so loved the world that he gave his one and only Son, that whoever believes in him shall not perish but have eternal life." Wesley's notes on this passage drive home the clear biblical truth that God's love of the world entails, "all men under heaven, even those that despise his love."[18] God's love is universal and embracing. Such a love bespeaks, once again, of who God is in terms of nature, essence and being. Love is God's darling attribute. Wesley, of course, had not forgotten.

Moreover, and this must not be missed, the Father gives the gift of the Son, knowing of course, precisely what such giving entails. Likewise the Son, out of his love of humanity, consents to such giving in utter harmony with the love and will of the Father: "This is love: not that we loved God, but that he loved us and sent his Son as an atoning sacrifice for our sins" (1 John 4:10). As Wesley, himself, put it, out of the Father's love for humanity, "God imputes our sins, or the guilt of them, to Christ. He consented to be responsible for them, to suffer the punishment due for them."[19] Again, the Father gave his only Son "truly and seriously,"[20] and the Son in turn gave himself, "truly and seriously."[21] Put another way, the Father and the Son took upon themselves, though in different ways, the enormous burden of sin and its cost, such that the Son as given by the Father was treated as sin and descended to the very depths, where darkness and alienation threatened—and all of this out of humble, sacrificial love. How greatly have both the Father and the Son loved humanity—and at what great cost! The recognition of such a holy love, resplendent in its power, caused John Wesley to respond in doxological praise:

> What manner of love is this wherewith the only begotten Son of God hath loved us so as to empty himself, as far as possible, of his eternal Godhead; as to divest himself of that glory which he had with the Father before the world began; as to take upon him the form of a servant, being found in fashion as a man; and then, to humble himself still further, "being obedient unto death, even the death of the cross!"[22]

Simply put, the cost of the Father's giving is unfathomable; the cost of the Son's consent is unmeasurable. Forgiveness then is free for humanity, lavish in its offering, though costly for God. This is how both justice and mercy play out in John Wesley's practical theology. God bears the punishments of justice; humanity is offered the sweetness of reconciliation and mercy. In short, here is a theology well-poised for thanksgiving and praise, for the glorification of the One who bore such a great cost precisely because God has so loved the world.

> Father, God, thy love we praise
> Which gave thy Son to die;
> Jesus, full of truth and grace,
> Alike we glorify;
> Spirit, Comforter divine,
> Praise by all to thee be given,
> Till we in full chorus join,
> And earth is turned to heaven.[23]

Happy Fault

If sinners could get a glimpse, even a small measure, of the kind of love of God displayed at Calvary, as well as the cost of reconciliation to God, then their opposition and rebellion against the very holiness of the Most High might melt way in powerful, human-ward consequences that could lead to a lasting transformation of both heart and mind. These subjective affects, for want of better language, look like the moral influences that Abelard described in his own theory of the atonement during the twelfth century. Viewed in another way, if Adam had not fallen then Christ would not have died with the result that humanity could never have known the height, depth and breadth of the love of God for humanity manifested in the passion of Christ at Golgotha, especially in terms of all that Christ bore. Simply put, they could not marvel at what they had never witnessed. In his sermon, "On God's Love to Fallen Man," Wesley described this "happy fault" (the Latin is *felix culpa*) that would not have come about if Adam had not fallen:

> So there would have been no room for that amazing display of the Son of God's love to mankind: There would have been no occasion for his being "obedient unto death, even the death of the cross." It could not then have been said, to the astonishment of all the hosts of heaven, "God so loved the world," yea, the ungodly world, which had no thought or desire of returning to him, "that he gave his Son" out of his bosom, his only-begotten Son, "to the end that whosoever believeth on him should not perish, but have everlasting life." Neither could we then have said, "God was in Christ reconciling the world to himself;" or, that he "made him to be sin," that is, a sin-offering, "for us, who knew no sin, that we might be made the righteousness of God through him." There would have been no such occasion for such "an Advocate with the Father," as "Jesus Christ the righteous;" neither for his appearing "at the right hand of God, to make intercession for us."[24]

One of the human-ward consequences of such an "amazing display of the Son of God's love,"[25] was the grace-empowered obligation now to love both the neighbor and the stranger as God has loved all of humanity in Jesus Christ. Wesley explained, "If God so loved us, how ought we to love one another! But this motive to brotherly love had been totally wanting if Adam had not fallen."[26] To insure that his point had been made abundantly clear Wesley continued: "Consequently, we could not then have loved one another in so high a degree as we may now. Nor could there have been that height and depth in the command of our blessed Lord, 'As I have loved you, so love one another.'"²⁷ In other words, the magnificent display of humble, sacrificial love at Calvary was not only an invitation to know God in a new way in which the vaunted characteristics of sinful pride, often mistakenly attributed to God, would be thrown off, but it was also an encouragement to love the neighbor, "the other," in a whole new fashion, animated by God's grace, love and mercy manifested in Jesus Christ. In the holy flame of such a divine revelation at the cross, the path of a distinctively Christian love was illuminated, and for Wesley there was nothing like it. Adam's fall then was a happy fault indeed. In the larger providence of God it became nothing less than an engine for love, the richest love imaginable. Charles Wesley expressed all of this so beautifully in a pithy verse:

> O Love divine! What hast thou done!
> Th'immortal God hath died for me!
> Bore all my sins upon the tree:
> Th'immortal God for me hath died,
> My Lord, my Love is crucified.²⁸

King

The last of the offices of Jesus, the Messiah, is that of king. This regal role indicates, first of all, the continuity of the moral law, and the order that it reflects, even after atonement has been made. In other words, the moral framework, expressive of the goodness of God, once again continues. In his sermon, "The Law Established Through Faith, Discourse II, composed in 1750, Wesley explains: "[Jesus is] a King forever; as giving laws to all whom he has brought with his blood; as restoring those to the image of God whom he had first reinstated in his favor; as reigning in all believing hearts until he has subdued all things to; until he hath utterly cast out all sin, and brought in everlasting righteousness."²⁹ So then, the proclamation of the moral law by the King, even after his blood had been spilled, is an instance of the very goodness of God who gives this great gift, "a copy of the eternal mind,"³⁰ full of wisdom and light, to all of the redeemed.

Second, the "principal role of Christ's royal work, that of victory,"³¹ Wesley maintained, entails overcoming the evils that plague humanity. Just what are those evils? They are none other than Satan, sin and death, the evil triad, that are all conquered by the power of Christ's death and triumphant resurrection. But there is more. Christ's victory at Calvary not only issues in "conquering death by the power of his resurrection,"[32] but it also results in "destroying death's fearful rule over the minds of believers."[33] As Wesley, himself, put it: "Every man who fears death is subject to bondage; is in a slavish, uncomfortable state."[34] But this wretched state no longer has to be the case for believers because Christ, the King, to use Wesley's own words, "delivers all true believers from this bondage."[35] The sons and daughters of God are now free, free indeed. And they are protected by no one less than the King, himself—a King who has suffered so deeply on their behalf. In the face of all of this, Charles Wesley broke forth in exuberant royal praise:

> Ye servants of God, your Master proclaim,
> and publish abroad His wonderful name;
> the name all victorious of Jesus extol,
> His kingdom is glorious and rules over all.[36]

7. The Church Is For All People

> *"Christ loved the church and gave himself up for her*
> *to make her holy, cleansing her by the washing with water through the word,*
> *and to present her to himself as a radiant church,*
> *without stain or wrinkle or any other blemish,*
> *but holy and blameless." (Ephesians 5:25b-27)*

One of the ways that Jesus Christ is still present in the world even after he had ascended into heaven is through the church which is otherwise known as the Body of Christ on earth. Indeed, at his ascension Jesus offered his followers the precious and comforting promise, "And surely I am with you always, to the very end of the age" (Matt. 28:20b). In light of this, how is the church best understood in the age of the Wesleys as well as today? For his part, John Wesley reproduced the nineteenth article of the historic Thirty-Nine Articles of the Church of England for the American Methodists in his *Sunday Service*, an article that reads as follows: "The visible Church of Christ is a Congregation of faithful men, in which the pure Word of God is preached, and the Sacraments duly administered according to Christ's Ordinance, in all those things that of necessity are requisite to the same."[1] As important as this definition is Wesley was not entirely satisfied with it.

Wesley's Definition of the Church

Given John Wesley's strong ecumenical sensibilities, in other words, his belief that the Church embraces all orthodox Christian traditions, he stated very clearly in his sermon, "Of the Church," produced late in his career, in 1785, that he would not defend the accuracy of the Anglican nineteenth article which he, himself, had reproduced![2] Knowing that such a definition emerged during the very polemical environment of the sixteenth century, Wesley recognized that by this definition "the Church of Rome is not so much as a part of the catholic church."[3] This was simply unacceptable. Making a distinction between basic doctrines and various opinions, Wesley chose a better, more generous, way: "I can easily bear with their holding wrong opinions, yea, and superstitious modes of worship: Nor would I, on these accounts, scruple still to include them within the pale of the catholic Church;"[4]

Wesley's well-worked definition of the church evident throughout his writings was both accurate (including all those who should be included) and catholic (or universal) in the best sense of that term. Again, in his sermon "Of the Church," Wesley explained:

> Here, then, is a clear unexceptionable answer to that question, "What is the Church?" The catholic or universal Church is, all the persons in the universe whom God hath so called out of the world as to entitle them to the preceding character; as to be "one body," united but "one Spirit;" having "one faith, one hope, one baptism; one God and Father of all, who is above all, and through all, and in them all.[5]

Such a definition in its emphasis on unity and oneness is emblematic of the gospel, itself, as the universal love of God manifested in Christ Jesus, which ever breaks down barriers, and in which "There is neither Jew nor Gentile, neither slave nor free, nor is there male and female, for you are all one in Christ Jesus" (Gal. 3:28). Having its unity in Christ, who transcends all, the church cannot be exclusively identified with any tribe, nation, language, or "chosen" people. All are welcomed to become a part of that body which is greater than themselves or the groups in which they participate. Bear in mind that the problem back in Genesis 1-3 was universal; the solution offered by Almighty God through the Son is universal as well.

Moreover, when Wesley described the first century New Testament Church in his *NT Notes* a few other characteristics emerged that illuminate the nature of the Body of Christ in the world: Wesley pointed out: "[The New Testament Church] is "a company of men, called by the Gospel, grafted into Christ by baptism, animated by love, united by all kind of fellowship, and disciplined by the death of Ananias and Sapphira."[6] To be called, grafted, animated, united and disciplined, all of these action words make up the rhythms of life in the church, this distinct way of being in the world, though not a part of it. Charles Wesley expressed this well in the following stanza:

> Happy the souls to Jesus joined,

And saved by grace alone;
Walking in all his ways, they find
Their heaven on earth begun.

The church triumphant in thy love,
Their mighty joys we know;
They sing the Lamb in hymns above:
And we in hymns below.[7]

The Word Rightly Preached

Though John Wesley was obviously not entirely comfortable with the definition of the church found in the Anglican Thirty-Nine Articles, he nevertheless, of course, underscored the importance of preaching as well as the administration of the sacraments in the life of the church. In terms of preaching, Wesley believed that the best approach was "To invite. (2.) To convince. (3.) To offer Christ. (4.) To build up; and to do this in some measure in every sermon."[8] Just what these first two steps of inviting and convincing entailed was revealed in a letter drafted in 1751 in which Wesley opined: 'I think the right method of preaching is this. At our first beginning to preach at any place, after a general declaration of the love of God to sinners and His willingness that they should be saved, to preach the law in the strongest, the closest the most searching manner possible; only intermixing the gospel here and there, and showing it, as it were, afar off."[9] Moreover, to offer Christ to the congregation, the third step, entailed preaching him in all of his offices, as prophet, priest and king, and to declare both the law and the gospel in a very balanced way. In all of this the church would be built up and edified to the glory of God.

Though Wesley did not have the rhetorical gifts of a George Whitefield, nevertheless his preaching was often both powerful and effective as he offered the free grace of God, the gift of the Most High, to all within earshot. On one such preaching venture Wesley observed: "I declared the free grace of God to about four thousand people, from those words, "He that spared not his own Son, but delivered him up for us all, how shall he not with him also freely give us all things?" At that hour it was, that one who had long continued in sin, from a despair of finding mercy, received a full, clear sense of his pardoning love, and power to sin no more."[10]

The Sacraments Duly Administered

Baptism

As one of the two major sacraments of the church that was instituted by Christ himself, baptism as an emblem of the New Covenant entailed an outward and sensible sign, in this case the water, and an inward and spiritual grace, namely, the forgiveness of sins (justification) and renewal (the new birth). Despite these strong associations of the outward sign and inward spiritual grace, Wesley insisted that they must be distinguished in the sense that baptism, itself, is *not* the new birth (or justification for that matter) but is that sacrament, that outward sign of the church, strongly associated with it. As a good Anglican Wesley believed that the new birth always accompanies the sacrament in terms of infants, though the two elements can of course be distinguished. To illustrate, he wrote: "It is certain, our Church supposes that all who are baptized in their infancy are at the same time born again."[11]

The reception of the sacrament of baptism looks very different, however, in terms of adults. Wesley did not believe, for example, that the new birth always accompanies the sacrament in terms of adults. In other words, both men and women may come up from the baptismal waters as unregenerated as when they first went under due to either hypocrisy or insincerity. And then, of course, there was the problem of Wesley encountering so many people in England and elsewhere who had been baptized in their youth but who, like Wesley himself, had washed away that cleansing they had earlier received in the sacrament. Of his own experience Wesley wrote: "I believe, till I was about ten years old I had not sinned away that 'washing of the Holy Ghost' which was given me in baptism."[12] Of the experience of others, Wesley recognized that large state churches, such as the Church of England, often left nominal Christianity in their wake. Accordingly, he wryly pointed out on one occasion: "It must be . . . allowed that the people of England, generally speaking, have been christened or baptized. But neither can we infer: these were once baptized, therefore they are *Christians* now."[13] Given these difficult and painful realities, the subsequent ministry of the Methodists precisely to this population of adults, in other words, to the already baptized, would indeed be warranted. Charles Wesley expressed in the verses below how the triune God honors this sacrament in nothing less than divine presence:

7. The Church Is For All People

Come, Father, Son and Holy Ghost,
Honour the means ordained by thee!
Make good our apostolic boast,
And own thy glorious ministry.

We now thy promised presence claim,
Sent to disciple all mankind,
Sent to baptize into thy name,
We now thy promised presence find.[14]

The Lord's Supper

It is helpful when reading the *Sunday Service* to be attentive to its specific language as clues to the overall sacramental theology offered therein especially in terms of the Lord's Supper. To illustrate, whereas the *Book of Common Prayer* (1662 edition) used the language of priests and tables, indicating a shift that had begun in the second century church (and the early church would eventually move on to priests and altars), Wesley's language employed in the *Sunday Service* reverted back to the original first century rhetoric of both ministers (or elders) and tables. To illustrate, observe Wesley's choice of words in the opening lines of "The Order for Administration of the Lord's Supper," found in the *Sunday Service*: "And the Elder, standing at the Table, shall say the Lord's Prayer, with the Collect following, the People kneeling."[15]

However, in the Prayer Book that Wesley was using during the eighteenth century, the word "priest," not "elder" was employed.[16] Wesley, himself, then made the change from "priest" to "elder" in his own setting and for sound theological reasons. Indeed, such a shift was very intentional on Wesley's part and indicated that he wanted to avoid the theological missteps that could occur when sinful human beings were considered to be New Covenant priests. Such a role, which can be distinguished in some sense from Old Covenant, Levitical priests always entailed the act of mediation between God and humanity, a clear impossibility for anyone who is not both divine and human. With such a misunderstanding in place, in which sinful human beings would now attempt to take on the singular role of a New Covenant priest, not realizing all that was entailed, the officiant at the sacrament would then *lift up* the elements of bread and wine to the Father thereby offering Christ on behalf of the people to God. Compare this, however, with the first Lord's Supper celebrated by Christ, which was a genuine fellowship meal, in which there was no vertical lift of the elements at all but the bread and wine were distributed in a horizontal fashion to those reclining at the table. Put another way, at the first Lord's Supper, the Father gave the gift of the Son who was then offered to waiting recipients by Christ, himself, the true and only mediator ("my body which is broken for you; my blood which is shed for you), and the response of those gathered around the table, with the exception of Judas, of course, was nothing less than εὐχαριστήσας, genuine and rich thanksgiving.

Accordingly, in Wesley's eyes the priestly role pertains to Christ *alone*, since only he is both divine and human. In other words, he is the only one who is without sin and who is therefore capable of being a priest in the New Testament sense of that term. Wesley did of course affirm a more generally conceived priesthood of all believers in the sense that believers can intercede for one another through prayer and fasting, but none of them, not one, ever mediates the divine and human relationship. That's a clear impossibility for sinners. Simply put, that is a role reserved for Christ alone, the God/human, as the Book of Hebrews so clearly teaches, and as Wesley's editorial judgment affirmed.

With this clarification in place, the strong observations and judgments made in Article XX of the Methodist Articles in terms of the sacrament of the Lord's Supper can now be more readily understood and properly appreciated. It reads as follows:

> The offering of Christ, once made, is that perfect redemption, propitiation, and satisfaction for all the sins of the whole world, both original and actual; and there is none other satisfaction for sin but that alone. Wherefore the sacrifice of masses, in the which it is commonly said that the priest doth offer Christ for the quick and the dead, to have remission of pain or guilt, is a blasphemous fable and dangerous deceit.[17]

In a similar fashion, Wesley and eighteenth-century Methodism, both British and American, rejected that understanding of the sacrament that maintained that the officiant, through supposed priestly powers, reserved for himself alone (sacerdotalism) the instrumental power, in some sense, to transform the elements of the sacrament itself. In other words, through the pronouncing of the words of consecration it was thought by some that the officiant would thereby, through the grace of God, cause a change in the elements of the Supper at that *point* such that they were no longer bread and wine but utterly the body and blood of Christ, a teaching that hails from the Middle Ages, and is otherwise known as transubstantiation. The second and third paragraphs of Article XVIII of the Methodist Articles, however, offer the following necessary corrective judgments:

> Transubstantiation, or the change of the substance of bread and wine in the Supper of our Lord, cannot be proved by Holy Writ, but is repugnant to the plain words of Scripture, overthroweth the nature of a sacrament, and hath given occasion to many superstitions.
>
> The body of Christ is given, taken and eaten in the Supper *only after a heavenly and spiritual manner*. And the means whereby the body of Christ is received and eaten in the Supper is faith.[18]

In a way similar to the language of the *Book of Common Prayer*, the feeding upon Christ as reflected in the hymns of John and Charles Wesley, was taking place in the heart as evidenced in the following stanzas:

> O let us on thy fullness feed,
> And eat thy flesh, and drink thy blood;
> Jesu, thy blood is drink indeed,
> Jesu, thy flesh is angels' food.
>
> The heavenly manna faith imparts;
> Faith makes thy fullness all our own;
> We feed upon thee in our hearts,
> And find that heaven and thou are one.[19]

In these corrections pertaining to the Lord's Supper, a sacrament that had the visible signs of bread and wine indicative of inward graces, Wesley was putting aside several erroneous teachings, many of them having to do with priestcraft and the like, that not only limited the scope of the sacrament, in other words, one in effect had to be holy *first* in order to receive it, but that also failed to understand the Supper as the important means of grace that it had always been from the first century forward. Indeed, few interpreters of Wesley's sacramental theology have pointed out the radical, though enormously helpful, teaching in this area, one that even took exception to the early practice of the church (though not the earliest practice of Christ).

For his part, Wesley criticized this early practice by correctly pointing out that even the disciples at the first Lord's Supper were unconverted and had not yet received the Holy Spirit who would not, of course, be given until Jesus was glorified. To illustrate, Wesley observed in his journal: "The falsehood of the other assertion appears both from Scripture precept and example. Our Lord commanded those very men (the disciples) who were then unconverted, who had not yet 'received the Holy Ghost,' who (in the full sense of the word) were not believers, to 'do this in remembrance of him'."[20] And then Wesley added with consummate effect: "Here the precept is clear. And to these he delivered the elements with his own hands. Here is example, equally indisputable."[21]

Beyond this, Wesley maintained that the sacrament of the Lord's Supper was a converting ordinance. In other words, it was a suitable means by which a diversity of graces could be received even those that issue in justification and regeneration. In his Journal of June, 1740, Wesley, for example, affirmed: "I showed at large, (1) that the Lord's Supper was ordained by God to be a means of conveying to men either preventing or justifying, or sanctifying grace, according to their several necessities. . . ."[22] Observe that the logic here played out during the stillness controversy that had erupted at Fetter Lane, London, in November, 1739. At that time, the Moravian leader Philipp Molther and John Bray, an associate, had contended that one ought not to use any of the means of grace, including the Lord's Supper, until one had saving faith. Wesley's response to such a troubled view was that it was *precisely through such means of grace* that aspirants could receive what graces they both lacked and needed. Wesley therefore offered the following corrective in order to turn back this misunderstanding: "But experience shows the gross falsehood of that assertion that the Lord's Supper is not a converting ordinance. Ye are the witnesses. For many now present know, the very beginning of your conversion to God (perhaps, in some, the first deep conviction) was wrought at the Lord's Supper."[23]

> Arise, my soul, arise,
> Shake off thy guilty fears;
> The bleeding Sacrifice
> In my behalf appears;
> Before the throne my surety stands;
> My name is written on his hands.
>
> He ever lives above
> For me to intercede;
> His all-redeeming love,
> His precious blood to plead:
> His blood atoned for all our race,
> And sprinkles now the throne of grace.[24]

7. The Church Is For All People

It was, however, not the case that John Wesley had taught that just anyone could come forward to receive the sacrament. That too would constitute a mistaken judgment. It was only those, as the *Sunday Service* had clearly stated, who "do truly and earnestly repent of your sins, and are in love and charity with your neighbors, and intend to lead a new life, following the commandments of God, and walking from henceforth in his holy ways; Draw near with faith, and take this holy Sacrament to your comfort. . . ."[25] A spirit of repentance then was ever in order. Moreover, to the claim that one ought not to receive the Lord's Supper until several more things were in place thereby rending one now worthy to receive it, Wesley shot back: "For if we are not to receive the Lord's Supper till we are worthy of it, it is certain we ought never to receive it."[26]

Here then is one of the principal ways in which John Wesley's practical theology was enormously generous, reflective of the goodness and mercy of God. Where other traditions and theologies had thrown numerous obstacles in the way, and restrictions galore left in the wake of priestcraft and sacerdotalism, even barring one Christian from a different theological tradition from communing with another, in other words thereby setting up a badly divided, even tribal, Lord's Table, in sharp contrast to all of this, John Wesley welcomed all people, that is, all who were heartily sorry for their sins as well as Christians from every theological tradition, and especially the poor, in other words, all those people who were in a state of repentance. All of these were invited to come forward and to receive the healing balm, the welcoming graces, of both forgiveness and renewal that are at the very heart of the Supper and of the cross of Christ that ever shines through it.

> Come, sinners, to the gospel feast;
> Let every soul be Jesu's guest;
> Ye need not one be left behind,
> For God hath bidden all mankind.
> Sent by my Lord, on you I call;
> The invitation is to all:
> Come all the world; come, sinner, thou!
> All things in Christ are ready now.[27]

Wesley's Reading of the History of the Church

The way in which Wesley understood the history of the church is a key as to how he conceived its nature. As a good eighteenth century Anglican, informed by the writings of the Caroline divines of the preceding century, Wesley valued the primitive church as is evident in his following observation: "From a child I was taught to love and reverence the Scripture, the oracles of God; and, next to these, to esteem the primitive Fathers, the writers of the three first centuries. Next after the primitive church, I esteemed our own, the Church of England, as the most scriptural national Church in the world."[28] Moreover, Archbishop William Laud in the seventeenth century widened the scope somewhat and observed that the first four or five centuries were the time when, "the church was at the best."[29]

Of the four great marks of the church affirmed at the second ecumenical council in Constantinople in AD 381, that is, the church is one, holy, catholic and apostolic, John Wesley believed that the heaping of riches and honors upon the church by Constantine in the fourth century had undermined in particular the very holiness of the church. In other words, considerations of wealth and privilege had edged out concerns for humility and sanctity. Indeed, Wesley penned several sermons throughout his career that warned of the danger of riches to the vital Christian faith. Constantine, then, struck not at the branches of the church, at some peripheral or non-consequential matters, but at its very roots. The church should of course be holy, if it is carefully following its Master, simply because Christ is holy. In Wesley's reflections on the nature of the church as well as its history, he came to the conclusion that something would have to be done about this.

Real Christianity

Remarkably, Wesley tied together his love of the ancient church with his concern for the reform of the existing church in eighteenth century England through his well-developed motif of real or genuine Christianity. In a letter to Conyers Middleton, for example, Wesley elaborated:

> I reverence these ancient Christians (with all their failings) the more, because I see so few Christians now; because I read so little in the writings of later times, and hear so little, of genuine Christianity; and because most of the modern Christians, (so called,) not content with being wholly ignorant of it, are deeply prejudiced against it, calling it enthusiasm, and I know not what.[30]

This particular rhetoric or idiom was developed across the decades and revealed Wesley's ongoing concern for what role Methodism should play

7. The Church Is For All People

within the Church of England as an agent of reform and renewal. Indeed, Wesley employed the vocabulary of real, true, proper, Scriptural Christianity (he used all of these terms) throughout his writings, in a way that gave focus to his larger purpose in ministry. It is not that the Church of England in the eighteenth century was especially lacking or that it had failed to meet the definition of a true church in which the gospel was properly preached and the sacraments were duly administered. Services with the *Book of Common Prayer* as the chief liturgical instrument as well as regular preaching and the celebration of the Lord's Supper offered numerous occasions in which grace could be rightly conferred to the faithful. Nevertheless, despite a church that had a rich history, regular services, articles of religion, sacraments, preaching from the Bible, prayer as well as service to the poor, John Wesley believed that something vital was yet lacking. This perceived lack, which also characterized other churches as well, eventually led to the rise of Methodism, itself. Just what did John Wesley see in this area that so many others had not?[31] Observe the earnest concern about the truthfulness of the church in contrast to its mistaken substitutes in the following stanzas that Charles wrote and John published:

> The men who slight thy faithful word
> In their own lies confide;
> These are the temples of the Lord,
> And heathens all beside!
>
> The temple of the Lord are these,
> The only church and true,
> Who live in pomp, and wealth, and ease,
> And Jesus never knew.
>
> O wouldst thou, Lord, reveal their sins,
> And turn their joy to grief,
> The world, the Christian world, convince
> Of damning unbelief.[32]

One sure way that the church could remain on its proper course, faithful to the rich tradition that had preceded it, was to be mindful of the historical marks of the church, namely, one, holy, catholic and apostolic as noted earlier. Though appreciative of all the marks of the church, John Wesley especially valued the holiness of the Body of Christ, and he therefore strongly associated sanctity with the very identity of Methodism itself.

The Rise of Methodism

After Methodism was already in place, its first conference held in 1744 considered what was the *design* of God in raising up the preachers called Methodists in the first place: "Not to form any new sect; but to reform the nation, particularly the Church; and to spread scriptural holiness over the land."[33] Beyond this, when this same conference reflected upon the question, "What was the rise of Methodism, so called?" it offered the following helpful reply:

> In 1729, two young men, reading the Bible, saw they could not be saved without holiness, followed after it, and incited others so to do. In 1737 they saw holiness comes by faith. They saw likewise, that men are justified before they are sanctified; but still holiness was their point. God then thrust them out, utterly against their will, to raise a holy people.[34]

In light of such evidence, it is clear that both the design and the rise of Methodism had to do with holiness, a mark of the church that may fall through the cracks, so to speak, even in large, very institutionalized churches like the Church of England in the eighteenth century. Again, it is not the case that Anglicanism in Wesley's day was particularly bad, morally deficient, or neglectful in terms of its basic institutional life. The rounds of what ministry had come to be were indeed occurring. However, Methodism's design and purpose was much more focused than that. It recognized at its very beginning that the fostering of holiness in any church setting, whether Protestant, Roman Catholic or Eastern Orthodox, is a very intentional and deliberative activity that requires much additional effort and care beyond the usual operations of institutional church life.

So then Methodism as John Wesley and the first Methodist Conference had defined it was very intentional in a way that so many reforming movements are as well. Since holiness is a mark of the church and essential to its very nature, Methodism placed Christian sanctity, especially in terms of simplicity and purity, at the heart of its mission and purpose. And yes it was a matter of *reform*, after all, for Wesley affirmed that the original design of the Church was "to save each his own soul, then *to assist each other in working out their salvation.*"[35] And Charles Wesley, for his part, showed the importance of community as well:

> Two are better far than one
> For counsel or for fight;

> How can one be warm alone,
> Or serve his God aright?
> Join we then our hearts and hands,
> Each to love provoke his friend,
> Run the way of his commands,
> And keep it to the end.
>
> Woe to him whose spirits droop,
> To him who falls alone!
> He has none to lift him up,
> To help his weakness on.
> Happier we each other keep,
> We each other's burdens bear;
> Never need our footsteps slip,
> Upheld by mutual prayer.[36]

Moreover, when John Wesley, himself, explored the office and duties of a Christian minister from this celebrated communal vantage point, notice the many levels of labor-intensive activity, with ongoing service and care, that should be a part of the life of the church, any church. Wesley elaborated:

> To 'seek and save that which is lost;' to bring souls from Satan to God; to instruct the ignorant; to reclaim the wicked; to convince the gainsayer; to direct their feet in the way of peace, and then keep them therein; to follow them step by step, lest they turn out of the way, and advise them in their doubts and temptations; to lift up them that fall; to refresh them that are faint; and to comfort the weak-hearted; to administer various helps, as the variety of occasions require according to their several necessities: These are parts of our office.[37]

In this list of activities, ever vital to the life of the church, Wesley, among other things, remarkably enough criticized that minister "who imagines he has little more to do than to preach once or twice a week; that this is the main point, the chief part of the office, which he hath taken upon himself before God?"[38] With such a mistake in place, Wesley then added his resounding, trenchant judgment: "What gross ignorance is this! What a total mistake of the truth! What a miserable blunder touching the whole nature of his office!"[39]

The Church Is For All People

In the eyes of the early Methodists not only was there far more to do in the local church then some Anglican priests had imagined, but there was also an entire population of people, namely the poor, who were reluctant for a host of reasons to participate in Sunday services. Given the social and political stratification of English society during the eighteenth century in which certain seats in various churches would be marked for the rich, the poor at times were hardly welcomed. William Hogarth's overly criticizing work of the period, *The Sleeping Congregation*, displays a church service that is "dominated by royal, rather than divine images,"[40] and yet the poor were hardly Tories.[41]

For his part, John Wesley exclaimed "I love the poor; in many of them I find pure, genuine grace, unmixed with paint, folly, and affection."[42] Then as now the poor were largely hidden in English society but Wesley made their acquaintance by actually going to them, being among them, and thereby witnessing their plight first hand. In his journal of February 1753, for example, Wesley recounted one such occasion in which he spent considerable time with the poor: "On Friday and Saturday I visited as many more as I could. I found some in their cells underground, others in their garrets, half starved both with cold and hunger, added to weakness and pain. But I found not one of them unemployed who was able to crawl about the room."[43] Given this painful and challenging reality, and no doubt with considerable exasperation, Wesley then added to his account: "So wickedly, devilishly false is the common objection, 'They are poor only because they are idle.'"[44]

Many of the rich in English society during the eighteenth century were hardly aware of the poor and their mean conditions, and they could ease their consciences at least somewhat by remembering the Poor Laws, first established in 1601, which their taxes of course supported. Heitzenrater explored this particular social and economic policy by highlighting the threefold approach of the Poor Laws as evidenced in the following: "The idle and able-bodied poor were put to work or punished, the infirm and impotent who could not work were given cash support, and begging and casual almsgiving were banned."[45]

Though cash support in the form of funds from the public treasury was indeed available, Wesley, for whatever reason, refused to tap into the provisions offered in the Poor Laws as he and the Methodists ministered to the destitute.[46] Instead, Wesley had the stewards of the class meetings gather up money from its members which was then distributed to the down and out among them. Indeed, the early Methodists loved the poor so much so that they welcomed them into the very life of Methodism, itself, treating them like the brothers and sisters that they were. Put another way, the early Methodists did not just send money "to them" and then get on with their normal routines. Instead the poor, as bearing the image and likeness of God, were fully embraced in the Methodist household and welcomed. It was in that special setting, marked by an abundance of grace and love, and not through any impersonal government dole, in which all of the needs of the poor, both temporal and spiritual, would be addressed.[47] Economic, social and cultural divisions simply melted away in a Methodist class meeting. Identity, real identity, was to be located elsewhere.

Barred from many Anglican pulpits as was John Wesley, himself, George Whitefield, the grand itinerant, encouraged Wesley and others to take up the practice of field preaching. At first Wesley was very reluctant to participate in this "strange way of preaching"[48] but Whitefield in the end was persuasive. Wesley recorded his first venture into the fields in his journal of April 2, 1739: "At four in the afternoon I submitted to 'be more vile,' and proclaimed in the highways the glad tidings of salvation, speaking from a little eminence in a ground adjoining to the city, to about three thousand people. The Scripture on which I spoke was this . . . 'The Spirit of the Lord is upon me, because he hath anointed me to preach the gospel to the poor.'"[49] Moreover, because the harvest was plentiful but the laborers were few, Wesley encouraged laypeople under his care to take up the practice of preaching, though some of Wesley's lay preachers actually preached in chapels, so that more people would hear the good news of Jesus Christ than otherwise would.

With such a broad approach in place, John Wesley and the early Methodists insured that the universality of the Gospel would not only embrace a diversity of Christian traditions in a charitable spirit but that it would also welcome those well beyond the walls of the church, even a population that would be loath to set a foot therein. With all sorts of barriers in place, both visible and invisible, such folk would not come to church, any church. Given this stubborn and baffling reality, the Methodists in turn would simply have to go to such a needy people, their brothers and sisters, who were currently beyond the church doors. Charles Wesley opined:

> With grace abundantly endued,
> A pure, believing multitude,
> They all were of one heart and soul,
> And only love inspired the whole.
>
> Ye different sects, who all declare,
> Lo, here is Christ, or Christ is there,
> Your stronger proofs divinely give,
> And show me where the Christians live.[50]

The Creation of the Methodist Infrastructure

It should be clear by now that the purpose (focused on holiness) and extent (reaching the poor, the least of all) of Methodism, as John Wesley and others had conceived it, called for an entirely new approach to ministry, one that assumed the normal rounds of ministry in Anglican churches were, in fact, taking place. However, to all of this labor must be added the special care and oversight over souls that could lead them into the chambers of holiness while all the while ensuring that the impoverished were heartily welcomed as well. In a real sense, the Methodist way, and it was indeed distinct, entailed the operationalization of holy love, making it effective, and of deep consequence, in the warp and woof of life, for all people.

The rise of the United Society, first in London and then elsewhere, had to do with "a company of men having the form and seeking the power of godliness, united in order to pray together, to receive the word of exhortation, and to watch over one another in love, that they may help each other to work out their salvation."[51] For Wesley, then, true religion was not an individual or a private affair. Going to church and hardly talking to anyone was an aberration of the faith and not its norm. "Christianity is essentially a social religion and that to turn it into a solitary religion is indeed to destroy it."[52] Put another way, Christians need both the accountability as well as the responsibilities that are very much a part of group life. No one is a Christian alone. Charles Wesley expressed this well in the following verses:

> By thy reconciling love
> Every stumbling-block remove,
> Each to each unite, endear:
> Come, and spread thy banner here!

7. The Church Is For All People

> Make us of one heart and mind,
> Courteous, pitiful, and kind,
> Lowly, meek in thought and word,
> Altogether like our Lord
>
> Let us each for other care,
> Each the other's burden bear;
> To thy church the pattern give,
> Show how true believers live.[53]

Though John Wesley could boast that the only requirement for joining the United Society was "a desire to flee the wrath to come, to be saved from their sins"[54] once people were placed in a class meeting, then they would be introduced to *The General Rules of the United Societies* that offered three major counsels: 1) do no harm, 2) do good and 3) attend upon all the ordinances of God such as "The public worship of God; the ministry of the Word, either read or expounded; the supper of the Lord; family and private prayer; searching the Scriptures; and fasting and abstinence."[55] These same three counsels also emerged in Wesley's writings, as well as in discussions of the early Methodist conferences, when the topic of repentance was in view.[56] This fact demonstrates clearly that Methodism at its very beginning was, once again, about repentance, the willingness to turn around, to go a different way, in order to participate in the very life of God through mediated grace. And it was an invitation offered to all.

The class meeting of about a dozen people, meeting regularly and watching over each other's souls, was to be the chief organ of discipline and accountability in Methodist life. Wesley had written on one occasion, "'The soul and the body make a man; the spirit and discipline make a Christian;' implying that none could without the help of Christian discipline."[57] Accordingly, discipline in the form of regular class meetings would be the suitable instrument to actualize the very purpose of Methodism in terms of the inculcation of holiness and of its extent by reaching the poor. Comparing a ministry that simply focused on preaching to one that incorporated preaching along with the discipline of group life, Wesley observed:

> I was more convinced than ever, that the preaching like an Apostle, without joining together those that are awakened, and training them up in the ways of God, is only begetting children for the murderer. How much preaching

has there been for these twenty years all over Pembrokeshire! But no regular societies, no discipline, no order or connexion; and the consequence is, that nine in ten of the once-awakened are now faster asleep than ever.[58]

Though leaders were appointed for each class, Wesley reserved the larger supervisory role for himself, aided of course by the class leaders as well as by the stewards who reported regularly to him.[59] Wesley's disciplinary and supervisory authority included the right to examine the classes carefully, and "to prune" them as needed, in other words, to remove from the graces of fellowship, those who were not walking in accordance with the Gospel. In his *Principles of a Methodist Farther Explained*, Wesley cautioned: "When any members of these, or of the United Society, are proved to live in known sin, we then mark and avoid them; we separate ourselves from every one that walks disorderly. Sometimes, if the case be judged infectious, (though rarely,) this is openly declared."[60] As a gifted pastoral leader, Wesley recognized that not to remove self-willed and recalcitrant sinners, those, for example, who beat their wives or who repeatedly engaged in evil speaking, was to run the risk of corrupting the entire class.

In some respects the social arraignments of a Methodist class meeting offered a sharp contrast to class-conscious eighteenth-century British society. Both women and the poor, for example, did indeed emerge as leaders within the classes, and it was not because John Wesley had either strong democratic or egalitarian leanings.[61] He had neither. Rather women as well as the indigent could emerge as guides and mentors within the class structure due to what might be suitably called their "soteriological status," in other words, how they had received the transformative grace of God in their own lives and in what manner they had taken up the prudential disciplines of Methodist life. All of this, of course, was grounded in solid theological reasoning in that what counted in a Methodist class meeting was not money, education, rank, social status or other kinds of privilege or preferment. What mattered was that one was created in the glorious image of God and was now walking the arduous and narrow path of the obedience of faith in a fallen world. Upon entering a Methodist class meeting, women as well as the poor were recognized and appreciated in terms of what really mattered. For many folk the Methodist class meeting was now in a real sense their home, their haven. Charles wrote:

> How good and pleasant 'tis to see
> When brethren cordially agree,
> And kindly think and speak the same!
> A family of faith and love,

> Combined to seek the things above
> And spread the common Saviour's fame!⁶²

The infrastructure of societal life within Methodism was graded in terms of advances in grace as well as in earnestness as one moved from the class meeting to the voluntary band meeting or even on to the select society, the latter embracing those who were knocking on the door of heart purity. In terms of the band meeting, itself, Wesley defined its purpose in the following way: "The design of our meeting is to obey that command of God, 'Confess your faults one to another, and pray one for another that ye may be healed."⁶³ The increasing illumination of band life, so helpful for spiritual growth and transformation, entailed the willingness to be told one's shortcomings by the group in a very frank and honest manner. To illustrate, people were questioned *before* they were admitted into the band meeting along the following lines: "Do you desire to be told of all your faults, and that plain and home?"⁶⁴ And again, "Do you desire that in doing this we should come as close as possible, that we should cut to the quick, and search your heart to the bottom?"⁶⁵ If one was admitted to the band, then the following questions would be posed *every week*:

1. What known sins have you committed since our last meeting?
2. What temptations have you met with?
3. How was you delivered?
4. What have you thought, said, or done, of which you doubt whether it be sin or not?
5. Have you nothing you desire to keep secret?⁶⁶

Such probing questions entailed an increasing vulnerability in the bands. Confidentiality in the meetings was therefore very important. Moreover, due to the intimate nature of what might be confessed, women were separated from men and the married from single people in the bands. Such increasing illumination and vulnerability was, however, too much for some and so in American Methodism, for example, the band meeting was one of the first things of the Methodist infrastructure to be dropped.

Serious Christian Formation

Consider for a moment a couple of eighteenth-century Anglicans who, upon hearing either John or Charles Wesley preach, decided to become a member of a class meeting and thereby to identify as a Methodist. Recognize the vast array of the instruments of Christian formation that would be a part of their everyday experience. As good Anglicans, they would be guided by the rhythms of liturgical life as offered by the *Book of Common Prayer*. It's language, even in terms of its cadence and rhythms, would fill their minds with praise and adoration. Worship would be an avenue to respond to the grace of God already received in deep gratitude and thanksgiving. Preaching in its best sense would open up the Bible and offer the grandest narrative of all to every hearer. Beyond this, Baptism and the Lord's Supper, as sacraments of the church, emblems of the New Covenant, as well as an important means of grace, could communicate the very presence of God to participants. Moreover, such a church life would of course be marked by the rounds of prayer, fasting, and various ministries of the parish, all genuine means of grace.

As important as this ecclesiastical setting would be for the serious Anglican, John Wesley obviously believed that more was required in order to foster the raising up of a holy people in which sanctity was ever the focus and in which the poor would be heartily embraced. So then, to all of these elements of Christian formation that eighteenth-century Anglicanism had already offered, Methodism added more preaching, both in the fields and in numerous chapels, as well as the creation of an infrastructure of class meetings, bands and select societies, laced throughout the land, in order to insure that Christians would, after all, travel along the highway of holiness and watch over each other's souls as those who would have to give an account.

> I hope at last to find
> The kingdom from above,
> The settled peace, the constant mind,
> The everlasting love;
> The sanctifying grace
> That makes me meet for home;
> I hope to see thy glorious face
> Where sin can never come.[67]

Accordingly, the elements of Christian formation for Anglicans, as well as for members of other theological traditions, who embraced the Methodist way of being a Christian by entering a class meeting, for example, would

7. The Church Is For All People

be nothing less than "thick." Indeed, it is the Methodists, under the careful leadership of John and Charles Wesley, who called for an ecclesiastical and small group environment, *ecclesiola in ecclesia* (the small church within the larger church) that would be greatly conducive not only to spiritual growth and maturation over time but also, more particularly, to the inculcation of holiness for all people. Indeed, the rich and memorable hymns of Charles Wesley would bathe the congregations in the heart-felt expressions of sanctity whereas instructional materials in the form of sermons, as a distinct literary form, and penny tracts would offer the Methodists both instruction and helpful clarity for the way forward into the deeper graces of God. Moreover, service to as well as embracing the poor in holy love, in the form of numerous works of mercy, would be held up to all as a genuine means of grace. In other words, the Methodist way historically insured that the instruments of Christian formation, whereby God might become both deeply known and loved, would be nothing less than robust. There was no lack here.

8. God Has Forgiven All People of Everything

> *"If we confess our sins,*
> *he is faithful and just and will forgive us our sins*
> *and purify us from all unrighteousness." (1 John 1:9)*

When the church takes her mission seriously by going out into the world to bring the fragrance of Christ to all people, without being compromised by any worldly and ultimately alien narrative, then the consequence of all of this labor is that those beyond the walls of the church finally enter in. Indeed, it is the context of the church in general, and for the early Methodists the class meeting in particular, that ultimately became the grace-filled setting in which many people embraced a living faith in Jesus Christ. Since after being placed in a class meeting its members would be introduced to the *General Rules of the United Societies* (leave off evil, do good and employ the means of grace), as noted earlier, then this was a clear indication that such members where indeed open to repentance, in other words, they were open to that transformation of being entailed in the reception of the forgiveness of sins and the renewal of their natures, otherwise known respectively as justification and the new birth. The focus in this current chapter then will be on justification, the forgiveness of sins, and the assurance associated with this gift of grace. The next chapter will take up the new birth and election, two doctrines that though they are clearly distinct are often confused.

John Wesley referred to justification, the forgiveness of sins, first of all as one of "our main doctrines," as for example, in his treatise *The Principles of a Methodist Farther Explained*. He wrote: "Our main doctrines, which include all the rest, are three, that of repentance, of faith, and of holiness. The first of these we account as it were, the porch of religion; the next, the door; the third, religion itself."[1] Second, in his sermon "The New Birth," drafted in

1760, Wesley employed slightly different language to underscore the importance of justification: "If any doctrines within the whole compass of Christianity may be properly termed fundamental, they are doubtless these two, — the doctrine of justification, and that of the new birth: The former relating to that great work which God does *for us*, in forgiving our sins; the latter, to the great work which God does *in us*, in renewing our fallen nature."[2] Whether justification is seen as a main or as a fundamental doctrine, it is hard to get more basic or more important than this.

All Can Be Saved (The Gospel as a Universal Offer)

At times John Wesley utilized the phrases "justifying faith" and "saving faith" interchangeably as for example in his sermon, "Salvation by Faith." Beyond this he maintained, in contrast to George Whitefield, that such a faith, since it is the gift of God, is offered to all, that is, to all sinners who are in need of such grace. To illustrate, in his sermon "Free Grace," produced in 1739, Wesley affirmed that the grace or love of God, "whence comes our salvation is free in all and for all."[3] Interestingly enough, Wesley and Whitefield actually agreed on the "free in all" language which meant that justification or salvation, more broadly speaking, is not dependent on any human working or merit. They differed, however, on the "free for all," language which as Wesley understood it meant that the graces of justification (and regeneration as well) are offered to all people. In other words, salvation is a *universal offer* made by God through Christ as revealed in the following language from this sermon as cited by Wesley: "He is 'the Lamb of God, that taketh away the sins of the world'; He is 'the propitiation, not for our sins only, but also for the sins of the whole world. He (the living God) is the Saviour of all men; 'He gave himself a ransom for all; 'He tasted death for every man.'"[4] Moreover, at the end of this sermon, "Free Grace," it is likely Charles Wesley who composed the following memorable lines that encapsulate the basic truth of the Gospel that John as well was trying to communicate:

> For every man he tasted death,
> He suffered once for all
> He calls as many souls as breathe
> And all may hear the call
>
> Who'er to God for pardon fly

> In Christ may be forgiven,
> He speaks to all, 'Why will ye die,
> And not accept my heaven?'⁵

Justifying Faith

Whenever Wesley wanted to emphasize the significance of a particular doctrine such as justifying faith, he would engage, literally speaking, in a *via negativa*. In other words, he would go through a litany of what a doctrine is not before he took up the positive task, the *via positiva*, of describing what a doctrine actually is. Indeed, justifying faith is not just any faith as Wesley had learned from his own earlier experience. To illustrate, it is not the faith of a heathen in that it goes far beyond acknowledging that "God is; that he is a rewarder of them that diligently seek him."⁶ Simply put, a theistic belief, mere acknowledgement that God exists, is not enough. Moreover, justifying faith surpasses "a careful practice of moral virtue, of justice, mercy, and truth, toward their fellow-creatures."⁷ Personal and social uprightness and integrity, as important as they are, fall short as well.

Second, justifying faith is not the faith of a *devil*. This is admittedly an odd expression since most people are not used to the words "devil" and "faith" in the same sentence. However, as Scripture points out, "You believe that there is one God. Good! Even the demons believe that—and shudder" (James 2:19). In his *Explanatory Notes Upon the New Testament* concerning this particular passage Wesley observed: "So far is that faith from either justifying or saving them that have it."⁸ Beyond this, in his sermon, "Salvation by Faith," Wesley declared that even the devils believe that "Jesus is the Son of God, the Christ, the Savior of the world."⁹ And so belief *that*, intellectual *assent* to the truth about Jesus Christ revealed in Scripture, though important, is not enough. It too clearly falls short.

Third, justifying faith is not the faith which the Apostles themselves had while Christ was yet upon earth. This observation may come as a surprise to some readers, but upon further reflection it is clear that such an apostolic faith, since Christ had not yet been crucified and raised from the dead, is unable to acknowledge, as Wesley himself pointed out, "his death as the only sufficient means of redeeming man from death eternal, and his resurrection as the restoration of us all to life and immortality; inasmuch as he 'was delivered for our sins, and rose again for our justification.'"¹⁰ In a real sense the Apostles are distinct, transitional figures: they knew Christ both before and after his death and resurrection. However, all people in Wesley's age, as is the case today, are on the other side of these potent realities.

After this three part *via negativa* Wesley took up the positive work of distinguishing justifying faith from the faith of a heathen in that it is specifically "faith in Christ: Christ and God through Christ, are the proper objects of it."[11] Again, justifying faith is different from the faith of a devil in that "it is not barely a speculative, rational thing, a cold, lifeless assent, a train of ideas in the head; *but also* a disposition of the heart."[12] Observe the careful balance of Wesley's view: justifying or saving faith is not only *assent* to the truths of the Gospel surrounding Christ but it is also, in a very conjunctive way (both/and), a hearty *trust* in Christ, a disposition of the heart that engages the entire person. And justifying faith is different from the faith of the Apostles when Christ was on the earth because the crucifixion and resurrection, a dying and rising, are essential to what this faith is all about. Such a faith, then, is a full reliance on the blood of Christ; "a trust in the merits of his life, death, and resurrection; a recumbency upon him as our atonement."[13] Justifying faith then is not a thing of nature but of grace, and it ever has Christ as its object.

All Can Be Forgiven of Everything

Justification: The Definition

Wesley considered the nature of justification itself in his treatise *The Principles of a Methodist*, drafted in 1742, in the following way: "I believe, three things must go together in our justification: Upon God's part, his great mercy and grace; upon Christ's part, the satisfaction of God's justice, by the offering his body, and shedding his blood; and upon our part, true and living faith in the merits of Jesus Christ.[14] Observe that each of these roles highlights the importance of restoring a relationship shattered by sin and the alienation left in its wake. All parties are involved in such a setting for reconciliation always entails many, not simply one. Simply put, God's justice is satisfied in the atoning work of Christ such that believers receive a rich and abundant mercy through a true and living faith. Moreover, human rebellion and resistance are overcome in the display of holy, sacrificial love at Calvery as an earlier chapter has maintained.

Justification, itself, however is "not the being made actually just and righteous. This is sanctification," Wesley pointed out. "The one implies what God does *for us* through his Son; the other, what he works *in us* by his Spirit."[15]

Justification: The Definition

Wesley made an important observation in terms of his own Christian journey in that he confessed prior to 1738 he was "utterly ignorant of the nature and condition of justification."[16] In fact, he humbly admitted that "Sometimes I confounded it with sanctification; (particularly when I was in Georgia) . . ."[17] Why is it then so important to make a logical distinction between justification as the work that God does *for us* and sanctification or the new birth as the work that God does *in us*? If these two doctrines are not clearly distinguished, then some may mistakenly conclude that a measure of sanctification or holiness is necessary in order to receive justification or the forgiveness of sins. However, one does not have to be holy first in order to be forgiven. That remains a clear impossibility, given the realities of sin and grace, for it places an enormous burden on all people that no human being is able to bear. Justification implies only a relative change not a real one; it restores one to the favor of God. It transforms one's outward relation to God such that "of enemies we become children,"[18] as Wesley, himself, forthrightly affirmed in his writings.

Moreover, as "an act of God's free grace,"[19] justification is an utter gift and Wesley therefore emphasized the height, depth, breath and length of the mercy of God in that the Most High, "pardoneth all our sins and accepteth us as righteous in his sight."[20] In short, all sins have already been forgiven. In other words, there is no sin or evil that human beings have committed, no matter how wicked, perverse or debased, that has not already been forgiven in Jesus Christ. But that forgiveness must be *received*. And though Wesley affirmed that the blasphemy of the Holy Spirit is indeed an unpardonable sin, and even declared that "the judgment of God shall overtake him, both here and hereafter,"[21] is it actually the case that God refuses to forgive the sinner or is it rather that the sinner is now in a position in which such forgiveness could never be received? In other words, the result of eternal loss would be the same in each instance (and no one is denying this), though the cause of such a loss could be viewed as remarkably different. That is, if sinners judge the Holy Spirit to be evil, then they would not be open to the very agency by which forgiveness would be received in the first place. In this speculative consideration of the cause of the unpardonable sin, which admittedly John Wesley never entertained, God remains good, loving, merciful and forgiving throughout. In short, the problem is not with God but with sinners. Their sin is "unpardonable" simply because they reject the very ministrations of the Holy Spirit, who is judged to be evil, which would lead to forgiveness.

8. God Has Forgiven All People of Everything

Consider then the wide mercy of God and the enormous freedom entailed in justification: freedom from the very *guilt of sin*. That heavy burden of guilt, one that can crush the human spirit, is thrown off and believers are marvelously free whereby they can now look up and cry, "Abba Father." As Wesley noted in Article IX found in the *Sunday Service*, citing Anglican materials, this was "a most wholesome doctrine, and very full of comfort."[22] And Charles Wesley expressed this same truth in the following stanza:

> Jesus, I believe thee near:
> Now my fallen soul restore!
> Now my guilty conscience clear,
> Give me back my peace and power;
> Stone to flesh again convert,
> Write forgiveness on my heart.[23]

Wesley offered an additional counsel in terms of the nature of justification. This doctrine is suitably defined as the forgiveness of all sins, to be sure, but it is the forgiveness or the "remission of the sins that are *past*."[24] This one little word "past," that Wesley added makes a huge difference, and it keeps his doctrine of justification from being misunderstood in antinomian or lawless ways. So misunderstood, justification would mean that any ongoing committing of sin is not really much of a concern since one is already justified, as if justification were like an insurance policy in terms of all past, present and future sins. Such a mistaken approach fails to take into account both the seriousness and the deceitfulness of sin, that ongoing, unrepented sin changes the heart and stupefies the soul in terms of the things of God and eternity. Again, justification is the forgiveness of those sins that are *past* such that if there is any current breach of faith, a stubborn and willful violation of a known law of God, a disruption of the fellowship of holy love, then the way forward is marked by repentance not presumption.

Who Are Those Who Are Actually Justified?

At the beginning of this current chapter it was affirmed that the Gospel is offered to all. In other words, it held up the deep and rich scriptural truth that Christ died for all people, past, present and future; none are excluded. However, this universal dimension of the good news has to be properly understood lest there be misunderstanding. Wesley was not a universalist in the sense that in the end every human being will be saved. Not everyone will be redeemed. There is, after all, such a thing as loss, eternal loss, and no one less than Jesus Christ spoke about it (Matt. 7:13-14). The universal dimension that Wesley, the Arminian, did indeed have in mind in his various writings is that provision has already been made for the forgiveness of sins for the entire world, past, present and future, in the atoning work of Jesus Christ. In other words, the Savior's life and death is the *meritorious cause* of human salvation in the sense that a universal provision has already been made. But again that forgiveness must be received. To be sure, it is the transition from the provision made for all people, the universal dimension, to the limited, much smaller number of people who will actually receive this benefit that is behind the question "Who are those who are actually justified"?

Remarkably enough, this shift from the broad universal provision that has been made by Christ to the more limited reception of this same provision is mirrored in an important conversation that Wesley had with August Spangenberg while he was in Georgia. The inquisitive Moravian leader asked: "'Do you know Jesus Christ?' I paused, and said, 'I know he is the Savior of the world.' 'True', replied he, 'but do you know he has saved you? I answered, 'I hope he has died to save me.' He only added, "do you know yourself?' I said, 'I do.' But I fear they were vain words."[25] In other words, the shift from Spangenberg's particular question, "Do you know Jesus Christ," to Wesley's more general, even evasive, reply, "I know his is the Savior of the world," is at the heart of the difference presently in view.

Rigorous moralists of any age, both within and outside the church, those who think that the opposite of sin is virtue, and not the appropriate answer faith, may have a difficult time embracing the radical Pauline teaching that Almighty God justifies not the righteous, the personally and socially respectable or virtuous, but sinners: "However, to the one who does not work but trusts God *who justifies the ungodly*, their faith is credited as righteousness" (Rom. 4:5). And so when John Wesley, himself, posed the question, "Who are they that are justified?" he immediately responded, "the ungodly;" the ungodly of every kind and degree; and none but the ungodly."[26] Wesley's last phrase "none but the ungodly," was not only emphatic but it was also yet another way that he could underscore that holiness cannot in any way, in any sense, be the basis upon which one is forgiven. Again, Wesley maintained that God justifies "him that, till that hour, is totally ungodly; — full of all evil, void of all good. . . ."[27] Moreover, Charles Wesley wrote as follows:

> Nothing have I, Lord, to pay,
> Nor can thy grace procure;
> Empty send me not away,
> For I, thou know'st, am poor
> Dust and ashes is my name,
> My all is sin and misery:
> Friend of sinners, spotless Lamb,
> Thy blood was shed for me.[28]

Not only is justification (and the new birth) one of the two foci of the Wesleyan *ordo salutis*, but also the nature of this doctrine, along with its actualization in the warp and woof of life, reveals that the whole matter of justification has important consequences for so many other of John Wesley's theological emphases. Three such elements can now be explored. First of all, since it is sinners who are justified, that is, those who *are* or *have* nothing by themselves that could possibly issue in the forgiveness of sins, then justifying faith itself is a sheer gift of God lavished upon those willing to receive it. In citing a sermon from Christian David, a Moravian leader, Wesley approvingly observed: "this faith also is the gift of God. It is his free gift, which He now and ever giveth to everyone that is willing to receive it."[29] Again, "God freely gives faith, for the sake of Him in whom he is always 'well pleased,'"[30] as Wesley, himself, pointed out in his own *An Earnest Appeal to Men of Reason and Religion*. Remarkably, these declarations by Wesley are another way of affirming that the crucial doctrines in the Wesleyan order of salvation are fine examples of free grace, not cooperant grace, because justification, along with the faith that receives it, are sheer gifts of a good, gracious and merciful God. Indeed, the Holy One understands the painful realities of sinners and what appears to them as their baffling predicament. Indeed, they can neither alter their perplexing condition nor bring about their own justification. They are powerless to do so simply because they themselves are the problem, right down to a conflicted and corrupted will, as Wesley so clearly understood from his own belabored journey as amply recorded in his journal.[31]

Second, since it is sinners, those who are evil, who are justified, according to both the Apostle Paul and John Wesley, then this scriptural truth *necessarily* issues in the doctrine of justification by grace through faith alone *(sola fide)*. Simply put, the two theological truths imply one another. In other words, since sinners not only lack any good works, properly speaking, or holiness itself for that matter, then in the absence of such things, the very faith by which they will come to believe, as just pointed out above, is itself a gift from God. Accordingly, in his sermon, "The Scripture Way of Salvation," Wesley filled out this gracious theological truth as follows: "Faith is the condition, and the only condition, of justification. It is the condition: None is justified but he that believes: Without faith no man is justified. And it is the only condition: This alone is sufficient for justification. Every one that believes is justified, whatever else he has or has not."[32] To be sure, how could it be otherwise with sinners who are in need of such grace? In other words, to balk at the theological truth of justification by grace through *faith alone* is to fail to recognize the serious and troubled condition of sinners, even those who have measures of prevenient and convincing grace, and how it has left them void of anything from themselves that could possibly justify. In his comments on Galatians 6:12 Wesley therefore offered a pointed corrective: "faith in a crucified Saviour is alone sufficient for justification,"[33] precisely because of who Christ is and what he has done on behalf of sinners. Or as Charles Wesley likely put it:

> He would that all his truths should own,
> His gospel all embrace,
> Be justified by faith alone,
> And freely saved by grace.[34]

Third, stunning, practical consequences emerge from Wesley's understanding that saving faith itself is a gift from God and that whosoever is justified has received such forgiveness by grace through faith alone. In other words, justifying or saving faith is a species of free grace. To illustrate, after embracing what Wesley had referred to as "this new doctrine,"[35] in March 1738, it is highly significant that the first person to whom he offered "salvation by faith alone,"[36] was a certain Mr. Clifford, a condemned criminal about to be executed. Six months earlier, Wesley would not have made such an offer to any sinner about to die, much less to a criminal. Indeed, prior to March 1738, Wesley was still under the influence of strains of seventeenth-century Anglican theology that would not have offered Mr. Clifford and those like him either much comfort or hope. Though Wesley, himself, had profited much from reading the Caroline divine, Jeremy Taylor, he also picked up some troubling theology as well. Precisely because Taylor had an overwrought fear of antinomianism or lawlessness, like many Anglicans of his day, he flatly denied the possibility of death-bed conversions. This topic of dying, death-bed conversions and glorifying grace will be taken up in detail in a later chapter.

One of the several things that Wesley had learned from Böhler was that saving faith can be received instantaneously. At first Wesley was very reluctant to embrace such a teaching, and he noted at the time, "But I could not comprehend what he spoke of *an instantaneous work*. I could not understand how this faith should be given in a moment."[37] However, after consulting Scripture, and upon hearing the testimony of several living witnesses, Wesley was convinced. Several important streams of his emerging theology (the year 1738 truly made a crucial difference), now started to come together. Whereas some people, upon hearing that the conversions recorded in Scripture are instantaneous ("[I] found scarce any instances there of other than *instantaneous* conversions—scarce any other so slow as that of St. Paul . . ."[38]) are thereby perplexed and are therefore quick in their denials. However, they are likely only viewing this whole matter simply in terms of chronology. That, of course, is a serious mistake. However, what Wesley had come to learn in 1738, in his reflections on death bed conversions and the like, was that the temporal elements of salvation can highlight not only the divine role in redemption, which is ever preeminent, but also that salvific graces are freely given. In other words, the instantaneous dimension of justifying grace, for example, underscores free grace, salvation as a sheer gift, and that justification by grace is through faith alone, a triad attesting to the utter beneficence and goodness of God.

> Followed by their works they go,
> Where their head had gone before;
> Reconciled by grace below,
> Grace had opened mercy's door;
> Justified through faith alone,
> Here they knew their sins forgiven,
> Here they laid their burden down,
> Hallowed, and made meet for heaven.[39]

It should be clear by now that Wesley's practical theological reasoning evidences an order, in other words there is a rhyme and reason to it, and that some doctrines may actually imply each other. Beyond this first level of structure, there is a higher one that has to do with the two major doctrines, themselves, of the Wesleyan order of salvation, namely, justification and entire sanctification. At Wesley's hands, these two foci of the *ordo salutis* clearly evidence the larger structure of parallelism, once one pays attention to Wesley's articulate use of language, his careful choice of words, in exploring each particular doctrine. Therefore, key insights from the one theological focus of attention can be readily applied to the other, especially in terms of such things as chronology, the role of God in redemption, as well as the place for faith, grace and works. To illustrate, in his sermon, "The Scripture Way of Salvation," Wesley considered the approach to entire sanctification in the following way:

> And by this token may you surely know whether you seek it by faith or by works. If by works, you want something to be done first, before you are sanctified. You think, 'I must first be or do thus or thus.' Then you are seeking it by works unto this day. If you seek it by faith, you may expect it as you are: and if as you are, then expect it now.[40]

This same theological reasoning can now be applied in an analogous way to justification. Accordingly, if sinners think they must *be* or *do* something else first in order to be justified then not only will they need more time for this being and doing (remember the counsel of Jeremy Taylor) but they will also, as Wesley put it, be seeking salvation by works. However, since salvation is after all a sheer gift from a gracious God, who seeks to bless, then sinners can expect it as they are, and they therefore can expect it now. In other words, the temporal dimension here, the chronology, is one of Wesley's favorite ways to underscore the divine role in redemption and that salvation is a sheer gift, and therefore can be received now. In short, chronology, the instantaneous, showcases the generosity and goodness of God, that the Most High is a wonderful gift giver without parallel. Wesley was therefore very appropriate, and on so many levels, in offering Mr. Clifford the glad tidings of salvation today. Observe the graciousness of the Gospel as reflected in the words of Charles Wesley as well:

> Outcasts of men, to you I call,
> Harlots and publicans and thieves;
> He spreads his arms to embrace you all,
> Sinners alone his grace receive.
> No need of him the righteous have;
> He came the lost to seek and save.[41]

What Is to Be Done in the Meantime?

One of the remarkable things about Wesley's practical theology is that it is carefully balanced. It ever avoids extremes. Albert Outler employed the language of "conjunctions," both/and; not either/or, for instance, to describe Wesley's theology. In other words, in terms of Wesley's own theological posture, it's always a matter of law *and* grace; justification *and* sanctification; faith *and* works; free grace *and* cooperant grace. This conjunctive nature of Wesley's theology, which itself is once again an important evidence of structure, emerges very clearly once the question is raised, "What is to be done in the meantime?" for those who are not yet justified (and born of God) but who would like to be. For Wesley, if people have not yet received the graces of justification, if there be time and opportunity, then they should not just simply sit on their hands and do nothing because they already have measures of grace in the form of prevenient grace.

Early in his career as a field-preaching evangelist, John Wesley helped to establish a joint Moravian/Methodist society at Fetter Lane in London. Late in 1739 Wesley realized that some of the Moravians there were teaching what constituted stillness or what came to be known as quietism. In others words, for those along the way to justification, they should do nothing, that is, "Not to go to church; not to communicate; not to fast; not to use so much private prayer; not to read the Scripture,"[42] lest they spoil the possibility of being justified with their works. This fanatical teaching of Molther and Bray led Wesley, along with several others, to make the transition to the Foundery in 1740,[43] where he could continue to stress the importance of the means of grace along the path of salvation.

The conjunctive balance that Wesley was holding together in this area, in terms of divine and human action, can be seen in his comments to Isaac Andrews made much later in a letter, drafted on January 4, 1784, in which Wesley articulated three maxims, each having to do with the utter graciousness and sovereignty of God, on the one hand, and human action, in some form or other, on the other hand.

The first maxim is as follows:

"Undoubtedly faith is the work of God; and yet it is the duty of man to believe."[44]

In this first statement Wesley pointed out the supernatural flavor of saving faith by noting that it is the work of God and therefore in a very real sense, a *gift*. But Wesley did not leave it at that. Though the source of faith is divine, its enactment is human. In other words, it is, after all, the duty of people to believe, having received the grace of God, since they are persons, not stones. Therefore, not even an omnipotent God would ever force or coerce belief in terms of a person, that is, one created in the *imago Dei*. Since it is, after all, the duty of people to believe, it makes eminent sense that they wait for such belief, whose source once again is divine, in the means of grace appointed to that end.

The second maxim, likewise made up of two key components, is as follows:

And every man may believe if he will, though not when he will.[45]

Observe that the first part of this maxim, "And every man may believe if he will," displays the Arminian flavor of Wesley's practical theology in that the possibility of coming to faith embraces all. That is, all people may be redeemed because Christ has made provision for each and every one. Here then is genuine human acting even if it is richly informed by the grace of God. However, the second part of the maxim, "though not when he will," reveals that human beings, though they can come to believe through grace, are never themselves in control. In other words, they are not at the center of things, but a sovereign God is precisely there, ever at the center. Accordingly, the Almighty will give the sheer gift of saving or justifying faith on a divine timetable, not a human one. In this way Wesley underscored, once again, the graciousness of saving faith.

The third maxim with its two key components is as follows:

". . . if he seek faith in the appointed ways, sooner or later the power of the Lord will be present whereby (1) God works, and by His power (2) man believes."[46]

Though John Wesley wanted to be second to none in his affirmation that faith is a gift from God and that justification is *received by grace through faith alone*, nevertheless unlike Molther and Bray at Fetter Lane, he also wanted to underscore that faith should be sought "in the appointed ways," which is another way in which Wesley could stress the value of the means of grace as the normal or ordinary channels through which the saving grace of God is communicated. In other words, praying, reading Scripture and receiving the Lord's Supper will not be the basis upon which anyone is justified, but they can and will be the means through which the justifying grace of God is communicated. This difference is very important though it was apparently lost on both Molther and Bray.

Repentance and Its Fruits

So then, in light of these three Wesleyan maxims above, it can now be affirmed as Wesley, himself, did in his sermon, "The Scripture Way of Salvation," that repentance (leave off evil, do good, use the means of grace) and its fruits are in some sense necessary for redemption or justification, that is, if there be time and opportunity for them. Such is the case because the prevenient grace of God ever shines through such working. Indeed, no human being ever works alone apart from all grace for God has already acted by sending, "The true light that gives light to everyone . . ." (John 1:9a). That is what prevenient grace is all about. Therefore, those who desire to receive the saving grace of God should not simply sit around and do nothing. Again, Wesley rejected all forms of fanaticism (and quietism) and especially the one playing out at Fetter Lane. In his sermon, "On Working Out Our Own Salvation, Wesley lifted up two key truths that amplify this point: "First, God worketh in you; therefore you can work. . . . Secondly, God worketh in you; therefore you must work. . . ."[47] In other words, the prior activity of God creates both ability and obligation. Repentance and its fruits, such as serving the poor, for example, will not be required *in the same sense* as faith nor *in the same degree*, for *faith alone* is ever the only thing that is absolutely required. However, if there be time and opportunity, and for most people that will indeed be the case, then repentance and its fruits are in some sense necessary on the way to the reception of the forgiveness of sins. Wesley held both of these truths together in a very careful, even artful, balance. One can study these distinctions more carefully by examining the summary sermon, "The Scripture Way of Salvation" in greater detail.

All Can Know That They Are Saved and Forgiven (Assurance)

Those who believe redemptively in Jesus Christ are not left in the dark in terms of their relationship to God. They are assured that they are nothing less than the beloved of the Lord and that Christ died for them, even them. Such assurance is expressed by the Apostle Paul in Romans 8:16, and it is no one less than the Holy Spirit who bears a direct witness to the redeemed: "The Spirit himself testifies with our spirit that we are God's children" (Romans 8:16). Beyond this, an indirect witness can be seen in terms of such things as a good conscience, the fruit of the Spirit, and walking in the obedience of faith.[48]

Repentance and Its Fruits

So important was the direct witness of the Holy Spirit to John Wesley because he saw an important connection between this teaching and the doctrine of justification itself. For example, in a "Letter to a Gentleman in Bristol," Wesley cited approvingly from one of William Romaine's works: "He [the Holy Spirit] evidences our being justified by bearing His testimony with our spirits that we are the children of God, and by enabling us to bring forth first the inward and then the outward fruits of the Spirit."[49] This emphasis on the direct witness of the Holy Spirit, in other words, that the living God actually testifies to the sons and daughters of God, got Wesley in trouble from time to time in eighteenth-century Enlightenment England with those detractors who considered such a witness evidence of "enthusiasm" or as it would be put today, "fanaticism." As Outler pointed out, the critics of Wesley and the Methodists on this score "varied from moderate and serious men like Josiah Tucker and Joseph Trapp to intemperate pamphleteers such as those listed in Richard Green's Anti-Methodist Publications."[50] Wesley, however, remained undeterred in the face of such criticism for he believed that so much was at stake. The Holy One of Israel, who offered the gift of the Son, the Messiah, wants the children of God to know that they are indeed the beloved. What a source of both comfort and strength is such a witness throughout the Christian life!

In an important letter to his brother, Charles, drafted in 1747, Wesley affirmed three basic truths in terms of the direct witness of the Holy Spirit: "I allow (1) that there is such an explicit assurance; (2) that it is the common privilege of real Christians; (3) that it is the proper Christian faith, which purifieth the heart and overcometh the world."[51] Though the witness of the Holy Spirit is indeed a common privilege of a child of God, nevertheless Wesley recognized that there are exempt cases or exceptions due to either "disorder of body, or ignorance of the Gospel promises."[52] In other words, disease as well as ignorance of Scripture may prevent one from realizing this precious gift from the Most High, freely given to those who are justified.

> How can a sinner know
> His sins on earth forgiven?
> How can my gracious Saviour show
> My name inscribed in heaven?
> What we have felt and seen
> With confidence we tell,
> And publish to the sons of men
> The signs infallible.[53]

Moreover, over time, throughout the 1740's, Wesley came to recognize that there are degrees of assurance. This means then that the assurance associated with justification (and the new birth) is not full assurance (which would pertain to entire sanctification) for it can occasionally be marked by doubt and fear. In a letter to Richard Thompson, written in 1755, Wesley explained: "I know that I am accepted: And yet that knowledge is sometimes shaken, though not destroyed, by doubt or fear. If that knowledge were destroyed, or wholly withdrawn, 1 could not then say I had Christian faith."[54] So then, with the reception of the forgiveness of sins, believers know that they are accepted by Almighty God and that this assurance will deepen as they grow from grace to grace in the direction of heart purity. To know that one is not a servant, but a family member, sitting at the table of the Most High, so to speak, to belong, to be included in this distinct family life, marked by holy love, is an enormous blessing and one of the precious fruits of a vibrant Christian faith. The gifts of the redeemed are so great because the Giver is so great.

Serving Every Neighbor: The Fruit of Generous, Saving Grace

Having been justified freely by the grace of God, having received the assurance of the Holy Spirit that they were indeed the beloved of the Lord, the early Methodists were eager to share what gifts, both material and spiritual, they had received from the Lord with others. Indeed, John Wesley understood that a life of faith and grace, marked by the reception of gifts in so many ways, would become the engine of all manner of good works, evidencing a faith that was ever active in love, a lively faith, as St. James had put it (James 2:26), and not a dead faith. Wesley expressed this basic gospel truth in the following manner: "It is by faith in the righteousness and blood of Christ that we are enabled to do all good works."[55] Indeed, God in Christ had been so generous to the Methodists, and so this people, in turn, and out of a fund of grace-informed gratitude and thankfulness, sought to be a blessing to others as well.

Methodist labors among the poor in the eighteenth century, in other words, among those who lacked the basic necessities of life, such as food, clothing, shelter, and medicine, grew out of not only a deep sense of gratitude for gifts already received, but also out of a well-developed understanding of stewardship that arose in the class meetings themselves as the stewards managed the financial affairs of the society, received weekly contributions, and sent relief to the poor among their own numbers first of all. Again, recognizing that every good and precious gift is from above, Wesley taught that the Methodists in a real sense actually owned nothing at all since "we are now God's stewards. We are now indebted to him for all we have."[56] Exploring the nature and extent of this broad stewardship in his sermon, "The Good Steward," Wesley pointed out that the Holy One has endowed the children of God with all of the following: "an immortal soul, an immortal spirit,"[57] "our bodies,"[58] including "the most excellent talent of speech,"[59] "a portion of worldly goods,"[60] "several talents,"[61] especially "the talent of time,"[62] and of course the most precious gift of all, "the grace of God, the power of his Holy Spirit, which alone worketh in us all that is acceptable in his sight."[63]

> Lo! I come with joy to do
> The Master's blessed will,
> Him in outward works pursue,
> And serve his pleasure still.
> Faithful to my Lord's commands,
> I still would choose the better part,
> Serve with careful Martha's hands,
> And loving Mary's heart.[64]

Abundantly equipped, endowed with so many gifts and graces, the Methodists were guided by the counsel of no one less than Jesus, himself, in their ministry among the poor and as reflected in some of the words of Wesley as well:

> *Let us do unto all as we would they should do to us.* Let us love and honour all men. Let justice, mercy, and truth govern all our minds and actions. Let our superfluities give way to our neighbour's conveniences; (and who then will have any superfluities left?) our conveniences, to our neighbour's necessities; our necessities, to his extremities.[65]

Wesley expressed these same basic ethical truths, which should guide the lives of all Methodists, in his sermon, "The Use of Money," in three memorable and often-quoted phrases: *gain all you can*, thereby being industrious; *save all you can*, evidencing a godly thrift; and finally *give all you can*, displaying a generosity marked by the very love of God.[66]

In light of such counsel, offered in various literary forms, how could a Methodist, any Methodist, in the eighteenth century or today, engage in needless self-indulgence, in effect wasting what gifts have been entrusted to them, when the extremities of their neighbors repeatedly go unmet. "Cut off all this expense! Despise delicacy and variety, and be content with what plain nature requires,"[67] Wesley warned. Even more emphatically, he accused the rich of his own day, who repeatedly neglected proper stewardship, of outright "robbing the poor, the hungry, the naked, wrongdoing the widow and the fatherless."[68] The Methodists, for their part, would decidedly go another way—at least while under John Wesley's care and supervision.

Employing what resources and talents were at their disposal, and guided by a generous sense of stewardship, the Methodists were to become a blessing to others in the eighteenth century by taking up numerous ministries that Wesley, himself, had outlined in order to serve the poor. In 1740, for example, Wesley saw the poverty within the Methodist societies themselves, and he therefore developed the project of carding and spinning cotton that helped to ease the financial plight of some of its members.[69] A few years later, in 1748, Wesley realized that he could help those struggling to make ends meet by creating a lending stock in which funds could be provided for the startup and continuation of small businesses with the hope that these enterprises would quickly become self-sufficient and the money loaned could therefore be repaid. Of course, the early Oxford Methodists had visited the workhouses, the ones at "Whitefriars in Gloucester Green and near Little High Bridge in the parish of St. Thomas."[70] Beyond this, the Oxford Methodists ministered to those "in the county prison (at the Castle) and the city jail at the north gate (Bocardo),"[71] though the later Methodists, Silas Told among them, were well known for their gracious ministries attending to the condemned at Newgate prison. Earlier, in September 1738, John Wesley, himself, had taken up this often-neglected labor, and he visited "the condemned felons in Newgate and offered them *free salvation*."[72]

> Let us each for other care,
> Each the other's burden bear;
> To thy church the pattern give,
> Show how true believers live.[73]

Laboring among many of the lower class, Wesley was well aware that in eighteenth-century England several lawyers and physicians had grown accustomed to fleecing the poor by delaying their cases and thereby collecting larger fees. Clearly out of his element in the legal area, Wesley turned his attention to medicine, and he established a medical clinic for the poor at the Foundery towards the end of the 1740s.[74] No doubt chaffing under the criticism that even in the area of medicine he was likewise out of his depth, Wesley "hired an apothecary and a surgeon to take the difficult cases."⁷⁵ Perhaps Wesley's greatest help to the destitute in the area of medicine, however, came with the publication of his well-intentioned *Primitive Physick* in 1747 that was filled with the popular medical wisdom of the day, along with Wesley's own preferred treatments. This particular medical guide was so well received by the people that it went through many editions.

Beyond all of these efforts, John Wesley yet honored the poor in so many other ways. For one thing, he recognized the dignity of those who had been created in the blessed image of God just as he had been. His ministry among the poverty-stricken, therefore, took into account the whole person: body, soul and spirit. Such balance, such anthropological depth, is clearly on display in Wesley's sermon, "On Visiting the Sick," that was drafted in 1786. Observe the two key elements in this, and in the other material that is cited below, drawn from Wesley's own writings.

First of all, Wesley ministered both to the body *and* to the soul; never the one without the other. In other words, meeting the maintenance needs of the poor, in other words, providing such things as food, clothing and shelter, for example, was never enough. It was only a beginning, though an important one at that. Having cared for the body then it was imperative to minister to the soul since Methodist ministers in the eighteenth century were not and never were simply glorified social workers. That is a modern fiction. Indeed, the Methodists, who were seasoned by grace, the heirs of so many spiritual blessings, could bring gifts and benefits of which social workers hardly knew. That is the first basic truth of Wesley's ministerial posture.

Second, in the material cited below observe also that Wesley clearly made some important *value judgments* in terms of what ministry to the penniless was most important of all, judgments that have often been forgotten or outright repudiated by some of his twenty-first century heirs. Consider, then, the balanced counsel that Wesley offered to those who took up the Methodist ministry of easing the plight of the poor:

- "But it may not be amiss usually to begin with inquiring into their outward condition. You may ask whether they have the necessaries of life. Whether they have sufficient food and raiment. If the weather be cold, whether they have fuel. . . . These little labours of love will pave your way to things of *greater importance*. Having shown that you a regard for their bodies you may proceed to inquire concerning their souls."[76]

- "While you are eyes to the blind and feet to the lame, a husband to the widow and a father to the fatherless, see that you still *keep a higher end in view, even the saving of souls from death*, and that you labour to make all you say and do subservient to that great end."[77]
- "He doth good, to the uttermost of his power, even to the bodies of men. . . . *How much more does he rejoice if he can do any good to the soul of any man!*"[78]
- "Over and above all this, are you zealous of good works? Do you, as you have time, do good to all men? Do you feed the hungry and clothe the naked, and visit the fatherless and widow in their affliction? Do you visit those that sick? Relieve them that are in prison? Is any a stranger and you take him in? *Friend, come up higher.* . . . Does he enable you *to bring sinners from darkness to light, from the power of Satan unto God?*"[79]

To be sure, John Wesley knew the difference between the temporal affairs that are fleeting, filled with both the necessities of life and its pleasures, and the things that endure, in other words, that find their source in God, in holy love, and in all eternity. Again, John was richly acquainted with the pleasures and satisfactions of earthly life as well as with that particular lasting treasure, of far greater worth, of adoring God both now and forevermore, the very completion, the perfection, of all human purpose. In light of such carefully-drawn judgments, which naturally found their way into Wesley's ministry among the poor, he was eager to translate a hymn from Gerhard Tersteegen, no doubt with Charles's approval, that expressed these very same brilliant truths but this time in rich poetic form as evidenced in the following lines:

> Gladly the toys of earth we leave,
> Wealth, pleasure, fame, for thee alone
> To thee our will, soul, flesh we give;
> O take! O seal them for thine own!
> Thou art the God; thou art the Lord;
> Be thou by all thy works adored![80]

9. All People Can and Must Be Born Again

> *"You should not be surprised at my saying, 'You must be born again.'*
> *The wind blows wherever it pleases.*
> *You hear its sound, but you cannot tell where it comes from or where it is going.*
> *So it is with everyone born of the Spirit."* (John 3:7-8)

When many people think of conversion they often include justification or the forgiveness of sins along with regeneration or the new birth. Since the last chapter already explored the forgiveness of sins in great detail, it is now time to consider the new birth. As it will become clear as this chapter unfolds, if believers simply received the forgiveness of sins, as important as this is, without also being born of God, then it would be simply impossible to live the Christian life with any integrity or peace. In other words, without a transformation of nature, a modification of *being*, then those just forgiven would almost immediately commit the very same sins for which they had just sought forgiveness in the first place. Such an approach would not lead to happiness but to ongoing spiritual defeat and failure.

Wesley rejoiced in the truth that God who is merciful enough to forgive sins is also good enough to transform the hearts of believers. He wrote: "And at the same time that we are justified, yea, in that very moment, sanctification begins. In that instant we are born again, born from above, born of the Spirit."[1] Like justification, regeneration is therefore a fundamental, not a minor, doctrine of the Christian faith. Recall the language of the last chapter on this score: "If any doctrines within the whole compass of Christianity may be properly termed fundamental, they are doubtless these two, — the doctrine of justification, and that of the new birth: The former relating to that great work which God does *for us*, in forgiving our sins; the latter, to the great work which God does *in us*, in renewing our fallen nature."[2] Beyond this, when the

9. All People Can and Must Be Born Again

main doctrines of the Christian faith are considered, as Wesley, himself, had expressed them, then it is abundantly clear that the new birth is neither the "porch" nor the "door" of religion; but as being the very substance of holiness, it is "religion itself."[3] It is that important.

The Foundation of the New Birth

When Wesley considered what is the reason for or the foundation of the new birth, he interestingly enough drew a tight connection between the doctrine of original sin, on the one hand, and the new birth on the other. "Know your disease! Know your cure!," he wrote, "Ye were born in sin: Therefore 'ye must be born again,' born of God."[4] In other words, the foundation of the new birth is "the entire corruption of our nature."[5] Again, "In Adam ye all died: In the second Adam, in Christ, ye all are made alive."[6] Here then sin and grace are drawn together in a problem/solution model. The current human condition has resulted in malaise, broad and wide. That is unmistakable. Therefore, an utterly good God, who aims at abundant life for all, offers the happiness of holiness, initially begun at the new birth. In short, sin results in misery; holiness results in bliss. Once again, "Know your disease! Know your cure!"[7]

Since Wesley drew this relation between original sin and the new birth, then the clear consequence of this judgment is that *all* people can and must be born again. That is, since original sin is universal, with of course the one exception of Jesus Christ, then the new birth, at least the offer of it, predicated on the atoning work of Christ, must be universal as well. To fail to discern the universality of the offer of the new birth to all sinners who are in need, due to the corruptions of original sin in their lives, is to fail to appreciate the extent of the goodness, mercy and the love of God. Again, to fail to discern the universality of the offer is to construct a theology that wallows in a sinful pessimism in which sin repeatedly triumphs over grace and in which so many are never offered what graces they actually need. In short, such a theology bespeaks neither of a God of holy love nor of generosity, but of a much different understanding of the Most High. Charles Wesley expressed this truth well:

> While dead in trespasses I lie,
> Thy quick'ning Spirit give:
> Call me, thou Son of God, that I
> May hear they voice and live.[8]

A Definition of the New Birth

The strength and power of the good will of God towards sinners is seen in the reality of the new birth, which by definition is not a minor, weak or empty change but is in the words of John Wesley, "a vast and mighty change; a change from darkness to light, as well as from the power of Satan unto God; as a passing from death unto life, a resurrection from the dead."[9] Indeed, the rich vocabulary that Wesley repeatedly employed in his writings to describe this life-giving grace bespeaks of its broad extent and empowering nature. Observe Wesley's descriptions of the new birth in the following language:

- "It is that great change which God works in the soul when he brings it into life: when he raises it from the death of sin to the life of righteousness."[10]
- "It is the change wrought in the whole soul by the almighty Spirit of God when it is 'created anew in Christ Jesus', when it is 'renewed after the image of God', 'in righteousness and true holiness.'"[11]
- "it is that change whereby the 'earthly, sensual, devilish' mind is turned into 'the mind which was in Christ'."[12]
- "that entire, general change, the new birth; that total change, from the image of the earthly Adam into the image of the heavenly; from an earthly, sensual, devilish mind, into the mind that was in Christ."[13]

The common word in each of the descriptions above is "change." The new birth, then, is that transformation of *being* that all believers receive through life-giving grace. Moreover, in a couple of instances above Wesley located such change in the "soul," in other words in the depth or heart of persons, the throne room of their being. If, however, sinners are not open to a change in being, simply because they privilege their own current sinful state or experience and thereby make it the center, then such a marvelous change is not in the offing.

As great as the new birth is, it is by no means the whole of sanctification or holiness but its very beginning. In his sermon, "The New Birth," for instance, Wesley explained: "This is a part of sanctification, not the whole; it is the gate to it, the entrance into it. When we are born again, then our sanctification, our inward and outward holiness, begins; and thenceforward we are gradually to "grow up in Him who is our Head."[14] As a good teacher,

Wesley illustrated this important truth of the temporal dimensions of the new birth by drawing an analogy with natural birth. He observed: "A child is born of a woman in a moment, or at least in a very short time: Afterward he gradually and slowly grows, till he attains to the stature of a man. In like manner, a child is born of God in a short time, if not in a moment. But it is by slow degrees that he afterward grows up to the measure of the full stature of Christ."[15] Put another way, the new birth, or what can be called regeneration or initial sanctification, is the beginning of holiness not its entirety. It is the gateway to sanctity not its summation. "The same relation, therefore, which there is between our natural birth and our growth," Wesley wrote, "there is also between our new birth and our sanctification."[16]

All Must Be Born Again

The Necessity of the New Birth

Around the turn of the twentieth century, William James, the great philosopher and student of human nature, published his classic book, *The Varieties of Religious Experience*. James was perhaps influenced in some way by the revivalism of nineteenth century America, as well as by Horace Bushnell's reaction to it, as evidenced in the latter's work, *Christian Nurture*. Indeed, Bushnell had claimed that "The child is to grow up a Christian, and never know himself as being otherwise,"[17] in which the socializing forces of hearth and pew would rule the day. In a similar fashion, James developed the distinction between the once-born and the twice-born in his own work as if not everyone had to be born again in order to live out the Christian life. He explained: "In spite of the unquestionable fact that saints of the once-born type exist, that there may be a gradual growth in holiness without a cataclysm; in spite of the obvious leakage (as one may say) of much mere natural goodness into the scheme of salvation; revivalism has always assumed that only its own type of religious experience can be perfect. . . ."[18]

There are a number of misunderstandings in the work of Bushnell and James that need to be cleared up before readers can appreciate the necessity of being born again for all people, whether they are well socialized or not, whether they are well educated or not, on no less than the authority of Jesus Christ, himself, who exclaimed: "Very truly I tell you, no one can see the

The Necessity of the New Birth

kingdom of God unless they are born again" (John 3:3). First of all, because both Bushnell and James view all spiritual change in a gradual manner as changes of degree, in other words, a little more of what already was, the stuff of ongoing socializing forces, then they are not prepared to embrace those *qualitatively* distinct changes that occur when something radically *new* is introduced. To be sure, the new birth, as both Scripture and Wesley understood it, is not a little more of what already was, it is not a change in degree, but it represents nothing less than a *qualitative* change that bespeaks neither of nature nor of some normal socializing process, but of grace, even supernatural grace, the very gift of God. Simply put, the new birth is that qualitative change that marks the transition from sin to holiness. It is something new, unmistakably new. For his part, Charles Wesley observed:

> Take away my darling sin,
> Make me willing to be clean;
> Make me willing to receive
> All thy goodness waits to give.
> Force me, Lord, with all to part,
> Tear these idols from my heart;
> Now thy love almighty show,
> Make ev'n me a creature new.[19]

Second, John Wesley was adamant on this score in his own day, having already encountered the champions of moralistic, social or ecclesiastical scripts, who mistakenly thought that because of them, the new birth was therefore optional and not required. Moreover, given the class consciousness of English society in the eighteenth century, many of England's supposed social betters thought that such a disruptive and turbulent change as the new birth should only find its way among the desperate, that is, among those who lived a mean existence and therefore required religion of this sort, in other words, a solution of this intensity. Wesley, of course, thought otherwise. Indeed, to claim that not everyone needs to be born again, that regeneration is simply required of those sin-sick souls who have grievously lost their way, is not only to fail to acknowledge the *universality* of original sin, as well as its *extent*, as noted earlier, but it is also to mistake some form of moralism or celebrated virtue for the very substance of holiness, initially received, which is not a natural work at all but a supernatural work, a sheer gift from a God of holy love. In his sermon, "The New Birth," written in 1760, Wesley explained: Go to church twice a day, go to the Lord's table every week, say ever so many prayers in private; hear ever so many sermons, good sermons, excellent sermons, the best that ever were preached; read ever so many good books—still you must be born again. None of these things will stand in the place of the new birth. No, nor anything under heaven."[20]

Moreover, of the person who claimed that "he always was a Christian,"[21] Wesley replied in a way that would dispel the illusion: "He knows no time when he had need of such a change. By this also, if he give himself leave to think, may he know, that he is not born of the Spirit; that he has never yet known God; but has mistaken the voice of nature for the voice of God."[22] Moreover, Charles Wesley likewise underscored the necessity of the new birth as revealed in the following:

> I must for faith incessant cry,
> And wrestle, Lord, with thee;
> I must be born again, or die
> To all eternity.[23]

The New Birth Is Necessary for Holiness and Happiness

The necessity of the new birth is championed by the author of the Book of Hebrews for the sake of holiness: "Make every effort to live in peace with everyone and to be holy; without holiness no one will see the Lord" (Hebrews 12:14). Likewise Wesley developed this theme in his writings by lifting up the biblical image of "the wedding garment" (an image that is a part of a parable found in the Gospel of Matthew), and by showing its relation to holiness that can have no beginning apart from the new birth. To illustrate, in his sermon, "The Wedding Garment," Wesley revealed a number of ways in which holiness is essential to the Christian life. First of all, after pointing out that the righteousness of Christ is necessary to enter into glory, Wesley then noted that so too is holiness.[24] Second, he continued this theme but now with a couple of variations: "But it is highly needful to be observed, that they [justification and the new birth] are necessary in different respects. The former is necessary to entitle us to heaven; the latter to qualify us for it. Without the righteousness of Christ we could have no claim to glory; without holiness we could have no fitness for it."[25]

The very last words of Wesley cited above that "without holiness we could have no fitness for it [heaven]," get at the heart of his practical theology and his basic understanding of redemption. Yes, salvation entails the forgiveness of sins, to be sure, what is referred to as justification, theologically speaking, as noted earlier. However, if that forgiveness of sins is not accompanied by a renewal of nature in holiness, which begins in the new birth, then believers would have no fitness for heaven. In other words, the new birth or initial sanctification transforms the very being of believers such that they are now fit for heaven in the sense that they can be in the glorious presence of God right now on earth and not turn away in shame but can look up and cry out, "Abba Father" (Rom. 8:16). The fullness of this holiness that makes one fit for glory will, of course, be realized in entire sanctification, a topic that will be explored in the following chapter.

Beyond this, to maintain that the new birth is necessary for holiness is also to make the claim that the new birth is required for happiness; the one reality is readily connected to the other. In his writings, for example, Wesley maintained that "except he be born again none can be happy even in this world."[26] Why is this so? It's simply because, as Wesley reasoned, "No wicked man is happy."[27] Put another way, "all unholy tempers are uneasy tempers."[28] Such dispositions of the heart were never meant in the larger scheme of things to make one happy. It is quite the reverse; such dispositions can only lead in the end to misery. Think for a moment of envy, jealousy, greed, revenge, lust and hatred in comparison to the fruit of the Spirit in terms of love, joy, peace, patience, kindness and the like, and a clear picture begins to emerge although such clarity is often lost on sinners caught in the grip of their own pet evils. Nevertheless, the way to happiness runs along the path of holiness. And that path begins with the new birth.

All Can Be Born Again

In order to appreciate in a deeper way the reality of the new birth, distinguished from entire sanctification, for instance, it is helpful to consider the following threefold distinction:

1. Initial sanctification or the new birth (qualitative difference)
2. The process of sanctification (changes of degree)
3. Entire sanctification (qualitative difference)

In terms of the new birth, the first distinction, it must be pointed out at the outset that this is not a human possibility at all. In other words, men and women, try as they may, they cannot make themselves holy. They are simply powerless to do so. That is, no amount of education will ever bring the new birth about. No reform program, however brilliantly devised, will ever bring it into being. No amount of wanting it, as if human desire were the proper engine in this setting, can ever make it happen. To be sure, the new birth is once again not a human work but a divine work. It is not a thing of nature but of grace, supernatural grace. As a consequence, the new birth must be *received* as the sheer gift that it is from the hands of a God of holy love. Indeed, in his treatise *An Earnest Appeal to Men of Reason and Religion* Wesley highlighted the gracious reception of the new birth in the following way: "'It is the gift of God.' No man is able to work it in himself. It is a work of omnipotence. It requires no less power thus to quicken a dead soul, than to raise a body that lies in the grave. It is a new creation; and none can create a soul anew, but He who at first created the heavens and the earth."[29] And Charles added:

> O my God, what must I do?
> Thou alone the way canst show.
> Thou canst save me in this hour;
> I have neither will nor power.
> God if over all thou art,
> Greater than the sinner's heart,
> All thy power on me be shown,
> Take away the heart of stone.[30]

In his practical theology John Wesley considered the relation between justification, on the one hand, and sanctification on the other hand, the one having to do with a change in *relation*; the other with a change *in being*. In his sermon, "The Scripture Way of Salvation," for instance Wesley remarked as follows: "Exactly as we are justified by faith, so are we sanctified by faith. Faith is the condition, and the only condition of sanctification, exactly as it is of justification. It is the condition: none is sanctified but he that believes; without faith no man is sanctified. And it is the only condition: this alone is sufficient for sanctification. Everyone that believes is sanctified, whatever else he has or has not."[31] Though Wesley is referring to entire sanctification in this context, the same relation holds between justification and the new birth; the logic is exactly the same. In other words, the new birth, just like justification, is an utter gift and therefore is to be received by grace through faith alone, *sola fide*.

The grace, then, that informs the reception of the new birth is not cooperant grace, as is sometimes mistakenly supposed, but free grace, highlighting the divine, sovereign role. In his sermon, "The Means of Grace," Wesley elaborated:

> Ye are saved from your sins, from the guilt [justification] and power [regeneration] thereof, ye are restored to the favour and image of God, not for any works, merits, or deservings of yours, but by the free grace, the mere mercy of God, through the merits of his well-beloved Son: Ye are thus saved, not by any power, wisdom, or strength, which is in you, or in any other creature; but merely through the grace or power of the Holy Ghost, which worketh all in all.[32]

Observe in the paragraph above that Wesley was continuing the Reformation by applying some of its keys insights, in terms of free grace and *sola fide*, not simply to justification and the forgiveness of sins, a forensic theme, but also to the new birth and entire sanctification, participatory themes. Simply put, the new birth, just like justification, is an utter gift from God and is therefore to be received by grace through *faith alone*. In other words, just as one does not have to be or do something else first in order to make oneself worthy to receive the forgiveness of sins, so too one does not have to be or do something else first in order to receive the new birth, to become a child of God as if it were absolutely required. Simply put, the new birth as the gift of God is ever received by grace through faith *alone*. How generous, how marvelous, then, is God such that "Whatsoever good is in man, or is done by man, God is the author and doer of it. Thus is his grace free in all; that is, no way depending on any power or merit in man, but on God alone, who freely gave us his own Son, and 'with him freely giveth us all things.'"[33]

All Can Be Set Free (From the Power and Dominion of Sin)

The generosity of John Wesley's theology is abundantly evident in his teachings on the new birth which reflect divine grace and empowerment. Indeed, the gifts of the Almighty lavished upon the sons and daughters of God can be seen, first of all, in terms of presence of the Holy Spirit, now tabernacling in their souls, aiding, comforting and empowering. The table has already been set, and all has been provided. In particular, as Wesley explored the marks of the new birth (faith, hope and love) in greater detail, in a sermon by the same name, he stressed the enormous freedom that those born of God enjoy, namely, a liberty that is so broad and expansive that it must be expressed in a twofold way as both *freedom from* and *freedom to*. One framework alone is simply not enough.

In terms of the first liberty that the children of God enjoy, namely *freedom from*, they are set free, as heirs of the kingdom, by invigorating, regenerating grace, from the very power or dominion of sin. The shackles of slavery are now thrown off. In his sermon, "The Marks of the New Birth," for instance, Wesley exclaimed: "An immediate and constant fruit of this faith whereby we are born of God, a fruit which can in no wise be separated from it, no, not for an hour, is power over sin; — power over outward sin of every kind; over every evil word and work; . . . and over inward sin; . . ."[34]

Notice in the affirmation above just cited that believers are set free from committing both outward *and* inward sins, in other words from a full range of actual sins (plural), both of omission and commission, that can plague the soul and keep it enslaved. This full range of liberty, precious in so many ways, is also reflected in Wesley's following cautions as he calls sinners to repentance and to the empowering graces of the new birth: "O repent, repent! Know yourself; see and feel what a sinner you are. Think of the innumerable sins you have committed, even from your youth up. How many wicked words have you spoken? How many wicked actions have you done? Think of your *inward sins*; your pride, malice, hatred, anger, revenge, lust!"[35]

> In God we put our trust;
> If we our sins confess,
> Faithful he is, and just,
> From all unrighteousness
> To cleanse us all both you and me:
> We shall from all our sins be free.[36]

Theologically speaking, the liberty entailed in the new birth can be seen in terms of the freedom of justification or the forgiveness of sins as Wesley related these two doctrines, and in some sense compared them, in accordance with their associated freedoms. In his sermon, "What is Man?" for example, Wesley wrote: "Believe in the Lord Jesus Christ, whom God hath given to be the propitiation for thy sins, and thou shalt be saved'; first from the *guilt of sin*, having redemption through his blood; then from the power, which shall have no more dominion over thee...."[37]

Remarkably enough, when Wesley in his own eighteenth-century setting proclaimed the glorious liberties of the children of God, a number of people immediately balked and began to qualify such bold statements in what was actually an exercise of unbelief. Some, for example, maintained that those born of God were not actually free from the power of sin in their daily lives, nothing so great as that, but that they only did not commit sin habitually. When Wesley heard that one word "habitually," he immediately recognized the evasion that it entailed, and he therefore responded with a measure of energy in the following manner: "'Whosoever is born of God doth not commit sin habitually.' Habitually! Whence is that? I read it not. It is not written in the Book. God plainly saith, 'He doth not commit sin'; and thou addest, habitually! Who art thou that mendest the oracles of God?"[38] Charles Wesley added his clear voice on this matter as well.

> For this in steadfast hope I wait;
> Now, Lord, my soul restore,
> Now the new heavens and earth create,
> And I shall sin no more.[39]

However, John and Charles Wesley's older brother, Samuel, Jr., balked at the liberty of the children of God as his brothers had proclaimed it. Thus, in a very revealing letter to John, Samuel, Jr. posed a number of qualifying questions: "Have you ever since continued sinless?"[40] he asked. "Do you never, then, fall? Or do you mean no more than that you are free from presumptuous sins?"[41] After these pointed questions, Samuel drew the only conclusion he knew how: "If the former, I deny it; if the latter, who disputes?"[42] So then, in his conclusion, Samuel, Jr. was evidently only willing to admit that a Christian believer can be free from presumptuous sins and the like, perhaps such things as adultery or public drunkenness, but that is about as far as gospel liberty goes according to some. This judgment, however, once again constitutes evasion. Not surprisingly, John Wesley, himself, had actually responded to others, though in this particular case not directly to his brother, who had raised similar objections and qualifications. To illustrate, he wrote to one of his detractors no doubt with some exasperation: "But if you would hence infer, that all Christians do and must commit sin as long as they live; this consequence we utterly deny: It will never follow from those premises."[43]

Even more emphatically, Wesley declared: "What; make Christ destroy his own kingdom? make Christ a factor for Satan? set Christ against holiness? talk of Christ as saving his people in their sins? It is no better than to say, He saves them from the guilt, and not from the power, of sin. Will you make the righteousness of Christ such a cover for the unrighteousness of man?"[44] Furthermore, on this particular theological issue Charles Wesley, once again, shared the same theological view of his brother John, and not Samuel, as is evidenced in the following stanza:

> With labour faint thou wilt not fail,
> Or wearied give the sinner o'er,
> Till in this earth thy judgments dwell,
> And born of God I sin no more.[45]

From the perspective of the self that in a real sense is still managing its own spiritual life, the liberty of the new birth looks like an impossibility, an unreachable *standard*—and it is! Indeed, nothing that the self is or does will ever bring it about. That is precisely the point. Therefore the best counsel is to abandon all attempts at self-justification as Wesley himself did in 1738. From the much different perspective of saving faith, the new birth looks like a precious *promise* that will be fulfilled by a gift-giving, generous God and realized in the soul by grace through faith alone—and therefore not an impossibility at all! The difference between these two viewpoints is so wonderfully important. "Wherever the Spirit of the Lord is there is freedom, real freedom (2 Cor. 3:17). And as Wesley, himself, noted in terms of this last passage: "liberty to behold with open face the glory of the Lord."[46]

All Can Be Set Free (To Love God and Neighbor)

The liberty of the new birth, as great as it is, is not exhausted in any measure of *freedom from*. That is only part of the story. There is also a *freedom to*, even a freedom to love God and neighbor. Accordingly, as believers make the transition, through the efficacious grace of God, from sin to holiness, not only is the blessed image in which they were created renewed in splendor, evidencing the very beauty of God in their souls, but they are also empowered, as the drag of sin is thrown off, to love God and neighbor as they ought.

Wesley described the liberating renewal of the *imago Dei* that takes place at regeneration in the following way:

> It is the change wrought in the whole soul by the almighty Spirit of God when it is "created anew in Christ Jesus;" when it is "renewed after the image of God, in righteousness and true holiness;" when the love of the world is changed into the love of God; pride into humility; passion into meekness; hatred, envy, malice, into a sincere, tender, disinterested love for all mankind. In a word, it is that change whereby the earthly, sensual, devilish mind is turned into the "mind which was in Christ Jesus."[47]

As the unholy and uncomfortable passions of the heart such as "hatred, envy, [and] malice,"[48] are transformed into "a sincere, tender, disinterested love for all mankind,"[49] by the grace and power of God, as Wesley carefully noted above, a genuine healing of the soul begins to take place, as the promise of Christian discipleship is embraced. Observe that it is precisely at this point of the *ordo salutis*, in other words, in terms of the healing graces of the new birth, when the therapeutic framework, that is, Christ as the Great Physician of the soul, really starts to come into its own. Again, in this very special setting of renewal and transformation, both the love and grace of God are the healing balms applied to the soul to bring about not only its healing but also its high purpose.

Moreover, in the process of sanctification, which can be distinguished from the new birth, as believers grow in holiness and are transformed by degrees, and as they are slowly healed by both grace and love, there is a genuine divine and human cooperation that takes place that is indicative of the flush of cooperant graces now filling the soul. Granted the new birth is and remains a species of free grace, an utter gift from God, and in a real sense the work of God alone. Only God can make a soul holy. Nevertheless, the process of sanctification that it begins, an invitation to love both God and neighbor ever more deeply, with so much healing along the way, is clearly a species of cooperant grace, that is, a genuine divine and human working together. In his sermon, "The Great Privilege of Those That are Born of God," Wesley explained:

> From what has been said we may learn . . . what the life of God in the soul of the believer is, wherein it properly consists, and what is immediately and necessarily implied therein. It immediately and necessarily implies the continual inspiration of God's Holy Spirit; God's breathing into the soul, and the soul's breathing back what it first receives from God; a continual action

of God upon the soul, and a re-action of the soul upon God; an unceasing presence of God, the loving, pardoning God, manifested to the heart, and perceived by faith; and an unceasing return of love, praise, and prayer, offering up all the thoughts of our hearts, all the words of our tongues, all the works of our hands, all our body, soul, and spirit, to be a holy sacrifice, acceptable unto God in Christ Jesus.[50]

Moreover, even in the context of cooperant grace, Wesley made it abundantly clear in his sermon, "On Working Out Our Own Salvation," that human working never eclipses the overarching goodness and agency of God that shines through all human working. On this matter, Wesley elaborated in considerable detail:

> First, we are to observe the great and important truth which ought never to be out of our remembrance. 'It is God that worketh in us both to will and to do of his good pleasure. . . . [This] removes all imagination of merit from man, and gives God the whole glory of his own work. Otherwise we might have had some room for boasting, as if it were our own desert, some goodness in us, or some good thing done by us, which first moved God to work.[51]

So then, once again, Wesley's theology is ever marked by a careful, conjunctive balance: both cooperant grace *and* free grace, the latter at times pointing to overarching divine agency (a window on providence as well) even in the midst of synergistic contexts.

Repentance and Works Suitable for Repentance

Such a conjunctive balance is also evident in the gracious truth, clearly articulated by Wesley, that if people are not yet born of God but wish to be so, then they should wait for such a wonderful gift in the repentance and works suitable for repentance on the way to the new birth. This point was developed in the last chapter in terms of justification in great detail. It is now stated here briefly and in a summary fashion in terms of the new birth. In other words, the same exact counsel applies to both justification, on the one hand, and to the new birth, on the other hand. Doing literally nothing, then, a form of quietism, is not the way forward, *if there be time and opportunity*, and for most people there will be. Remember Fetter Lane! Rather because God has *already* acted in granting prevenient grace, which is leading to convincing grace, than those who desire saving, regenerating grace in particular can do something. They should not simply fold their hands, so to speak. Consequently, leaving off evil, doing good and using the means of grace, a very Methodist thing to do, will ever be the way forward. Such things will not be the basis upon which anyone is born of God, but they will likely become the means through which such invigorating grace is received.

Moreover, cooperant grace, a genuine divine and human working, will mark the *process* leading up to the new birth, though the new birth, itself, will be received as the sheer gift that it is—and remains. It is a species not of cooperant grace, but of free grace. Repentance and its fruits then will not be required *in the same sense as faith nor in the same degree, for faith alone* in this context as well is the only thing that is absolutely required. Put another way, cooperant grace prepares the way for free grace. That is, the new birth is not a change in degree, a little more of what already was; it is something remarkably new as its very name clearly indicates. Accordingly, the role of entering in is reserved for another, even for the remarkable free grace of God. Wesley's theology, then, is marvelously generous through and through. To be sure, in the end the saints will cry out not what they have done or suffered, but what they have received at the hands of a gracious God of holy love as a sheer, utter gift. Such is the wonder of the new birth when all things are made new.

All Can Know That They Are Born Again (Assurance)

When many Methodists from the eighteenth century as well as from the twenty-first century thought about Christian assurance, they often did so in terms of justification and the forgiveness of sins but not specifically in terms of the new birth. This is actually a remarkable development simply because the principal text from the Bible that John Wesley often quoted in terms of Christian assurance related specifically not to the forgiveness of sins (though it was implied) but to the new birth whereby one becomes a child of God. Observe the language of the Apostle Paul in Romans 8:16, Wesley's often-cited verse: "The Spirit himself testifies with our spirit that we are God's children." Moreover, when Wesley considered one of the marks of the new birth, namely hope, he specifically cited the words of Paul once more with great effect: "It is, so to hope in God through the Son of his love, as to have not only the 'testimony of a good conscience,' but also the Spirit of God 'bearing witness with your spirits, that ye are the children of God;' whence cannot but spring the rejoicing in Him, through whom ye 'have received the atonement.'"[52] Beyond this direct witness of the Holy Spirit, there is an indirect witness as well that can be seen in terms of such things as a good conscience, the fruit of the Spirit, and walking in the obedience of faith, a point noted earlier in terms of justification.[53]

In light of such usage, it is clear from both Scripture and the writings of John Wesley that the redeemed are not only assured their sins are forgiven, but they are also assured that they are born of God, in other words, that they have become the very children of the Most High. Assurance then in the theology of John Wesley has a two-fold referent, not simply one. Moreover, such a direct witness of the Holy Spirit, as attested to by no one less than the Apostle Paul, is a great comfort and a blessed gift enjoyed by the saints as they walk in the challenging paths of serious Christian discipleship. To know that one is the "beloved," that one has a familial relationship with no one less than God Almighty, issues in a fund of confidence which is once again a remarkable gift given to those who have been transformed by regenerating grace in order to know Christ and his benefit. Charles Wesley waxed eloquently on this score as revealed in the following:

> Come, Holy Ghost, my heart inspire!
> Attest that I am born again!
> Come, and baptize me now with fire,
> Nor let thy former gifts be vain.
> I cannot rest in sins forgiven;
> Where is the earnest of my heaven?[54]

Election and Predestination

This section on election and predestination is appropriately placed in a chapter on the new birth because these doctrines are often confused and conflated in some other theological traditions. Put another way, in some Christian circles, beyond Wesleyanism, the new birth and election are effectively judged to be equivalent such that to be born of God is to be deemed to be a member of the elect especially when, in addition, it is claimed that those who are born of God can never fall away. Wesley, however, thought otherwise. In fact, he maintained that those who have enjoyed the miracle of the new birth and who have thereby become holy, may yet ultimately fall away and perish. In his treatise, *Serious Thoughts Upon the Perseverance of the Saints*, for instance, Wesley exclaimed: "I believe a saint may fall away; that one who is holy or righteous in the judgment of God himself may nevertheless so fall from God as to perish everlastingly."[55]

Beyond this, Wesley believed that even those who are entirely sanctified, in other words, those who have become pure in heart, may yet, oddly enough, turn away to take up a life of sin once more and therefore ultimately be lost. In this same treatise Wesley observed, no doubt with a measure of pain, "One who is endued with the faith that purifies the heart, that produces a good conscience, may nevertheless so fall from God as to perish everlastingly."[56] So then, the new birth is one thing and election is quite another. These doctrines must therefore be distinguished simply because those who are *genuinely* born of God may yet ultimately fall away revealing that they were never, after all, a part of the elect. The new birth and election are different doctrines, to be sure. They are therefore neither to be confused nor equated.

In terms of the ongoing issues of election and predestination, the welcoming nature of Wesley's practical theology, underscoring the generosity of God, is clearly evident in two grand truths of the Bible associated with these issues: the first concerns the divine nature itself and along with it God's agency with respect to election and redemption. The second concerns human nature, as created by God, as well as the human role with respect to receiving in freedom what precious gifts God has to offer the world in Jesus Christ.

First of all, in terms of the divine nature, Wesley started out with the basic affirmation that love is the darling, reigning attribute of the Most High, a truth that has already been noted in Chapter One.[57] In other words, love defines the very essence of who God is and this attribute is also related to the basic goodness of God, that is, the Almighty is without any touch of evil at all. In his treatise, *Predestination Calmly Considered*, for example, Wesley elaborated: "'God is love,' love in the abstract, without bounds; and 'there is no end of his goodness.' His love extends even to those who neither love nor fear him. He is good, even to the evil and the unthankful; yea, without any exception or limitation, to all the children of men."[58] Recall the language of Charles Wesley, drawn from Chapter One and recited here for emphasis, as he added his voice to this chorus of divine love:

9. All People Can and Must Be Born Again

> Thy darling attribute I praise
> Which all alike may prove,
> The glory of thy boundless grace,
> Thy universal love.[59]

With these basic, biblical truths in terms of the nature of God in place, John Wesley rejected the notion of unconditional election, in other words, that a Sovereign God determined the fate of all humanity, that is, who will be the elect and who will be the reprobate, a determination that has no other cause than the divine freedom itself. However, if the reprobate are the reprobate simply due to the sovereign freedom and determination of God, in other words, by the simple decree of the Almighty, then they are obviously never offered what graces they actually need in order to be redeemed in the first place. Not surprisingly, Wesley therefore referred to this teaching as a "horrible decree,"[60] and it is! With election and reprobation so understood, and with such horrific consequences, it must be immediately asked: how then is God just? More important, how is God even good? And who could worship such a god? In detracting from both the love and goodness of God, such a theology gets the theological basics wrong. That is, it fails to understand who God is in terms of essential being and purpose. As pointed out already in Chapter One, God cannot but will the redemption of all of humanity precisely because of who God is. It bears repeating, God is love. That is the glorious affirmation of Scripture and such a truth is of such great comfort to the saints. Moreover, that is a fundamental truth of the Gospel that should have consequence for every aspect of one's theology. It clearly did for John and Charles Wesley.

Viewing this problem of unconditional election in yet another way, beyond its detraction from the very goodness and love of God, much of this theological mischief (Wesley called it blasphemy[61]), which is so very harmful to the children of God who continue to suffer under it, can be cleared up in the basic recognition, as Scripture abundantly attests, that election is not after all unconditional, as some have mistakenly supposed, a function simply of divine freedom and sovereignty, but is and has always been conditional. What is the condition of election and therefore of redemption as well? It is none other than faith in Jesus Christ. It was Charles who likely observed:

> Whom his eternal mind foreknew,
> That they the power would use,
> Ascribe to God the glory due,
> And not his grace refuse;[62]

Second, in the chapters on the doctrine of humanity, it was clearly affirmed earlier that the Almighty created human beings in the very image and likeness of God. Simply put, the *imago Dei* is the glory and honor of humanity, a reflection of the One in whom their dignity consists. In creating human beings in this fashion, as genuine dialog partners who through grace have the freedom to worship God or not, to love God or not, the Most High took on a limitation, a restriction of liberty, that was explored in Chapter Two. More to the point, once humanity was created in this blessed and glorious image, then even the Holy One must take this image and its consequences into account. In other words, for the sake of aiming at holy love in all things, God has created human beings such that they are in some sense free (by divine grace), a freedom that even God must honor given precisely who God is. That is, the Most High cannot simply run roughshod over human will and desire, determine humanity in a way that renounces the freedom that pertains to personhood and to the *imago Dei*, itself. Other theologies may have faltered here simply because they fail to take into account what being created in the image of God actually entails in the context of ongoing grace. In such theologies human beings in their personhood, and all that this entails, are never actually allowed to come to the table, so to speak.

In light of the preceding, it should now be clear that irresistible grace or determinism, especially in terms of the new birth, is not a possibility in John Wesley's theology,[63] because as he puts it, "men should be saved, yet not as trees or stones, but as men, as reasonable creatures, endued with understanding to discern what is good, and liberty either to accept or refuse it. . . ."[64] By rejecting a strict determinism in which God irresistibly makes a person holy, with no concurrence of the human will in freely *receiving* such grace, Wesley believed he was not only preserving the very nature of God and the kind of creatures that were created in the blessed image of the Holy One, but he was also preserving the integrity of the moral order, itself, both in terms of honors awarded or condemnations deserved. Observe Wesley's reasoning the following:

> I cannot praise the sun for warming, nor blame the stone for wounding me; because neither the sun nor the stone acts from choice, but from necessity. Therefore, neither does the latter deserve blame, nor the former deserve praise. Neither is the one capable of reward, nor the other of punishment. And if a man does good as necessarily as the sun, he is no more praiseworthy than that; if he does evil as necessarily as the stone, he is no more blameworthy.[65]

If human beings are born of God, renewed in being through the inculcation of holiness, then this glorious change does not happen apart from the grace-informed freedom of the human hearts that receive it. Believers, then, receive the new birth almost in a passive way. If it were utterly passive then that would be Calvinism. Here then is the nexus of John Wesley's practical theology. Indeed, he had made the boast that his theology came to the very edge of Calvinism. And it did. However, it never crossed over due to the measure of freedom, a species of prevenient grace, that yet remained and that was strongly associated with the personhood of sinners. Moreover, this personhood was a reflection of the marvelous image of God that was ongoing. In other words, not even a sinful human condition could utterly destroy the image for God has *already* acted in Jesus Christ through prevenient grace. There is therefore now no human being, no matter how steeped in sin, who is utterly devoid of all grace. To argue otherwise can only constitute a well-worked theological myth. Again, even sinners have freedom enough to receive further graces beyond the prevenient grace that they have already received. Accordingly, saving, regenerating grace, the kind of grace that makes one both holy and beautiful, must be *received* as the sheer gift that it is. And it can be!

> He now stands knocking at the door
> Of every sinner's heart;
> The worst need keep him out no more,
> Of force him to depart.
>
> Through grace we hearken to thy voice,
> Yield to be saved from sin,
> In sure and certain hope rejoice,
> That thou wilt enter in.[66]

10. Entire Sanctification: What It Is and Is Not

> *"May the God of peace himself sanctify you entirely; and may your spirit and soul and body be kept sound and blameless at the coming of our Lord Jesus Christ. The one who calls you is faithful, and he will do this." (1 Thessalonians 5:23-24; NRSV)*

For the church to flourish, as the living Body of Christ, in carrying out its high calling, it must not only bring those outside the church within, through evangelism and missionary activity, but it must also nourish its new members so that they will take up the mantel of serious Christian discipleship which will be ongoing. As John Wesley understood in his own eighteenth-century context, neither baptism nor confirmation for that matter, neither the forgiveness of sins nor the new birth, is the goal of the Christian life, its ultimate purpose, but these graces do mark its very beginning. In short, beginnings must not be mistaken for endings. However, many pastors, then as now, would be content simply to add such people to the rolls of the church and conclude that all is well. But such an attitude would constitute pastoral malpractice on so many levels as this current chapter will demonstrate. Indeed, the new birth is the beginning of sanctification or holiness not its perfection. It is a wonderful, grace-filled start, but an entire life yet awaits, to be lived across the decades, with numerous challenges strewn along the way. And the world, the flesh and the devil have not gone away—nor are they sleeping. It is one thing to become a Christian. It is quite another thing to remain and thrive as a Christian. Wesley being the good pastor that he was understood the difference.

As Wesley carried out his Holy Spirit-anointed mission and preached his way throughout key centers in England and elsewhere, he gathered up the harvest by placing those who had responded to his ministry in a class meeting. It was in this personal, social and accountable context, marked by numerous graces, that so many finally entered in. In other words, several people received the forgiveness of sins as well as the renewal of their natures in the new birth, which taken together would suitably be described as conversion, within a Methodist class meeting, itself. This part of the larger Methodist infrastructure, then, this small and engaged group in which names were known and faces remembered, proved to be in so many cases a precious instrument of grace.

For those within the Methodist household, who were by now so evidently born of God, their lives being marked by the fruit of the Holy Spirit, Wesley extended an invitation to them not to remain where they were but to go forward into the deeper graces of God. Though this theological concern of Wesley was clearly present early on, as demonstrated in his key sermon, "The Circumcision of the Heart," drafted in 1733, he did not take up the specific rhetoric of choosing "the more excellent way" of Christian living in sermon form until much later in his career. Thus, in his sermon by the same name, written in 1787, Wesley invited all the children of God to their high calling and purpose in the following manner:

> From long experience and observation I am inclined to think, that whoever finds redemption in the blood of Jesus, whoever is *justified*, has then the choice of walking in the higher or the lower path. I believe the Holy Spirit at that time sets before him the "more excellent way," and incites him to walk therein; to choose the narrowest path in the narrow way; to aspire after the heights and depths of holiness, after the entire image of God.[1]

Cooperating with God

Since believers now see a more excellent way of living before them, a higher Christian life, they realize that in this journey there can be no standing still. The call of God, as Wesley understood it, is ever to go forward. Indeed, to fail to improve the grace already received, through divine and human cooperation, is not to remain where one is but it is actually to go backward! In his sermon, "On Faith" (Heb. 11:6), composed in 1788, Wesley explained: "You cannot stand still; you must either rise or fall—rise higher or fall lower. Therefore the voice of God to the children of Israel, to the children of God is, 'Go forward.'"[2] And Wesley then added to this helpful counsel, giving a specific Christian reference: "Forgetting the things that are behind, and reaching forward unto those that are before, press on to the mark, for the prize of your high calling of God in Christ Jesus!'"[3] Beyond this, when Wesley had encouraged a certain Mrs. Barton earlier, in 1770, he reminded her that the grace of God is "sufficient for you," and that "you must continue to grow if you continue to stand; for no one can stand still. And is it not your Lord's will concerning you that you should daily receive a fresh increase of love?"[4] Simply put, and as Wesley had advised Miss March that same year, "To use the grace given is the certain way to obtain more grace. To use all the faith you have will bring an increase of faith."[5]

When believers had received the forgiveness of sins and the renewal of their natures earlier, it was then that "the seed of every virtue . . . [was] then sown in the soul."[6] Now through divine and human cooperation, as displayed in Wesley's sermon, "On Working Out Our Own Salvation,"[7] those implanted seeds are beginning to grow from one *degree of grace to the other*. In other words, believers are advancing slowly by increments, a little more of what already was is now coming into being. The fruit of the Spirit are growing, prospering, filled with divine grace and favor. Accordingly, believers are becoming more patient, kind and peaceful by degrees as they are situated in all the means of grace in community and as they take up the works of mercy in serving their neighbors, especially the poor among them. With such growth in grace underway, much healing of the soul is taking place in this process of sanctification, as believers become holier and holier over time. To be sure, it is at this point of the Christian journey in which Wesley's paradigm of salvation as therapy, a genuine healing of the soul *(therapeia psuches)*, and one in which Christ emerges as the Great Physician, begins to blossom beyond the new birth to embrace the healing entailed in the process of sanctification itself.

To be sure, Wesley affirmed not only a legal and moral paradigm of redemption but a therapeutic one as well. Granted the children of God, those justified and born of God, are indeed redeemed, that is, they are reconciled to a God of holy love and renewed in nature, but if everything was well, then why would they need a physician at all as well as therapy in an ongoing fashion, that is, throughout the *process* of sanctification? In considering salvation as therapeia psuches, Wesley pointed out that it is indeed "the only true method of healing a distempered soul."[8] However, he then added, filling out his meaning: "But what need of this, if we are in perfect health? If we are not diseased, we do not want a cure. If we are not sick, why should we seek for a medicine to heal our sickness?"[9] Again, though the children of God are clearly both forgiven and holy, further and necessary transformation yet awaits. This is precisely what so many pastors then as now have missed. One of the greatest enemies of both God and humanity is still very much in place. For many, however, this corrupted nature is either hidden or when it is even recognized at all, it is often ignored. However, the carnal mind or inbred sin ever lurks within, even in the hearts of the children of God. As such, a *second kind of repentance* is needed before believers are prepared to see Christ in glory face to face.

Evangelical Repentance

Earlier, in the chapters on justification and the new birth, what Wesley called *legal repentance* was in some sense necessary, if there were time and opportunity, as sinners repented of their actual sins, that is, sins of omission and commission, outward and inward sins. In other words, they repented of all the those sins that one *commits*. In this current setting, however, as believers are cooperating with God in grace, actual sins are not the problem. Indeed, Wesley observed: "The question is not concerning outward sin, whether a child of God commits sin or no. We all agree and earnestly maintain, 'He that committeth sin is of the devil. We agree, 'Whosoever is born of God doth not commit sin.'"[10] Rather believers, those who have all the marks of the new birth, of faith, hope and love, repent not of actual sins (plural) but of inbred sin (singular), the latter which is a state or condition. In other words, the sin problem for all of humanity is not singular but twofold. Therefore, an *evangelical repentance* will point the way to that additional cleansing of the soul that is necessary before one sees God face to face in glory. Moreover, Wesley's frank recognition of the twofold nature of sin as both "act" and "being" not only underscores the two foci of the Wesleyan *ordo salutis*, justification on the one hand and entire sanctification on the other, a well-developed conjunction in Wesley's practical theology, but it also demonstrates that entire sanctification is, after all, a second work of grace or what Wesley, himself, had referred to on numerous occasions as a "second blessing."[11] Simply put, salvation is not accomplished in one grand stroke.

Evangelical repentance, then, entails "a deep conviction that we are not yet whole; that our hearts are not fully purified; that there is yet in us a "carnal mind."[12] Healing must be ongoing and this second repentance, beyond a legal one, will involve a "deep conviction of our demerit, after we are accepted, which . . . is absolutely necessary in order to our seeing the true value of the atoning blood."[13] And thirdly, such a repentance will embrace "a deep conviction of our utter helplessness, of our total inability to retain anything we have received, much more to deliver ourselves from the world of iniquity, remaining both in our hearts and lives. . . ."[14] This need to be purified was expressed by Charles in the following lines that his brother, John, saw fit to publish as well:

> O grant that nothing in my soul
> May dwell, but thy pure love alone!
> O may thy love possess me whole,
> My joy, my treasure, and my crown!
> Strange fires far from my heart remove;
> My every act, word, thought, be love![15]

In light of these basic truths, such a repentance is necessary for believers, again if there be time and opportunity, simply because inbred sin or the carnal mind can neither be reformed nor forgiven. Listen to John Wesley's voice once more: "But if there be no such second change, if there be no instantaneous deliverance after justification, if there be none but a gradual work of God, (that there is a gradual work none denies,) then we must be content, as well as we can, to remain full of sin till death. . . ."[16] What's more, the carnal nature bars the way to that great blessing that God has in store for all believers. In other words, inbred sin as an active propensity to depart from the living God, as a corrupted nature in rebellion against a God of holy love, and as a seat of impurity within the soul that may repeatedly become the occasion of temptation for believers, this inbred sin, this carnal mind, again cannot be forgiven, not now, not ever; rather, it must *die*. To be sure, the carnal mind has no place in what is to come, in what awaits, and for Wesley the way is ever forward. In short, the soul must become nothing less than entirely sanctified, perfected in holy love. The need of such cleansing is evident once more in the following verse of which John, once again, heartily approved:

> Purge me from every sinful blot:
> My idols all be cast aside:
> Cleanse me from every evil thought,
> From all the filth of self and pride.
>
> The hatred of the carnal mind
> Out of my flesh at once remove:

> Give me a tender heart, resign'd,
> And pure, and full of faith and love.[17]

Entire Sanctification: What It Is Not

John Wesley employed a number of phrases to describe the second blessing which is none other than the second focus of the Wesleyan *ordo salutis*. That is, he wrote about entire sanctification, and sometimes perfect love, and at other times he waxed eloquently about Christian perfection. In other words, he employed all of these phrases interchangeably. The first two are the easiest on the ear but many people, both in the eighteenth century as well as in the twenty-first, react negatively whenever they hear the word perfection. In their minds, at least, the words human and perfect should never be in the same sentence. Wesley understood this reservation, and so he took great pains to describe in what ways Christians are not perfect.

First of all, Christians are *not perfect in knowledge*. "They are not so perfect in this life," Wesley observed, "as to be free from ignorance."[18] Human beings are ever dynamic, always capable of growing in wisdom and knowledge both now and throughout out eternity. Indeed, human knowledge of God and the goodness of the Almighty is inexhaustible. It will grow forever. "How astonishingly little do we know of God! How small a part of his nature do we know!"[19] Wesley exclaimed.

Second, the one limitation readily flows into another. Since Christians, those perfected in love, are not perfect in knowledge, then they will *not be free from mistake*. "Those who 'know but in part' are ever liable to err touching the things which they know not,"[20] Wesley pointed out. Put another way, out of ignorance those perfected in love may judge people to be better than they actually are, or worse than they actually are, thereby doing them real harm. However, not even a well-intentioned, pure heart will ever free one from such a mistaken judgment. Nevertheless, "'Tis true the children of God do not mistake as to the things essential to salvation. They do not put darkness for light, or light for darkness,"[21] Wesley affirmed clarifying his overall meaning. "But in things unessential to salvation they do err, and that frequently. The best and wisest of men are frequently mistaken even with regard to facts."[22]

Third, those whose hearts have been purified of all "filthiness of flesh and spirit"[23] (2 Cor. 7:1), a well-worked phrase on this topic for Wesley, are nevertheless *not free from infirmities* such as "weakness or slowness of understanding, dullness or confusedness of apprehension, incoherency of thought, irregular quickness or heaviness of imagination."[24] Mature Christian leader that he was, Wesley realized that there was room for serious misunderstanding in this area, and so he added the following caution: "Only let us take care to understand this aright. Let us not give that title to known sins, as the manner of some is. So, one man tells us, 'Everyman has his infirmity, and mine is drunkenness.'"[25] On the contrary, an infirmity is not a moral failure at all but is an amoral, temporal, finite limitation of embodied existence. Wesley understood, even in his own age, that the body can drag down the soul even in terms of the saints.

Fourth, those whose hearts have been washed by the blood of the lamb are *not free from temptation.*[26] Some have mistakenly thought that if the heart is pure, if the soul is utterly oriented to God in holy affections, then how could one possibly be tempted? The fault in such thinking is readily apparent once the additional question is raised, "Was Jesus Christ as a true human being actually tempted? The answer, of course, is "Yes," simply because all that is necessary for temptation is the following: a) freedom, b) knowledge of the will of God, and c) the circumstances of the temptation itself. All these elements were clearly in place for Jesus of Nazareth, even though he had a pure heart, just as they are in place for Christians of any age and of any measure of holiness.

Fifth, there is *no "absolute perfection on earth."* Wesley wrote, one that "does not admit of a continual increase."[27] The basic idea here is that perfection allows for an expansion, an enlargement, because human beings are dynamic persons who are constantly growing, becoming more than what they once were. But bear in mind that it is a pure heart that is increasing and growing, not an impure one. In other words, perfection and growth are not contradictory terms or mutually exclusive ideas. They do indeed belong together. This basic truth of salvation that plays out in the course of entirely sanctifying grace can be illustrated by the three beakers of increasing volume below:

10. Entire Sanctification: What It Is and Is Not

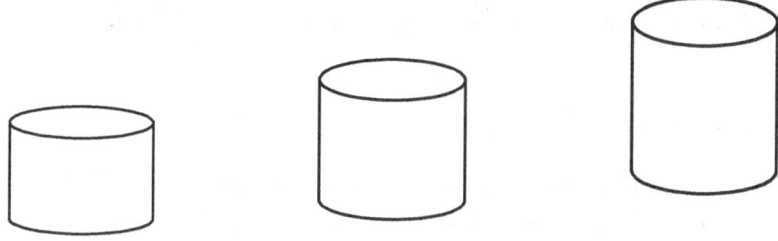

All of these beakers are filled to the top with water. And now for the first question: "Is any beaker more full than the other?" And the obvious answer is "No." No beaker is more full than the others. They are all equally full. Put another way, fullness is a *threshold change, a qualitative change*, and each beaker is filled to its capacity, to its very brim. And now for the second question, "Does one beaker contain more water than another?" And the answer is undoubtedly "Yes," because the beakers are of different sizes, different capacities. And so two of them do indeed contain more water than the smallest, and the largest of all contains more water than any other.

So then, the fullness of the beakers corresponds to the perfection of the heart, that it is *entirely sanctified*; in other words, it is of a *distinct qualitative* condition; it is in fact *pure*. The different volume of the beakers, however, corresponds to the growth, the changes in degree, that ever occur in persons as they thrive and become more over time especially in terms of knowledge, wisdom, and experience etc. But it will be persons who are pure in heart who are growing. That is precisely the point. In other words, these two ideas of qualitative distinctiveness and differences of degree due to growth are not contradictory. In fact, they point the way for the highest reaches of grace and being as Wesley taught and as the illustration above clearly affirms.

Entire Sanctification: What It Is

The doctrine of entire sanctification is so much a part of Scripture as well as the history of the Christian church that Wesley employed a number of different ways to describe this teaching. In fact, some of the distinct terminology, clearly not all, that Wesley used to describe this important teaching are so significant that each one will be listed separately and a brief observation will be offered in order to clarify its meaning. In this way, Wesley will be allowed to speak for himself which is especially important on this crucial topic.

The Doctrine of Jesus Christ

In his own day Wesley heard the claim that "This is Mr. Wesley's doctrine!" as if this teaching of entire sanctification was neither a part of Scripture nor of the Church but that it was simply his own idiosyncratic view. Wesley's reply to those who uttered this falsehood was brief and decisive: "it is the doctrine of Jesus Christ. Those are his words, not mine: . . . 'Ye shall therefore be perfect, as your Father who is in heaven is perfect.'"

Embracing the Two Great Commandments

In his sermon, "On Perfection," Wesley wrote as follows: "This is the sum of Christian perfection: it is all comprised in that one word, love. The first branch of it is the love of God: and as he that loves God loves his brother also, it is inseparably connected with the second, 'Thou shalt love thy neighbour as thyself.' Thou shalt love every man as thy own soul, as Christ loved us. 'On these two commandments hang all the law and the prophets:' these contain the whole of Christian perfection."[28]

The Humble, Gentle, Patient Love of God and Man

In a similar vein in terms of the preceding description, Wesley explored entire sanctification in a letter to his brother Charles as "the humble, gentle, patient love of God and man ruling all the tempers, words, and actions, the whole heart and the whole life."[29]

Having the Mind of Christ; Walking as Christ Walked

In the preface to a volume of hymns that was published in the early 1740s, the question was raised, "But whom then do you mean by 'one that is perfect?'" To which it was readily replied, "We mean one in whom is 'the mind which was in Christ,' and who so 'walketh as Christ also walked.'"

10. Entire Sanctification: What It Is and Is Not

The Circumcision of the Heart

Wesley lifted up entire sanctification in an early sermon, preached in 1733, utilizing a distinct rhetoric, and he employed similar language in his *A Plain Account of Christian Perfection* in the following way: "It is the circumcision of the heart from all filthiness, all inward as well as outward pollution."[30]

Holy Love

The one rhetoric of circumcision of the heart easily led to another well-worked one as is evident in the following excerpt drawn from Wesley's 1733 sermon just cited: "Here, then, is the sum of the perfect law; this is the true circumcision of the heart. Let the spirit return to God that gave it, with the whole train of its affections. . . . Let it be continually offered up to God through Christ, in flames of holy love."[31]

Cleansed from All Filthiness of Flesh and Spirit

In his treatise, *The Principles of a Methodist*, composed in 1742, Wesley reproduced material that he employed elsewhere but this time it is remarkably to the point: "But whom then do you mean by 'one that is perfect?' We mean one . . . that is 'cleansed from all filthiness of flesh and spirit'; one 'in whom is no occasion of stumbling. . . .'"[32]

Renewal of the Heart in the Whole Image of God

The first Adam despoiled the image in which he was created. The second Adam renewed it which led Wesley to observe in terms of Christian perfection: "It is a renewal of the heart in the whole image of God, the full likeness of Him that created it."[33]

Purity of Intention and Dedicating All the Life to God

One of the things that Wesley had learned from reading the writings of Jeremy Taylor, Thomas a Kempis, and William Law, early on in his career, is that the Christian life at its highest reaches is essentially devotion. As such, entire sanctification now emerges in his later writings as "purity of intention, dedicating all the life to God. It is the giving God all our heart; it is one desire and design ruling all our tempers. It is the devoting, not a part, but all our soul, body, and substance to God."[34]

Simplicity and Purity; Entire Devotion to God

Evil is complicated; goodness is simple. Liars have to have good memories to keep it all straight. Goodness is sincere: what you see is what you get. It is no surprise then that simplicity and purity make up the substance of what holiness at its highest reaches is all about. Wesley counseled a woman late in his career: "Always remember the essence of Christian holiness is *simplicity and purity*; one design, one desire—entire devotion to God."[35]

Perfect Love

In his commentary on 1 John 4:18, one of Wesley's favorite books on the topic of entire sanctification, he observed in a pungent, brief and very helpful way: "It is 'perfect love.' This is the essence of it."[36]

Deliverance from All Sin

And finally, in *A Plain Account of Christian Perfection* Wesley declared: "Christian perfection is that love of God and our neighbour, which implies deliverance from all sin."[37] Such a truth was expressed in this same account but this time in verse:

> From every evil motion freed,
> (The Son hath made us free,)
> On all the powers of hell we tread,
> In glorious liberty.[38]

Entire Sanctification and Freedom.

The clear majority of the preceding twelve descriptions of the essence, the very heart, of entire sanctification are expressed *positively* in terms of "freedom to." In other words, Christian perfection is the freedom to love God and neighbor as we ought. And what a freedom this is! It is only the last description, however, deliverance from all sin, that actually begins to move in a different direction: not freedom to but *freedom from;* the one a positive expression, the other a negative one.

So then what kind of sin are those who are entirely sanctified freed from? As the children of God they have *already* been set free from the guilt (justification) and power (regeneration) of sin earlier when they received redemptive graces, properly speaking, that is, through the forgiveness of sins and the renewal of their natures. Remarkably, Wesley took great pains to insure that these earlier liberties, as precious as they are, would not be confused with that of perfect love, a common mistake. He therefore reminded the Methodists of the following basic, gospel truth: ". . . even babes in Christ are in such a sense perfect, or born of God, . . . as, First, not to commit sin."[39] Observe in this last phrase that Wesley is not writing about those who are entirely sanctified, a common mistaken interpretation, but about "babes in Christ," in other words, about the children of God. And even they enjoy such a liberty, such a freedom, as not to commit sin. They are "saved from sin;"[40] Wesley remarks, "yet not entirely: It remains, though it does not reign."[41] In short, the freedom entailed in entire sanctification is something even *greater* than this.

By his clarifying comments Wesley was trying to make sure that the Methodists would parse the freedoms of the gospel in the right way, making the proper distinctions in the area of *freedom from in terms of guilt, power and being*. To illustrate, in his sermon, "On Sin in Believers," composed in 1763, Wesley explained: "The guilt is one thing, the power another, and the being yet another. That believers are delivered from the guilt and power of sin we allow; that they are delivered from the being of it we deny."[42] When exactly then are believers set free from the being of sin? Only when they are perfected in love. That is freedom from at its height, a gospel truth, that Charles Wesley so aptly expressed in a few memorable lines:

> Breathe, O breathe thy loving Spirit
> Into every troubled breast,
> Let us all in thee inherit,
> Let us find that second rest;
> Take away our bent to sinning,
> Alpha and Omega be,
> End of faith, as its beginning,
> Set our hearts at liberty.[43]

Entire Sanctification and Freedom.

Entire sanctification, setting our hearts at liberty as Charles had put it, is about freedom in a double sense: freedom *from* and freedom *to*. Such a celebrated freedom, as the Wesley brothers had explored it in their writings throughout the years, is ever in the service of love, that is, the holy love of God and neighbor.

11. All the Children of God Can Receive Entire Sanctification

> *"For by a single offering he has perfected for all time those who are sanctified."*
> *(Hebrews 10:14; NRSV)*

The balance of John Wesley's practical theology is readily seen when the two foci of his order of salvation, that is, justification, on the one hand, and entire sanctification on the other hand, are considered. Informed by some of the key insights of the Reformation, Wesley maintained that the precious gift of entire sanctification is received in a parallel way, when compared to the reception of justification and the new birth, as a previous chapter has already made clear. Nevertheless, is there a sense in which entirely sanctifying faith is different from justifying faith? The answer, for Wesley, is of course "Yes," a topic now to be considered in its own right.

What Is Entirely Sanctifying Faith?

Entirely sanctifying faith is in some sense different from regenerating and justifying faith. It is and remains, after all, distinct. For one thing, it takes into account the growth in grace that has already occurred, and that it is a person who is already *holy* that seeks heart purity. In his sermon, "The Scripture Way of Salvation," one of Wesley's most important ones, he lays out four key dimensions of this particular faith.

1. "First, that God hath promised it in the Holy Scripture."[1]
2. "Secondly, that what God hath promised he is able to perform."[2]

3. "Thirdly, a divine evidence and Conviction that he is able and willing to do it now."[3]
4. "[Fourthly] there needs to be added one thing more, — a divine evidence and conviction that he doeth it."[4]

In order to rightly interpret these four basic characteristics of entirely sanctifying faith, as noted above, it must be recognized at the outset that all Christians of whatever tradition believe that there is no sin in heaven, none at all. Indeed, if there were sin in such a setting then it would not be heaven, period! The differences, then, between the various Christian traditions on this score come about in terms of *when and by what means* are believers entirely sanctified. Roman Catholics, for example, believe that the soul will be purified after death in a place known as purgatory. Lutherans and Calvinists reject any purification beyond death and instead insist that death itself brings about heart purity. Wesley rejected the first option because the idea of purgatory cannot be found in Scripture, at least not in the Protestant Bible,[5] and he put aside the second one because death is an enemy of God to be judged, and so how can that which will be condemned by the Holy One bring about holiness? It makes no sense, none at all.

So then, all of the four characteristics of entirely sanctifying faith listed above point to the reality that heart purity occurs *in this life* by means of the grace of God that is ever predicated on the atoning work of Jesus Christ. Such grace is therefore *sufficient* for the needs of believers *now*. If, however, the first two descriptions above are outright denied, in other words, that entire sanctification is indeed promised in Scripture and that God is able to offer it, then the conversation is simply over. Unbelief bars the way. The soul in such a state or condition will never be entirely sanctified—by its own refusal. Oddly enough, that person in effect has told God what the Most High can and cannot do. However, is this ever the proper posture for Christian believers? Would it not be far better to be open to what God can do, or better yet, to believe in particular that the Almighty can entirely sanctify a believer, any believer, in this life, a truth that Wesley repeatedly held before the Methodists as the grand depositum?[6]

All Can Be Saved to the Uttermost

Entire Sanctification as a Gift

When Wesley considered how those who are born of God can receive entirely sanctifying grace, he did so once again in a very balanced and conjunctive manner. If there is time and opportunity along the way, believers should cooperate with God, improve the grace already received, and thereby repent and do works suitable for evangelical repentance as noted earlier. That is one half of the conjunction. The other half of the conjunction is that none of these works suitable for repentance are or could ever become *the basis* upon which one is entirely sanctified. In other words, such works can lead up to the door of entire sanctification but entirely sanctifying grace, being the sheer gift that it is and remains, is received not on the basis of cooperant grace, that is, in terms of what we have done, but of free grace, underscoring that this is a sheer gift. In this setting, then, Wesley did something remarkably new. That is, he took the insights of the Reformation in terms of sola fide (free grace) and he applied them not simply to justification and the new birth but also to entire sanctification! No one had ever done that before: not any Roman Catholic divine or even an Eastern Orthodox one. Indeed, Wesley made the connection explicit in his following parallel construction, a literary form that is broadly theologically significant: "Exactly as we are justified by faith, so are we sanctified by faith. Faith is the condition, and the only condition, of sanctification, exactly as it is of justification. It is the condition: None is sanctified but he that believes; without faith no man is sanctified. And it is the only condition: This alone is sufficient for sanctification. Every one that believes is sanctified, whatever else he has or has not."[7] Once more Wesley observed: "'that we are saved by faith,' will never be worn out, and that sanctifying as well as justifying faith is the free gift of God."[8] Moreover, the offer of such a free gift, as well as the recognition that God is a generous gift giver, will surely evoke joy. But one, of course, must be willing to *receive* what gifts are genuinely offered.

The Temporal Dimensions as a Clue to Entire Sanctification

These considerations of faith and works just outlined above are a window on the temporal dimensions of entire sanctification, in other words, what place is there for both process and the instantaneous in the reception of entirely sanctifying grace. Observe the connections made by John Wesley along these lines in his following observation: "And by this token you may surely know whether you seek it by faith or by works. If by works, you want something to be done first, before you are sanctified. You think, I must *first be or do* thus or thus. Then you are seeking it by works unto this day. If you seek it by faith, you may expect it as you are; and if as you are, then expect it now."[9] The instantaneous language in this context reveals that God, not human beings, is the principal actor here, and that precisely because entire sanctification is after all a gift, lavished upon the saints by an almighty and generous God, then it can be received *now*. In other words, process in the sense of what one may possibly become by the grace of God must issue in actuality, in the instantiation of grace in the here and now. In short, the question must eventually be raised, "what is one actually today?"

The first interpretive error, then, with respect to entire sanctification that Wesley addressed consists in the mistaken assumption that one must "first be or do thus or thus,"[10] in order to be entirely sanctified as if this were *the basis* for receiving such grace. This approach suggests entire sanctification is after all by works, that is, by human working, whether it is fully recognized or not. Such a mistake can easily characterize those who simply take up Wesley's cooperant understanding of grace, with its divine and human working, without ever embracing, in a conjunctive way, the salvific realities of free grace that underscore the sovereign role of God as well as the sheer graciousness of the gift.[11] Again, those who commit this error, of which Wesley was well aware, may be baffled, and that's the right word, by their lack of progress along the path of divine and human working ("haven't I done enough?" "was not *my consecration* thorough?"), for the bright and shiny horizon of entire sanctification appears to be ever receding from them precisely as they make incremental progress and are growing from one degree of grace to the other. In short, they never arrive at the desired destination. The prospect of entire sanctification simply baffles them. It is always just beyond their reach, just beyond the horizon. Indeed, cooperant grace brings them up to the door of entire sanctification but Christian perfection, to employ Wesley's preferred idiom, is not, after all, the last degree of a process of incremental change. Such an understanding would describe the process of sanctification, to be sure, but not entire sanctification, itself. Put another way, perfect love is not a little more of what already was but something new is actually in place, namely heart purity. Christian perfection, then, just like the new birth, represents *a qualitative change*, not a change in degree.

11. All the Children of God Can Receive Entire Sanctification

The second interpretive error with respect to entire sanctification is to consider the temporal dimensions of this highest grace in yet another unbalanced and therefore in an un-conjunctive way, by simply focusing on the instantaneous aspects, themselves, of this larger complex of grace. This too constitutes error. No one doubts that Wesley placed a premium on the truth that the gift of entire sanctification is available now (for all those who are already born of God) precisely because it is a gift of grace as just noted above. John wrote to his brother Charles, for example, in 1762 and affirmed: "As to the manner, I believe this perfection is always wrought in the soul by faith, by a simple act of faith; consequently in an instant."[12] But he then added in a very balanced way, clarifying his meaning: But I believe a gradual work both preceding and following that instant."[13] If Wesley had rejected the gradual working preceding that instant then the result would have been a quietism that Wesley had already rejected at Fetter Lane. So then, just as it is a mistake to focus simply on divine and human cooperation, on process, in terms of the actualization of entire sanctification in the warp and woof of life, so too it is a mistake simply to focus on the instantaneous of the actualization of this grace as if this too was the only pertinent consideration. Simply put, neither temporal dimension tells the whole story. Nor is one by itself the simple corrective of the other. Rather, Wesley's theology is actually far more balanced then either option can allow. It entails the conjunction of both process and instantaneous, of both divine and human working as well as the sovereign gift of God that best characterizes the artful balance of Wesley's carefully-drawn theology.

Moreover, as Wesley balanced the temporal dimensions of process and instantaneousness in the new birth through the image of natural birth, he employed a much different image in fleshing out the temporal dimensions in entire sanctification, not the image of birth but that of death. Wesley and the Methodist Conference explained: "A man may be dying for some time; yet he does not, properly speaking, die, till the instant the soul is separated from the body; and in that instant he lives the life of eternity. In like manner, he may be dying to sin for some time; yet he is not dead to sin, till sin is separated from his soul; and in that instant he lives the full life of love."[14] Charles Wesely expressed this blessed hope well in the following verse:

> O may thy quick'ning voice,
> The death of sin remove,
> And bid our inmost souls rejoice
> In hope of perfect love![15]

A Helpful Temporal Distinction

In terms of the temporal dimensions surrounding entire sanctification it is helpful to make a twofold distinction. The first one concerns what can be called the *narrow usage* of the temporal difference between process and instantaneous. In this setting the narrow usage refers to such matters as *the manner and the basis of the reception* of such grace as already pointed out above in Wesley's comments to his brother, Charles. It focuses therefore on the realization of entirely sanctifying grace in the lives of believers as well as what immediately precedes this event and what follows. It is a time frame, in other words, that is quite small or narrow. As such it will also pick up the spiritual and psychological dimensions of the realization of entirely sanctifying grace, of what it means, of what it feels like, for the person to actually become pure in heart. In the narrow usage of the temporal difference of process and instantaneous, Wesley places a premium on the instantaneous, as pointed out earlier, without denying the importance of preceding process. In his sermon, "The Scripture Way of Salvation, composed in 1765, he observed: "But it is infinitely desirable, were it the will of God, that it should be done instantaneously; that the Lord should destroy sin "by the breath of his mouth," in a moment, in the twinkling of an eye. And so he generally does; a plain fact, of which there is evidence enough to satisfy any unprejudiced person. Thou therefore look for it every moment."[16]

The second distinction concerns the *broad usage* of the temporal difference between process and instantaneous, and it is much different. It does not focus on the small length of time in terms of the manner of reception, from process to instantiation, from being in works of mercy and charity and the like, to actually becoming entirely sanctified in a moment. Nor does it consider the spiritual or psychological dimensions of receiving such grace today. Rather it focuses on the broad sweep of salvation, *the duration that exists between the new birth and entire sanctification*. And here the time period of the process is not short but long, very long. In fact, for many people, by Wesley's own admission, it will last nearly a lifetime. To illustrate this last truth, Wesley declared that "the greater part of those we have known, were not sanctified throughout, not made perfect in love, till a little before death."[17] And in a letter to George Lavington, the Bishop of Exeter, Wesley affirmed: "A man is usually converted long before he is a perfect man."[18] Beyond this, the Methodist Conference acknowledged with one voice: ". . . we grant . . . That the generality of believers whom we have hitherto known were not so sanctified till near death."[19] Moreover, in 1762, in a letter to his brother Charles, John stated: "As to the time, I believe this instant *generally* is the instant of death, the moment *before* the soul leaves the body. But I believe it may be ten, twenty, or forty years before death."[20]

This last observation made to Charles is doubly interesting because it contains both forms of the rhetoric: the narrow usage in that John focuses on instantiation, "the moment before the soul leaves the body," and the broad usage in that he maintains that the reception of this grace is, after all, shortly before death though admittedly it could have occurred "ten, twenty, or forty years before death."[21] Here the lengthy duration between the new birth and entire sanctification is also in view. In light of this, the following chart should prove to be helpful:

	Temporal Rhetoric Developed by John Wesley in Terms of the Focus of Entire Sanctification		
	Process/Instantaneous Difference	Cooperant/Free Grace	Duration of the Process
Narrow Usage	Underscores Instantaneous Do not have to "be" or "do" something else first	Stresses Free Grace Avoids works righteousness	Very Brief; Even Now; an Instant Receiving Entire Sanctification as an utter gift
Broad Usage	Underscores Process If there be time and opportunity: repent and do works suitable for repentance	Stresses Cooperant Grace Avoids Quietism	Very Lengthy; Just Prior to Death; Prepares the way for the reception of free grace and divine gifts

How to Avoid Confusion Concerning Entire Sanctification

Though John Wesley was very careful in his own observations on the topic of entire sanctification, employing two distinct forms of rhetoric to display its temporal dimensions, his heirs, especially his North American ones, have not been so careful. Not only did they neglect the role of repentance and works suitable for repentance on the way to entire sanctification in their celebration of the narrow usage of the temporal difference between process and instantaneousness, such that Wesley emerges at times almost as a quietist, but they also entirely neglected Wesley's careful development and numerous comments about the broad usage of the temporal difference between process and instantaneousness, his repeated affirmation that the *duration* between the new birth and entire sanctification is *generally* long.

One other piece of the puzzle has to be put in place before the errors of Wesley's heirs can be properly understood along with their very troubling consequences. When Wesley affirmed that one does not have *"to be* or *do "*[22] something else first in order to be entirely sanctified, he was not repudiating the basic truth that for most people they will not be entirely sanctified until just prior to death. Instead he was highlighting the truth of the narrow usage of the rhetoric that entire sanctification is a sheer gift, predicated on the atoning work of Christ, not on human works or merit, and therefore it could be received now, by faith alone, precisely because it is a gift. All of this, of course, is and remains true.

The problem, however, is that many believers cannot receive this gift now, for a whole host of reasons, even though it is genuinely offered now, simply because of who they are as a person (with a soul thirty thousand fathoms deep) and what beliefs they hold at this point in their Christian journey. For example, if they do not actually believe that entire sanctification is a possibility in this life, after all is said and done, then the conversation is over as noted earlier. It has been shut down by an unbelief that bars the way. As a good pastor, Wesley clearly recognized this baffling reality as well the duration of time on the way to entire sanctification. In other words, the way forward for such believers will likely entail the lengthy process of repenting of the carnal mind, and doing works suitable for repentance on the way to entire sanctification. Again, if there be time and opportunity (and for most people there will be) "though it be allowed that both this repentance and its fruits are necessary to full salvation, yet they are not necessary either in the *same sense* with faith or in the *same degree.*"[23]

Such working, of course, will not and could never be the *basis* on which one is entirely sanctified, but it may nevertheless become the *means* that will lead up to the door through which heart purity will be received as the sheer gift that it is, in other words, through the ministrations not of cooperant grace but of free grace. Indeed, Wesley once again, and it bears repeating, clearly applied the insights of the Reformation in terms of *sola fide* not simply to justification, a forensic theme, but also to the participatory theme of entire sanctification. Earlier, in the chapter on the new birth, the parallels with respect to the reception of justification, on the one hand, and entire sanctification, on the other hand, were noted and are now repeated for emphasis. "Exactly as we are justified by faith, so are we sanctified by faith. Faith is the condition, and the only condition of sanctification, exactly as it is of justification. It is the condition: none is sanctified but he that believes; without faith no man is sanctified. And it is the only condition: this alone is sufficient for sanctification. Everyone that believes is sanctified, whatever else he has or has not."[24] Clearly literary form, in this case parallelism, once again has significant theological consequences. Accordingly, the reception of perfect love is ever marked by grace through faith *alone*, that is, such an honor is reserved in Wesley's theology for the free grace of God underscoring the truth that entire sanctification is and remains an utter gift from a God of holy love.

What might repentance and works suitable for repentance look like on the way to heart purity? For one thing believers may even speak strongly against Christian perfection arguing that the words "human beings" and "perfection" never belong in the same sentence. If this is the case, then impediments clearly bar the way to the reception of this highest reach of grace, and evangelical repentance has now become necessary, in some sense, even in terms of casting aside false and confused beliefs. Second, given the baffling power of inbred sin, some Christian believers may mistake dimensions of the carnal nature, itself, for their own identity, the very substance of who they are as a person. When this is the case, repentance and works suitable for repentance are again in some sense necessary for entire sanctification, if there be time and opportunity, as the Holy Spirit illuminates the soul and casts light on its true condition. Again, elements of inbred sin may masquerade as the very identity of the person. Through the *process of sanctification*, with its transformations of degree, such elements, such accretions to the soul, will be stripped away under the superintending, illuminating and cleansing power of the Holy Spirit.

So then Wesley did indeed recognize that there may be impediments to the reception of entirely sanctifying grace that must be cleared away in the *process of sanctification* on the way to perfect love. Evangelical repentance is, after all, important. That is, believers may have to repent of various forms and levels of inbred sin, and do works suitable for repentance, if there be time and opportunity, so that they may then become open to receive the entirely sanctifying grace which is freely and genuinely offered. Again, none of this emphasis on evangelical repentance detracts in the least from the sheer gratuity of entirely sanctifying grace as Wesley had understood it or from the atoning work of Christ as the only suitable basis upon which this grace is freely given. Perfect love is and remains a gift, lavished upon the saints by a God of holy love who is generous beyond imagination. To be sure, when the grace of entire sanctification is finally received it will not be on the basis of any human working at all, as its substantiating factor, but it will be received as the utter gift that it is, in other words, by grace through faith alone. Accordingly, the broad usage of a lengthy duration will eventually make room for the narrow usage of a brief period of time at the very end of the process of sanctification if the actualization, the realization, of entire sanctification will finally occur.

> Ever fainting with desire,
> For thee, O Christ, I call!
> Thee I restlessly require,
> I want my God, my all.
> Jesu, dear redeeming Lord,
> I want thy coming from above:
> Help me, Saviour, speak the word,
> And perfect me in love.[25]

When the narrow and the broad usages of the temporal differences between process and instantaneousness, however, are confused or not properly recognized, then this can only result in significant error. Take the example of a 25-year-old seminarian in a North American Wesleyan denomination who must give a testimony of being entirely sanctified *before* he or she can be ordained. Are most young adult believers entirely sanctified? John Wesley did not think so. Here the narrow usage of the temporal difference between process and instantaneousness has washed out a consideration of the broad usage. However, the early British Conferences of which Wesley was a part did not make this kind of error at all. Instead they posed a series of questions to determine the sincerity of believers as well as their usefulness for ministry.

> Have you faith in Christ?
>
> Are you "going on to perfection?"
>
> Do you expect to be "perfected in love" in this life?
>
> Are you groaning after it?
>
> Are you resolved to devote yourself wholly to God and to his work?

11. All the Children of God Can Receive Entire Sanctification

Do you know the Methodist plan?

Have you read the "Plain Account?" the "Appeals?"[26]

One only needed to affirm the expectation to be perfected in this life and to be groaning after it in order to be ordained. A twenty-five year old believer in Wesley's day did not have to chronicle an experience of entire sanctification in order to become a lay preacher as if this experience itself were some type of union card in order to gain entrance to ministry. This approach represents a serious misunderstanding of this lofty grace—and on so many levels.

Or what of the sincere young woman who is groaning after heart purity, is cooperating with God in the process of sanctification, and is becoming holier by degrees, and some measure of inbred sin has recently been cleansed away, through the illuminating and cleansing power of the Holy Spirit. She now thinks she is on the very doorstep of heart purity but she eventually realizes that her recent cleansing was just another layer of the onion, so to speak, that has been removed, and that there are likely to be so many more layers to go. Inbred sin can be downright baffling at times. Consequently, the heart, once again, is by no means pure, not yet anyway. However, this woman is clearly growing in grace and for that reason she should not be discouraged, either by herself or by others. She should be called to go forward into the deeper graces of God.

Or consider the situation of an earnest young man who wants to be entirely sanctified, who takes up both works of mercy and charity in serving the poor as a genuine means of grace, but who fails to enter in. In this case, the bewildering power of the carnal mind or inbred sin may have deceived this man into thinking that if he loves God with all of his heart, mind, and soul then he will become nothing, a zero—or very much "less." This prospect in turn evokes considerable fear in him because it looks like death—and in a sense it is. "If God is all and all in the highest reaches of grace, then where will I be? What will become of me?" Fear now bars the way.

Or what of the middle-aged woman who has consecrated all that she is and all that she has to God and yet her heart too still contains the enemy of inbred sin within. A good pastor would counsel this woman along the lines that consecration is, after all, a human work, it is something that we do, but that entire sanctification is a divine work, something that God does. Entirely sanctifying grace then is unswervingly a species of free, sovereign grace as Wesley repeatedly affirmed. It is therefore not humanity who sets the timetable for the reception of this wonderful gift but Almighty God does. Observe what Wesley, himself, wrote on this score demonstrating the divine, sovereign role in the giving of this grace: "We know not why he bestows this [entire sanctification] on some even before they ask for it (some unquestionable instances of which we have seen); on some after they have sought it but a few days; and yet permits other believers to wait for it perhaps twenty, thirty, or forty years; nay, and others till a few hours or even minutes before their spirits return to him."[27] By way of analogy, though the dynamics of grace are the same, Wesley reflected upon just how initially sanctifying grace is received as noted earlier in the chapter on the new birth. He observed: "That every man may believe *if he will* I earnestly maintain, and yet that he can believe *when he will* I totally deny. But there will be always something in the matter which *we cannot well comprehend or explain.*"[28] Applying this same reasoning to the reception of perfect love, one can conclude that believers can be entirely sanctified if they will but *not when they will.*

Beyond this, some approaches to entire sanctification today are almost formulaic, akin to reciting the four spiritual laws: do w, x, y and z and you are in! Or take all of the four instances of entirely sanctifying faith that Wesley, himself, described above. Believe *that* and you will enter in, as some people mistakenly counsel even today. The problem, though, is that Wesley's four statements of entirely sanctifying faith noted above can be viewed in a minimalist way. In other words, they clear out various levels of unbelief that may bar the way. Entirely sanctifying faith, however, in a full-orbed sense, includes not simply belief *that* but also *belief in* just as justifying faith does. It always entails a disposition of the heart, that is, to believe in Jesus Christ in a new and deep way, one that saves to the uttermost.

Moreover, John Wesley's own approach, in contrast to the ruminations of his nineteenth-century North American heirs, takes into account the *mystery* of personhood as well as the *glory* of the *imago Dei*. Shorter ways, especially when they take on a cherished formula or a popular slogan, seem both flat and superficial, anthropologically speaking. They do not fully recognize the depth of human personhood, and that the realities which Christian believers will confront in the process of sanctification, on the way to entire sanctification, can at times be either downright frightening or frustratingly baffling. They are growing increasingly holy but they have not yet entered in. However, in the world of sloganeering twenty five year olds should, of course, already be entirely sanctified. This flat and superficial view of the depth and reality of a human soul, any human soul, along with a superficial understanding of inbred sin, a form of sin that is interlaced even in the very words of the saints must of course be cleared away. To that end Wesley forthrightly observed: "how much sin cleaves to the best conversation of believers! The conviction of which is another branch of the repentance which belongs to them that are justified."[29]

Yes, perfect love precisely because it is a gift of grace is clearly offered to believers *now*. That is and remains one part of Wesley's careful teaching, and he stressed it as illustrated in an admonition made to his brother, Charles in 1766: "O insist everywhere on full redemption, receivable by faith alone. Consequently to be looked for *now*."[30] The problem, however, is that many believers are evidently not willing to receive what grace is genuinely offered today. That is the other part of Wesley's teaching, a well-developed temporal rhetoric, that has been neglected or outright repudiated by some of his heirs. However, this part, this other half of the conjunction, if you will, has to be taken up once more if a balanced and more accurate picture is ever to emerge, one that can both encourage and bless the saints, and one that in the end is fully truthful just as the gospel is fully truthful. Charles Wesley, for his part, held forth the promise of the gift:

> Spare me, till I my strength of soul,
> Till I thy love retrieve,
> Till faith shall make me spirit whole,
> And perfect soundness give.
>
> Faith to be healed, thou know'st, I have,
> From sin to be made clean;
> Able thou art from sin to save,
> From all indwelling sin.[31]

All Can Know That They Are Saved to the Uttermost

When Christian believers are finally pure in heart, the balanced nature of John Wesley's practical theology is revealed in his teaching on the direct witness of the Holy Spirit to the soul that it has been entirely sanctified, perfected in love. Once again God does not leave believers in the dark but assures them that their hearts are indeed pure, cleansed of all filthiness of the flesh and spirit. This is a specific demonstration of both the love and favor of God. Observe the *parallel language*, a literary device that is theologically significant, that Wesley once again employed, but this time in terms of the assurance of this second work of grace: "None therefore ought to believe that the work is done, till there is added the testimony of the Spirit, witnessing his entire sanctification, *as clearly as* his justification."[32]

> The word of God is sure,
> And never can remove;
> We shall in heart be pure,
> And perfected in love;
> Rejoice in hope, rejoice with me,
> We shall from all our sins be free.[33]

This full assurance of faith is not only "the privilege of God's children,"[34] as they receive entirely sanctifying grace, but it also "utterly excludes all doubt and fear, and leaves them no place, no, not for an hour."[35] Such an assurance, then, is in some sense different from that which pertains to a child of God because the latter is occasionally marked by doubt and fear; the former, however, is not so marked at all. As the author of 1 John 4:18 writes: "perfect love drives out fear." So then, as believers grow in grace, the assurance that characterizes their lives deepens, ever deepens. They know in a new and powerful way that they are indeed the beloved of the Lord. And the indirect witness, that of their own spirit, deepens as well in that the fruit of the Spirit are not only full but they also endure. Wesley pointed out, for instance, that "love, joy, [and] peace, [are] *always* abiding; by *invariable* longsuffering, patience, resignation; by gentleness, triumphing over all provocation. . . . "[36] What a gift and grace this is in that the holy love of God fills the heart, reigns without a rival, and empties it of all fear! Such a gift will be a helpful preparation for all that lies ahead. To be sure, the journey is not yet over, not even with a pure heart in place, for salvation embraces not simply the heart or soul but the body as well. And the body is about to encounter its greatest challenge of all.

12. Death and the Greater Powers of Grace

"Jesus said to her, "I am the resurrection and the life. Those who believe in me, even though they die, will live, and everyone who lives and believes in me will never die. Do you believe this?" (John 11:25-26)

As believers walk in the light and truth of the Holy Spirit, as they seek deeper levels of wisdom, of having the mind of Christ, in all of their activities, they will become increasingly aware of the frame of their own life on earth, of its extent and limitations, as well as of the high goal towards which they are ever called. To live in this wide-awake fashion is to take up the self-examined life, a practice employed by the early Methodists as well. In fact, a "Scheme of Self Examination," which focused on the love of God and humanity, was used at Oxford to great effect.[1]

Some Christians today, however, are hardly mindful of the limits of their own existence, even as believers, with the result that the specter of death, especially when it intrudes into their lives suddenly and unexpectedly, sometimes catches them off guard and in a way that evokes many disturbing and painful emotions. Caught up in cultures that can barely tolerate even the mentioning of personal death, much less factor into present life the consequences of such knowledge, these believers are deeply emotionally troubled in terms of the impending reality of their own demise. Pastoral counselors who work in hospice settings[2] reveal that orthodoxy or believing the right things or even chronicling an earlier conversion experience is at times of little comfort in a Christian life that has drifted throughout the years and that never took up the important work of self-examination on an ongoing basis, that is, of preparing to die.

The eighteenth-century Methodists, in contrast to some modern examples, were known far and wide as a people who died well.[3] To illustrate, a medical doctor once quipped to Charles Wesley: "Most people die for the fear of dying; but I never met with such people as yours. They are none of them afraid of death, but calm, and patient, and resigned to the last."[4] Beyond this, through his numerous pastoral experiences, John Wesley, himself, realized that "The last scene of life in dying believers is of great use to those who are about them. Here we see the reality of religion and of things eternal; and nothing has a greater tendency to solemnize the soul and make and keep it dead to all below."[5] To be sure, John marveled at the calm and steady assurance displayed at so many Methodist death bed scenes. He therefore gathered up these and many other uncanny accounts and subsequently published around two hundred and eighty of them in *The Arminian Magazine*,[6] for the edification of all Christians, Methodist or otherwise. The following journal account, to cite just one example, shows that at the deathbed of the faithfully departing, John Wesley was both a teacher and a student. He observed: "The next day I went to Leeds; and, after preaching in the evening, pushed on to Otley. Here I found E— R— weaker and happier than ever. Her life seemed spun out to the last thread. I spent half an hour with her, to teach her, at once, and learn of her, to die."[7]

These differences in approaching death can be understood, in part, in light of the Methodist practices of discipleship, beyond the new birth and any conversion experience, that oriented believers to the hope and promise of the highest reaches of grace, that is, of Christian perfection. This direction of growing in grace, this process of sanctification with utter holiness of heart and life as its goal, entailed along with it the process of evangelical repentance that was ever mindful of the reality of inbred sin, and sometimes in a very painful way. In other words, the Methodists, as the genuine children of God, were yet aware of the inward corruption, as the last chapter has demonstrated, the impurity, the carnal mind, that yet remained even in the hearts of the children of God.

> Show me, *as my soul can bear,*
> The depth of inbred sin![8]

Such an awareness, distressing at times, issued in numerous rounds of self-examination which resulted in increasing self-knowledge. In short, the Methodists were not absentees in terms of their own spiritual lives, but they understood, in a very realistic way, of how their relationship with a God of holy love faired, with the One whose eyes are too pure to behold evil. The specter of death would not catch them unaware. Indeed, they had been preparing for it all along.

The Threefold Nature of Death

The earlier chapter on the fall of humanity considered the reality of *spiritual death* in pointing out that Adam and Eve were alienated from God, separated from the Most High, the very *day* that they had disobeyed. This manner of death, then, must form the heart of what is meant by the warning given by God, "but of the tree of the knowledge of good and evil you shall not eat, for *in the day* that you eat of it you shall die" (Genesis 2:17, NRSV). Or as Wesley, himself, had put it, "Not only thou shalt become mortal, but spiritual death and the forerunners of temporal death shall immediately seize thee."[9]

When most people think of death today, however, they have in mind what Wesley simply called *temporal death,* in other words, the heart stops, brain function ceases, and the body begins to decay. However, by his understanding of temporal death Wesley actually meant much more than this. Death was not simply the cessation of all bodily functions and then subsequent decay. It was all this, to be sure, but it also entailed something else because in Wesley's estimation human beings are not and never were simply bodies. Rather, they are more suitably described in a full orbed way as embodied souls, in other words, as complex creatures, created in the image and likeness of God. With this deeper understanding in place, Wesley considered temporal death, then, as entailing *the separation* of the soul from the body. That is, just as spiritual death entails a separation from God so too does temporal death entail a separation as well but this time it is the soul, itself, which is separated from the body. In his sermon, "What is Man," for example, Wesley explained: "Therefore we can say no more, than that death is the separation of the soul and body; but in many cases God only can tell the moment of that separation."[10]

So then temporal death not only entails the cessation of the body in the realization of the biblical declaration, "dust you are and to dust you will return" (Gen. 3:19), but it also involves the separation of body and soul with one important difference. Unlike the body in several respects, the soul can never die—at least not in the sense implied by temporal death, that is, in terms of decomposition and the cessation of being. Put another way, the soul is not a material thing, a piece of stuff or an object. It is not tangible but intangible; it is not visible but invisible. Unlike a body, it does not and cannot decompose. Accordingly, on the topic of temporal death, Wesley clearly taught that the soul, itself, cannot die because as spirit, its given nature, the soul is immortal. To illustrate this basic truth, Wesley pointed out:

> I? But what am I? Unquestionably I am something distinct from my body. It seems evident that my body is not necessarily included therein. For when my body dies I shall not die. I shall exist as really as I did before. And I cannot but believe this self-moving, thinking principle, with all its passions and affections, will continue to exist although the body be mouldered into dust.[11]

Here then is a clear affirmation, even in the face of sin and death, that the kind of human being that the Creator had intended and fashioned, even before the foundation of the world, was one that would never die, as noted in an earlier chapter. Duration without end, therefore, is "not an incommunicable attribute of the great Creator," Wesley maintained, "but he has been graciously pleased to make innumerable multitudes of his creatures partakers of it."[12] Again, Wesley declared, "Their bodies, indeed, are 'crushed before the moth;' but their souls will never die. God made them, as an ancient writer speaks, to be 'pictures of his own eternity.'"[13] These affirmations, expressive of the nature of humanity, are ones that will have lasting consequences for both the redeemed and for the lost. Simply put, it is the immortality of the soul, as taught by Wesley, that emerges as both a gift and as a problem.

To be sure, all human beings will die, both saints and sinners alike; none are excluded. Temporal death will come to all. And while all human beings have at times experienced spiritual death, through their own personal rebellion against a holy God, manifested in numerous instances through the darkness and bondage of committing open willful sin, nevertheless not all people will ever experience what Wesley called, *eternal death*,[14] that separation from the Holy One, of which Scripture warns, an alienation that knows no end. "Banishment from the presence of the Lord," Wesley cautioned, "is the very essence of destruction to a spirit that was made for God. And if that banishment last forever, it is 'everlasting destruction.'"[15] Put another way, the lost, Wesley continued, "will then know and feel, that God alone is the center of all created spirits; and, consequently, that a spirit made for God can have no rest out of him."[16] The classic text that illustrates the nature of this kind of death is 2 Thessalonians 1:8-10 which reads as follows:

"He will punish those who do not know God and do not obey the gospel of our Lord Jesus. They will be punished with everlasting destruction and shut out from the presence of the Lord and from the glory of his might on the day he comes to be glorified in his holy people and to be marveled at among all those who have believed. This includes you, because you believed our testimony to you."

John Wesley's notes on this particular passage are helpful in filling out the utter emptiness, the great void, entailed in eternal death. In terms of the language of "everlasting destruction," for example, Wesley contended that those who are lost, who stubbornly reject the gifts of the Almighty, "must of necessity, therefore, be cut off from all good, and all possibility of it."[17] Since there is no good that does not have its source in God, as Wesley's doctrine of sin and grace has already amply demonstrated, then to be separated from God is likewise to be separated from almost every good imaginable,[18] though the good of *being* on some level yet remains. However, even the goodness of friendship finds no place in eternal death and Wesley, therefore, warned all who would listen:

> Thus are they totally separated from all the things they were fond of in the present world. At the same instant will commence another loss, — that of all the persons whom they loved. They are torn away from their nearest and dearest relations; their wives, husbands, parents, children; and (what to some will be worse than all this) the friend which was as their own soul. All the pleasure they ever enjoyed in these is lost, gone, vanished away: For there is no friendship in hell.[19]

Death as an Enemy

Some religions and philosophies maintain that death, itself, is an illusion, as in Christian Science, or that people only fear death because they suffer from the illusion of a persistent self, as in Buddhism. The Christian faith, however, is different on both counts in its frank recognition that death, though it is not the ultimate reality, is nevertheless *real* and that the self or personal identity does indeed exist in a new manner beyond the portals of death to experience either the bliss of God's presence or the loss of separation. Both of these moves give the Christian faith in general and Methodism in particular a very realistic feel to its practice in daily life such that death is seen for what it is, with all of its ghastly trouble and loss, in other words, as something that is nothing less than an outright enemy of God as the Apostle Paul had declared earlier in 1 Corinthians 15:25-26. Not surprisingly, Wesley's notes on this particular passage reveal that death is undoubtedly a formidable enemy, which along with Satan and sin, must be conquered by Christ. No wonder, then, that Wesley rejected the notion that death could ever bring about the immense good of sanctification by cleansing the heart and thereby making it utterly holy. Such a lofty and honored role for death is pure fiction.

The oppositional nature of death to God and to the things of God, which has the character of an enemy, can be readily seen once it is compared to the substance of Christian salvation in terms of relation, connection, fellowship, and even communion in the form of holy love between both God and humanity. Most of these precious goods, which deserve celebration, are cut off by death. They are put to an end in this life. Without a body that has now perished who could ever participate in the time/space world that remains? To be sure, the departed have been separated from all of the living; communication is now over; and the sweetness of fellowship is clean gone. Moreover, those who are left behind suffer under the weight of grief, with its psychological and spiritual pain, which oddly enough is at times magnified precisely by the depth of the relation and of the extent of the love that was once enjoyed in the light of face to face fellowship.

But there is more. The author of the book of Hebrews recognized that in terms of death there are not only physical concerns to be addressed but spiritual ones as well. Remember human beings are complex beings not simple ones. Again, no one is simply a body. And it is exactly this spiritual dimension of human life surrounding the specter of death that may be missed by any materialistic or secular culture—to its own peril. In other words, as a Christian believer who has discerned the invisible world, the author of Hebrews frankly recognized the spiritual *powers* in play surrounding death and that therefore the redeeming work of Christ is necessary, in part, to "break the power of him who holds the power of death—that is, the devil—and free those who all their lives were held in slavery by their fear of death" (Heb. 2:14-15). Commenting on this passage, Wesley pointed out that "Death is the devil's servant and serjeant,"[20] and acknowledging the spiritual powers that surround death in deep levels of fear and bondage, he cautioned: "And every man fears death, more or less, who knows not Christ: death is unwelcome to him, if he knows what death is."[21] But then Wesley added to these comments offering a ray of hope by revealing what God has already done in the face of this evil, fear and bondage through the very good gift of the Son: "But he [Christ] delivers all true believers from this bondage."[22] Charles Wesley knew the power of the blood:

12. Death and the Greater Powers of Grace

The world, sin, death, oppose in vain,
Thou by thy dying, death hast slain,
My great Deliverer, and my God!
In vain does the old dragon rage,
In vain all hell its powers engage—
None can withstand thy conqu'ring blood.[23]

Death as a Conquered Enemy

Though death is a formidable enemy, the serjeant of Satan, as John Wesley had put it, nevertheless it is an enemy that has been utterly conquered by the atoning work of Jesus Christ and by the power of his resurrection. Those who receive the free gift of forgiveness as well as the renewal of their natures through the Holy Spirit know that their rich inheritance, along with their true identity, comes not from Adam but from Christ. The Apostle Paul compares these two different legacies in Romans 5:12-21 by setting up a detailed contrast between Adam, on the one hand, and Christ on the other as the following chart reveals:

ADAM	CHRIST
"For if the many died by the trespass of the one man," (5:15)	"how much more did God's grace and the gift that came by the grace of the one man, Jesus Christ, overflow to the many!" (5:15)
"The judgment followed one sin and brought condemnation," (5:16)	"but the gift followed many trespasses and brought justification." (5:16)
"For if, by the trespass of the one man, death reigned through that one man," (5:17)	"how much more will those who receive God's abundant provision of grace and of the gift of righteousness reign in life through the one man, Jesus Christ!" (5:17)
"just as one trespass resulted in condemnation for all people" (5:18)	"so also one righteous act resulted in justification and life for all people." (5:18)
"For just as through the disobedience of the one man the many were made sinners," (5:19)	"so also through the obedience of the one man the many will be made righteous." (5:19)
"But where sin increased," (5:20)	"grace increased all the more," (5:20)
"just as sin reigned in death" (5:21)	"so also grace might reign through righteousness to bring eternal life through Jesus Christ our Lord." (5:21)

In commenting on this larger passage, in his *Notes Upon the New Testament*, Wesley once again underscored that the work of Christ results in abundant grace and gifts that are showered upon every believer. All of this bespeaks of the sheer goodness of God, and that death and evil, despite their roaring, are never the final word for those who receive what is freely offered in Jesus Christ. Commenting on Romans 5:14, for example, Wesley observed that Adam was a fountain "of sin and death to mankind by his offence," but that Christ was a fountain "of righteousness and life by his free gift."[24] Moreover, in terms of another key passage from the Apostle Paul on this topic, 1 Corinthians 15:54 ("Death has been swallowed up in victory"), Wesley affirmed that death was "totally conquered, abolished forever."[25]

Earlier when Wesley was on board the ship the *Simmonds* enroute to Georgia in 1736, he had seen what the reception of generous, divine love looked like in a very practical way as the Moravian community was worshipping the Lord in the midst of a horrific storm in which the threat of death was ever present. Wesley recounted this memorable event in his journal in the following words:

> In the midst of the psalm wherewith their service began the sea broke over, split the mainsail in pieces, covered the ship, and poured in between the decks, as if the great deep had already swallowed us up. A terrible screaming began among the English. The Germans calmly sang on. I asked one of them afterwards, 'Was you not afraid? he answered, 'I thank God, no! I asked, 'But were not your women and children afraid? *He replied mildly, 'No; our women and children are not afraid to die.*[26]

So greatly moved was Wesley, in seeing both the serenity and the courage of the Moravian community, that he wrote in his journal the following: "This was the most glorious day which I have ever hitherto seen."[27]

Upon subsequent reflection, Wesley came to believe that the embodiment of grace that he had witnessed on board the Simmonds among the Moravian faithful, especially in terms of freedom from the fear of death, was a gift to be enjoyed by every Christian believer, none excluded. There are, of course, many kinds of fears that are associated with human mortality (psychological and social pains that are indicative of finite, human existence; separation from loved ones, etc.), but Wesley had three particular types of fear in mind from which genuine Christian believers should indeed be free. To illustrate, in 1745, in his *A Farther Appeal to Men of Reason and Religion*, Wesley distinguished three kinds of fear that should no longer crush or harry the soul:

> Men commonly fear death, First, because of leaving their worldly goods and pleasures: Secondly, for fear of the pains of death: And, Thirdly, for fear of perpetual damnation. But none of these causes trouble good men, because they stay themselves by *true faith, perfect charity, and sure hope of endless joy and bliss everlasting.*[28]

Though Wesley listed three elements above, his focus throughout much of his subsequent ministry was largely on the third type of fear, that is, the one that feared condemnation, damnation, and eternal loss. In short, such a fear was none other than the fear of hell, however disguised. To be sure, a child of God should at the very least be free from this fear that has *torment* because not only is the gospel true in general but also Romans 8:1-2 is real in particular: "Therefore, there is now no condemnation for those who are in Christ Jesus, because through Christ Jesus the law of the Spirit who gives life has set you free from the law of sin and death." Of this key passage Wesley observed in his *NT Notes* that there is no condemnation "for things present or past."[29] Here emerges, in other words, the utter gift of "deliverance and liberty,"[30] a gift to be enjoyed by all the children of God.

Such a liberty, marked by rich and satisfying grace, became a part of the gospel of freedom that Wesley proclaimed in his rounds of ministry throughout England and elsewhere. Thus, for example, shortly after his Aldersgate experience in June, 1738, Wesley declared in St. Mary's church, Oxford, on June 11, 1738, that believers are now free from both the guilt of sin and from sinful fear: "Not indeed from a filial fear of offending;" Wesley cautioned, "but from all servile fear; from that *fear which hath torment;* from fear of punishment; from fear of the wrath of God."[31] Elsewhere in his sermon, "The Way to the Kingdom, preached in 1746, Wesley articulated the great liberties enjoyed by the children of God, even babes in Christ who had a *measure of assurance:* "It is a peace that banishes fear," Wesley declared, "all such fear as hath torment; the fear of the wrath of God; the fear of hell; the fear of the devil; and, in particular, the fear of death."[32]

Much later in his career Wesley continued to highlight the gracious freedom that those who are justified and born of God enjoy at the hands of a God of holy love who sets the captives free. Thus, in a letter to Ms. Cummins, penned in 1773, Wesley offered the following to-the-point and even trenchant spiritual counsel: "O make haste. Be a Christian, a real Bible Christian now! You may say, 'Nay, I am a Christian already.' I fear not. (See how freely I speak.)

A Christian is not afraid to die. Are not you? Do you desire to depart, and to be with Christ?"[33] The continuity of Wesley's affirmations in this area are nothing less than striking. Something, therefore, very important was at stake.

Beyond this, and late in his career in his "A Thought on Necessity," Wesley was insistent once again that this precious liberty, this gracious gift, which God offers to all the children of God, as a part of their rich inheritance, marks them as nothing less than *the beloved of the Lord*. As the children of God, heirs to every good and lasting promise; they are free indeed. By now, however, the language of triumph and victory marked Wesley's ever bold proclamation: "O what advantage has a Christian (a real Christian) over an Infidel! He sees God! Consequently . . . He tramples on inexorable fate, and fear, and death, and hell!"[34] For his part, Charles Wesley expressed the joy of the children of God, who already delight in the wonders of salvation on so many levels, and who therefore wait to praise the Lord for "thy great salvation," in new ways in glory. Recall the words of the very memorable verse:

> Finish, then, thy new creation;
> Pure and spotless let us be;
> Let us see thy great salvation
> Perfectly restored in thee;
> Changed from glory into glory,
> Till in heav'n we take our place,
> Till we cast our crowns before thee,
> Lost in wonder, love and praise.[35]

A Troubling Inheritance for Pastoral Ministry Among the Dying

In an earlier chapter on the doctrine of justification and assurance, the theological contribution of Jeremy Taylor for pastoral ministry to the dying was briefly assessed, but now a more detailed examination is clearly warranted in light of the current topic. Given John Wesley's very balanced, conjunctive theology, it is expected that there will be both similarities and differences when the theologies of these two key Anglican leaders are compared. And that is precisely what is found. First of all, a couple of similarities can be noted. Both Anglicans leaders, one from the seventeenth century, the other from the eighteenth, taught that repentance and works suitable for repentance were in some sense necessary on the way to the forgiveness of sins (justification) and the renewal of nature entailed in the new birth, though they may have disagreed on the nature and extent of that necessity as will be evident shortly. Second, both Anglican leaders lifted up the importance of self-examination in an ongoing way, and for Wesley this self-examination was so thorough, as noted earlier, even to the point of repenting of inbred sin, such that the suffering left in the aftermath of sin would not likely make itself evident in the most inappropriate of settings, namely, at the death bed, itself. But here the similarities of these two theologies in this particular area come to an end.

Clearly, the theology of Jeremy Taylor took a different trajectory than that of John Wesley's because Taylor, as a seventeenth century Caroline divine, feared the lawlessness or the antinomianism that could emerge in the wake of *sola fide*, improperly understood, in which such a "faith" would simply presume upon the favor of God, regardless of how one was actually living. As a consequence, Taylor took up a project of theological correction which in Wesley's eyes could only later be viewed as an overcorrection, a theme that has played out so many times and in other venues in the long history of the church. In particular, Taylor's overcorrecting tendencies can be seen in three major areas, all of which will distinguish his practical theology from that of Wesley's: repentance, forgiveness, and the question of death bed conversions.

In terms of the first issue of *repentance*, Taylor surmised that "No man is to reckon his pardon immediately upon his returns (sic) from sin to the beginnings of a good life. . . ."[36] Why couldn't the forgiveness of sins be immediately enjoyed? Simply because such a forgiveness was subsumed under the dictates of cooperant grace, of divine and human working, and Taylor maintained that there was so much yet to be done before such forgiveness could ever be enjoyed. And some folk would simply run out of time.

Of the second issue of *forgiveness itself*, Taylor insisted that pardon, the forgiveness of sins, is doubtful throughout most of the Christian life and along with it the witness of the Holy Spirit which should issue in the assurance that normally accompanies forgiveness. Taylor reasoned: "For we must know that God pardons our sins by parts; as our duty increases, and our care is more prudent and active, so God's anger decreases."[37] Again, Taylor in trying to keep the supposed lawlessness of *sola fide* in check, ends up undermining the potency of free grace as well expressed as the power of a generous and gift-giving God. He wrote: "A true penitent must all the days of his life pray for pardon, and never think the work completed until he dies. . . . And whether God hath forgiven us or no, we know not, and how far we know not."[38] With respect to the third issue of death bed conversions, once again there was a considerable difference between the theologies of Taylor and Wesley in certain respects. Both religious leaders agreed that it was wildly imprudent to delay repentance until one's last days.[39] For his part, Wesley observed: "But this holy faith is the gift of God, and he is never straitened for time. He can as easily give this faith in a moment as in a thousand years. He frequently does give it on a death-bed, in answer to the prayer of believers, but rarely if ever to those who had continued unholy on the *presumption* that he would save them at last."[40] Though Wesley expressed some caution in this area, nevertheless he clearly rejected, both in thought and in action, Taylor's claim of the *impossibility* of death bed conversions. To illustrate just why repentance was now an impossibility, at least in his estimation, Taylor reasoned along the following lines:

> . . . on a Man's Death bed the day of Repentance is past: for Repentance being the renewing of a holy life, a living the life of grace, it is a contradiction to say that a man can live a holy life upon his Death bed: . . . *Nothing that is excellent can be wrought suddenly.*[41]

Not content with this outright rejection of death-bed repentance, thereby making judgment on what the grace of God can and cannot do, Taylor proceeded to engage in what can only be described as caustic criticism on this very sensitive and important topic: "A Repentance upon our Death-bed, is like washing the Corps (*sic*), it is cleanly and civil, but make (sic) no change deeper than the skin."[42]

Death and the Greater Powers of Grace

Though John Wesley had undoubtedly profited much from the writings of Jeremy Taylor, as the chapters on holiness as the end or goal of religion have clearly demonstrated, nevertheless Wesley's meeting with Peter Böhler in February, 1738 ("a day much to be remembered"[43]), brought about important shifts in Wesley's own theology, some of them away from those of Taylor, especially in terms of Wesley's newly found appreciation of free grace and its practical applications to a needy and desperate population, in other words, to those sinners who were now in extremis. It is remarkably and wonderfully telling that when Wesley first preached "this new doctrine,"[44] as taught by Böhler, he offered this to a condemned criminal who was about to be executed: "The first person to whom I offered *salvation by faith alone* was a prisoner under the sentence of death. His name was Clifford."⁴⁵ This is something that Jeremy Taylor would not and in fact had not done. The condemned criminal would not have the time for the lengthy and belabored rounds of repentance that Taylor had clearly envisioned. Here, in other words, was a genuine parting of the ways. To use the rhetoric identified in an earlier chapter, Taylor only had the broad sense of the temporal distinctions in play (between process and instantaneous) and not the narrow one. The process of repentance was accordingly lengthy, very lengthy, with its numerous changes of degree. In such a theology, there was little room left for either the sovereign action of God or for the ministrations of free grace. How then was this good news?

The ground-breaking shift that Peter Böhler had precipitated in John Wesley's theology at the time was to re-acquaint him with the clear Pauline teaching of *sola fide*, celebrated by Martin Luther and other Reformers, and by Wesley's own Anglican tradition, itself. Later Wesley came to realize in a deeper way the wonders of saving faith when in the fall of 1738 he "began more narrowly to inquire what the doctrine of the Church of England is concerning the much controverted point of justification by faith. And the sum of what I found in the Homilies [of Thomas Cranmer] I extracted and printed for the use of others."⁴⁶ Put another way, the young Moravian (around ten years Wesley's junior) had communicated the favor and power of *free grace* so much so that when Wesley proclaimed the gospel in his sermon, "Salvation by Faith," in June of 1738, shortly after his crucial Aldersgate experience (as attested *literally*, by the way, by the ten-page-long narrative insert in his journal), the words of "*free grace*," were almost immediately on his lips.⁴⁷ He then had a message of good news to proclaim for all people whatever their condition. The gift of redemption could indeed be received today by the likes of Mr. Clifford. He was not out of time in terms of either the love or the generosity of God. The only thing absolutely necessary, after all, was faith. Mr. Clifford would have time for that. Böhler had done his work well.

> I hope at last to find
> The kingdom from above,
> The settled peace, the constant mind,
> The everlasting love;
> The sanctifying grace
> That makes me meet for home;
> I hope to see thy glorious face
> Where sin can never come.⁴⁸

13. The Emblems of a Very Generous Theology

"What do you have that you did not receive?" (1 Corinthians 4:7b)

"Heal the sick, raise the dead, cleanse those who have leprosy, drive out demons. Freely you have received; freely give." (Matthew 10:8)

In order to appreciate the incarnational depth and breadth of John Wesley's practical theology, how it reaches out to the very least of all, even to the condemned, it is necessary to demonstrate, through a careful examination of his own language, how redemption in Jesus Christ, from first to last, is bountifully free, giving new and powerful expression to the word gift. Indeed, the word "free" or "freely" emerges repeatedly in Wesley's theology and specifically in terms of all of the following phrases: free love, free mercy, free forgiveness, free pardon, free justification, free salvation, free redemption, and free sanctification—all of which highlight the importance of *free grace* and the generosity of a God of holy love.

> O Come, thou radiant Morning Star,
> Again in human darkness shine!
> Arise resplendent from afar!
> Assert thy royalty divine:[1]

Beyond this, the substance of the word free in this theological context, has two principal referents, not just one. First of all, the word free in this setting means "without cost." In other words, such things as the forgiveness of sins and the transformation of being entailed in the new birth and entire sanctification come at no cost to those in need. It is a benefit freely offered because Christ has *already paid* the huge price of such a benefit through his atoning blood. Second, the word free in this setting refers to the effects, the consequences, of receiving these gracious benefits, such that one is now free, for example, from the *guilt and power of sin* in being freely justified and born of God or from the *being of sin* in terms of entire sanctification. Moreover, one is now free, positively speaking, to love both God and neighbor as one ought. This is the greatest liberty of all, and it is filled with the Holy Spirit. In light of these gracious dynamics, it will be helpful to give a few examples of each phrase, associated with the word "free," so that the cumulative effect of these two senses can be properly appreciated, and the generosity of Methodist theology can so readily be revealed.

Free Love

The source of all is, of course, the outreaching, value creating, holy love of God. Such a love, which is freely given in Jesus Christ, is behind everything as the following examples from John Wesley's writings demonstrate:

- "And what unworthiness can hinder the *free love* of God? his love in and through Christ Jesus? So that all the promises lie fair before you. The land flowing with milk and honey, the Canaan of his perfect love, is open. Believe, and enter in!"[2]
- "'So then it is not of him that willeth, nor of him that runneth,' to choose the condition on which he shall find acceptance; 'but of God that showeth mercy;' that accepteth none at all, but of his own *free love*, his unmerited goodness."[3]
- "As a fruit of the *free, undeserved love* and favour of God, may you enjoy all blessings, spiritual and temporal; all the good things which God hath prepared from them that love him."[4]
- "We have nothing but what is owning entirely to thy *free and bounteous love*, O most blessed Creator, and to the riches of thy grace, O most blessed Redeemer."[5]

Free Mercy

The love of God manifested in Jesus Christ is often expressed in free mercy in the sense that those who have rebelled against a holy and righteous God, and who have grievously harmed their neighbors, are not given what

Free Forgiveness

they deserve but are surprised by the lavish mercy of God as the following examples from John Wesley's writings illustrate:

- "For we claim nothing of right, but only of *free mercy*. We deserve not the air we breathe, the earth that bears, or the sun that shines upon, us. All our desert, we own, is hell: But God loves us freely; therefore, we ask him to give, what we can no more procure for ourselves, than we can merit it at his hands."[6]

- ". . . trust in Him for happiness as well as for help. All the springs of happiness are in him. Trust 'in Him who giveth us all things richly to enjoy,' . . . who, of *his own rich and free mercy*, holds them out to us, as in his own hand, that, receiving them as his gifts, and as pledges of his love, we may enjoy all that we possess."[7]

- "I rejoice in him, who, of his own unmerited love, *of his own free and tender mercy*, 'hath called me into this state of salvation,' wherein, through its power, I now stand."[8]

- "Some measure of this faith, which bringeth salvation, or victory over sin, and which implies peace, and trust in God through Christ, I now enjoy by *his free mercy*; though in very deed it is in me but as a grain of mustard-seed:"[9]

Free Forgiveness

If forgiveness is free, if sinners, not the righteous, are forgiven, then sinners can come just as they are right now. In other words, they don't have to clean themselves up first in order to receive this wonderful bounty:

- "About three in the afternoon, I came to Mr. Benjamins Soward's. . . . At Five I expounded in his house, (part of the thirteenth chapter of the first of Corinthians,) and at seven, in the school-house; where I invited all who 'had nothing to pay,' *to come and accept of free forgiveness. In the morning*, I preached near Mr. Seward's house, to a small serious congregation, on those words, 'I came not to call the righteous, but sinners to repentance.'"[10]

- "At seven I invited all guilty, helpless sinners, who were conscious they 'had nothing to pay,' *to accept of free forgiveness.*"[11]
- "'For they being ignorant of God's righteousness,' (of the justification that flows from his mere grace and mercy, *freely forgiving our sins* through the Son of his love, through the redemption which is in Jesus)."[12]

Free Pardon

The language of forgiveness that Wesley employed is also expressed in the theological terminology of "pardon," and "justification" as the following examples demonstrate:

- "Regarding Mr. Grimshaw being under conviction of sin—. . . 'being in the utmost agony of mind,' there was clearly represented to him, Jesus Christ pleading for him with God the Father, and gaining a *free pardon f*or him. In that moment all his fears vanished away, and he was filled with joy unspeakable."[13]
- "Here then is the sole meritorious cause of every blessing we do or can enjoy; — in particular of our pardon and acceptance with God, of our *full and free justification.*"[14]
- "Justification is the act of God, *pardoning our sins*, and receiving us again to his favour. This was free in him, because undeserved by us; undeserved, because we had transgressed his law, and could not, nor even can now perfectly fulfil it."[15]

Free Salvation and Redemption

If forgiveness and justification are free, since the cost was once again paid by Jesus Christ in the atonement at Calvary, then salvation and redemption are free as well.

- "I preached in the morning at St. Ann's, Aldersgate; and in the afternoon at the Savoy chapel, *free salvation* by faith in the blood of Christ. I was quickly apprized that at St. Ann's, likewise, I am to preach no more."[16]

- "So I stood in the yard, and proclaimed *free salvation* to a loving, simple people. Several were in tears, and all of them so thankful that I could not repent of my labour."[17]
- "On Easter Monday and Tuesday I preached there again, the congregation continually increasing. And as most of these had never in their lives pretended to any religion of any kind, they were the more ready to cry to God as mere sinners, *for the free redemption* which is in Jesus."[18]

Free Sanctification

Even the highest reaches of grace in this life, that is, heart purity, is a benefit that is freely offered as well. The carnal mind, which is yet in place before the reception of such a lofty grace, has such a difficulty at times recognizing the lavish generosity of God and the sheer, radiant goodness behind this highest offer of grace. Recall the language of Wesley offered in the preceding chapter: "And by this token may you surely know whether you seek it by faith or by works. If by works, you want something to be done first, before you are sanctified. You think, 'I must first *be or do* thus or thus.' Then you are seeking it by works unto this day. If you seek it by faith, you may expect it *as you are*: and if as your are, then expect it *now*."[19] The only suitable basis for the reception of this gift is by grace through *faith alone*. Such *a free offer*, if it can be received now, is illustrated in the following two accounts:

- "Now surely *sanctification is one of 'the things which are freely given us of God.'* And no possible reason can be assigned why this should be excepted, when the Apostle says, 'We receive the Spirit' for this very end, 'that we may know the things which are' thus *'freely given us.'*"[20]
- "Why should devout men be afraid of devoting all their soul, body, and substance to God? Why should those who love Christ count it a damnable error, to think we may have all the mind that was in him? We allow, we contend, that we are *justified freely* through the righteousness and the blood of Christ. And why are you so hot against us because we expect *likewise to be sanctified wholly through his Spirit*?"[21]

13. The Emblems of a Very Generous Theology

Free Gift as a Well-Developed Theme

The freedom of God is the source of every redemptive benefit which is showered upon recipients, who are surprised by such forgiveness, often in expressions of joy, when earlier there was a serious fault. The freedom of God is also the source of the invitation to a family relationship, to sit at the table, when earlier there was alienation, estrangement and even fear. What is freely offered, then, can be understood in another way, that is, through the language of "gift" and "gift giving," a rhetoric that plays a very handsome role in Wesley's practical theology as well. To illustrate this theme Wesley points out: "In every state we need Christ in the following respects. (1.) Whatever grace we receive, it is a *free gift from him*. (2.) We receive it as his purchase, merely in consideration of the price he paid. (3.) We have this grace, not only from Christ, but in him."[22]

The following examples then will serve to fill out the many ways in which the very elements of redemption, which are freely given, are nothing less than sheer, utter *gifts* offered by a God of holy love whose generosity is inestimable. Indeed, there is nothing that either sinners or the saints lack along the highway of salvation that God has not already made ample provision for in Jesus Christ. The sufficiency of grace, broad and deep, in this life is a recurring theme in Methodist theology.

Repentance as a Free Gift

In his affirmation of the free gifts that are graciously received, Wesley is mindful, in his conjunctive theology, that repentance and works suitable for repentance are *in some sense necessary*—if there be time and opportunity. As noted earlier Wesley clearly rejected quietism. None of this, however, detracts in the least from the basic and ongoing truth that even repentance and the works suitable for repentance are and remain free gifts from God.

- "It is true, *repentance and faith are privileges and free gifts*. But this does not hinder their being conditions too. And neither Mr. Calvin himself, nor any of our Reformers, made any scruple of calling them so."[23]
- "But if repentance and faith are *the free gifts of God*, can they be the terms or conditions of our justification? Yes: Why not? They are still something without which no man is or can be justified."[24] [Although they are not necessary in the *same sense as faith nor in the same degree*.]

Faith as a Free Gift

Even the very faith that is exercised to receive the benefits of salvation is itself a gift given by a merciful God who delights to give but who will never coerce. The exercise of such a faith, marked by grace, bespeaks of the personhood of the believer through which the *imago Dei* shines through in freedom.

- "'There is one faith;' which is the *free gift of God*, and is the ground of their hope."[25]
- "This faith, indeed, as well as the salvation it brings, is the *free gift of God*. But seek, and thou shalt find. Strip thyself naked of thy own works, and thy own righteousness, and fly to him. For whosoever cometh unto him, he will in no wise cast out."[26]
- "They added with one mouth, that *this faith was the gift, the free gift of God*; and that he would surely bestow it upon every soul who earnestly and perseveringly sought it. . . . By absolutely renouncing all dependence, in whole or in part, upon my own works, or righteousness; on which I had really grounded my hope of salvation, though I knew it not, from my youth up."[27]
- ". . . *this faith also is the gift of God*. It is his free gift, which He now and ever giveth to everyone that is willing to receive it."[28]

Justification as a Free Gift

Justification as the forgiveness of sins that are past is a boon, a free gift, that must be received. It comes from God, has divine markings and graces all over it, and is the work that the Most High does for sinners since it is first of all against a holy and righteous God that one has sinned in the first place.

- "And thus, 'as by the offence of one judgement came upon all men to condemnation, even so by the righteousness of one *the free gift came upon all men unto justification.*'"[29]
- "But 'as by the offence of one, judgment came upon all men to condemnation; so by the righteousness of one, *the free gift came upon all men, to justification of life.*' And the virtue of this *free gift*, the merits of Christ's life and death, are applied to us in baptism."[30]

13. The Emblems of a Very Generous Theology

- "'His righteousness:'——This is all His righteousness still: It is his own *free gift to us*, for the sake of Jesus Christ the righteous, through whom alone it is purchased for us: And it is his work; it is He alone that worketh it in us, by the inspiration of the Holy Spirit."[31]

The Process of Sanctification Is Itself a Free Gift

Adherents of cooperant theologies sometimes mistakenly teach that human working in effect merits an increase in holiness such that one becomes holier on the basis of human doing, thereby treating holiness as if it were simply just another *virtue* along the way, understood in an utterly moralistic manner. It is not. Holiness is not nature, but supernature. It is and remains a gift of God in every instance. It is neither a merit nor an achievement, and it is never given because human working in some sense has now obligated God to give "more." Not one of these carefully-drawn distinctions, found in Wesley's theology, contradicts the counsel, already cited in the chapter on entire sanctification, that he offered to Miss March in 1770: "To use the grace given is the certain way to obtain more grace. To use all the faith you have will bring an increase of faith."[32] Again, neither sinners nor saints ever put God in their debt. That is a serious though popular misunderstanding of Wesley's articulation of cooperant grace. Rather, in the midst of divine and human working, which Wesley clearly affirmed, God *freely gives the gift* of an increase in holiness through the very instrument of human working which is never *the basis* on which such grace is given, but is the well-appointed occasion, *the means*, for its reception.

- "That great truth, 'that we are saved by faith,' will never be worn out; and that *sanctifying as well as justifying faith is the free gift of God.*"[33]
- "His invariable will is *our sanctification*, attended with 'peace and joy in the Holy Ghost.' These are his own *free gifts;*"[34]
- "His indwelling Spirit makes them both *holy in heart*, and holy in all manner of conversation. But still, seeing all *this is a free gift*, through the righteousness and blood of Christ, there is eternally the same reason to remember, 'He that glorieth, let him glory in the Lord.'"[35]

Salvation Itself as Free Gift

Salvation itself, broadly speaking, is a gift to be received. Think of this marvelous gospel reality by way of analogy. God, the Holy One of Israel, given who the Almighty is, has prepared for a great wedding feast that will honor his Son, Jesus Christ. All the arraignments for this fabulous feast have *already been made*. White linen cloth lines the table, plates and silverware have been set, and there is a tiny card at each place setting, and one of them has our exact name written on it. And underneath the name it has but one word: "Come"!

- "With what is past, or what is to come, we have little to do. Now is the day of salvation. The great *salvation is at hand, if you will receive it as the free gift of God.*"[36]
- "'O mother, if all the world believed in Christ, what a happy world would it be! — And they may; for Christ died for every soul of man: I was the worst of sinners, and *he died for me*. O thou that callest the worst of sinners, call me! O, *it is a free gift*! I am sure I have done nothing to deserve it.'"[37]
- "O it is *a free gift;* it is free for every soul, for *Christ has died for all.*"[38]
- "... so by the righteousness of one, '*the free gift*' might come upon all unto justification of life ... and it should be particularly observed, that 'where sin abounded, grace does much more abound.' For not as the condemnation, so is the *free gift*; but we may gain infinitely more than we have lost. We may now attain both *higher degrees of holiness*, and *higher degrees of glory*, than it would have been possible for us to attain."[39]

The Application of a Very Generous Theology

With the preceding material in mind, we are now in a place in which we can begin to appreciate the very generous nature of Methodist theology, especially in light of the following practical application. Remarkably enough, the eighteenth century Methodists were not only a people who had a reputation for dying well, as noted earlier, but they also distinguished themselves with a ministry among the dying and the condemned that few, even in the church, were willing to undertake. Since there were over two hundred capital offenses in eighteenth-century England for which one could be executed, for such things as arson, forgery, stealing horses or even for cutting down trees, the ministry to the condemned taken up by the Methodists was both necessary and considerable, and some key figures took up this particular calling.

Attitudes among Anglican clergy with respect to the condemned, however, were remarkably different.[40] One of the several duties of the Anglican ordinary was to watch over the condemned at Newgate prison where the convicted were housed until the day of execution. Andrea McKenzie points out that several of the ordinaries, such as "James Guthrie, and later Samuel Rossell, John Taylor and John Wood, complained vehemently of the interference, 'officiousness' and indecorous behaviour of Methodist preachers and visitors, referring to them as 'intruding, busy and unqualified zealot[s]' and 'ignorant busy people.'"[41] The hope of Anglican clergy was that the Methodists would simply go away and leave the ordinaries free to carry out their duty—as *they* saw fit. This conception of duty by the ordinaries, judging from various accounts, did not underscore the value of free grace at all or the descending, ever-reaching out, incarnational love of God.

McKenzie offers some insight in terms of what might have been behind the Anglican reluctance to welcome a Methodist ministry among the condemned. For one thing, many Anglicans "had more and more difficulty with the traditional notion that one's final moments were of critical spiritual significance, and that a 'good death' could outweigh a less than exemplary life."[42] Like Jeremy Taylor who had preceded them, Anglican ordinaries in the eighteenth century hardly believed in death bed conversions or that any event which occurred at the end of life could possibly undo decades of evil, debauchery and wretchedness. The very idea to them was simply preposterous. "Stephen Roe," for example, "thought it was a 'dangerous delusion' to teach that sins were forgiven without fulfilling the conditions of repentance. . . ."[43]

Empowered by an understanding of sovereign grace, separated from its Calvinists moorings that mistakenly limited it to a humanly-construed "elect," Wesley, a few months after his Aldersgate experience on September 17, 1738, went "to the condemned felons in Newgate and offered them *free salvation*."[44] Here, in other words, was the flesh and blood enactment of the gospel truth that God's grace is *free for all*, for everyone, even for condemned felons. In short, the reach of the good news of the gospel is not limited by social or even ecclesial conventions, but is universal; its breadth is wide; none are excluded.

John Wesley also recognized that free grace entailed that salvation was *free in all*, meaning that one did not have to be or do something else first in order to be forgiven, especially if time was short, but that folk could come just as they were, even condemned criminals, to be forgiven by a Savior who is the source of every good and gracious gift. This is once again Wesley's narrow sense of the temporal rhetoric that he developed, and it underscores that salvation can be received *today* especially by folk who are in a dire, life-threatening condition. In other words, faith, as well as the forgiveness of sins and the new birth, were *free* precisely because they were utter gifts to be received by those in need.

Consider now the following line of theological reflection: the approach of rank, abject sinners in order to receive the gift of forgiveness and the new birth is *exactly the same* (in a certain sense) as the approach of the saints, the genuine children of God, in order to receive the gift of entire sanctification. That is, the generosity of God's grace is so great, the love of God is so magnificent and embracing, as expressed in John Wesley's practical theology, that both saint and sinner receive the precious gifts of the Most High, in each case, in accordance with their respective needs, in precisely the same way, that is, *by grace through faith alone*, whether it be the justification of the sinner (Rom. 4:5), on the one hand, or the entire sanctification of the saint (1 Thess. 5:23-24), on the other hand. Granted the state of the redeemed as the forgiven and holy children of God is glorious and must be distinguished from that of those who are yet in their sins and are therefore under bondages of which they are ashamed. That much is clear. A qualitative difference, after all, remains. However, the point being made here is not about humanity and its condition, but about God and the divine goodness, generosity and glory. In other words, the Holy One is so great and glorious, surprisingly so, the divine Being is so awe-inspiring and generous, that whatever gifts are received from on high must come through the very same humble path of by grace through faith alone whether in terms of sinners receiving forgiveness and renewal or in terms of the saints receiving heart purity.

Moreover, like the workers hired first in the parable of the vineyard, those knocking on the doors of heart purity may grumble that they must approach the throne of grace in deep humility similar to those wretched sinners who are soon to become the children of God. Put another way, regardless of need, all must approach in the same way *by grace through faith alone*. That is after all Wesley's point in his employment of *parallel structures and expressions* on this score, one of which is now repeated for emphasis: "Exactly as we are justified by faith, so are we sanctified by faith. Faith is the condition, and the only condi-

13. The Emblems of a Very Generous Theology

tion, of sanctification, exactly as it is of justification. It is the condition: None is sanctified but he that believes; without faith no man is sanctified. And it is the only condition: *This alone is sufficient* for sanctification. Every one that believes is sanctified, whatever else he has or has not.[45] Therefore, any sort of grumbling posture on the part of those approaching heart purity, can only demonstrate, as in the parable, that they are in the end taking offense at the very generosity and goodness of God! How odd is that? Again, whether one is a saint or a sinner, the greatest gifts of the Holy One (justification, regeneration and entire sanctification, in other words, the foci of the Wesleyan *ordo salutis*) are received in only one way: *by grace through faith alone* in Jesus Christ. There is no other way. There are no other paths, other than those clogged up with self-righteousness, however gussied up, however well disguised. Simply put, in the end, it is not about us in terms of who we are and what we do. It is about God. It has always been about God and precisely who the Most High is in relation to humanity as Wesley, himself, had finally came to realize. In short, there is a rich *receiving* of gifts before there is ever any responding.

Accordingly, John Wesley's practical theology is generous at every turn. And even if one had much time and opportunity, unlike condemned criminals, so that the rounds of repentance and works suitable for repentance were in fact in place, then the result would once again be exactly the same. The gifts of God, in terms of the forgiveness of sins, the new birth or entire sanctification are not and never were given *on the basis* of any prior working. That remains a spinning-your-wheels myth. That is the broad sense of the temporal rhetoric once again eliminating the narrow sense in which ongoing process may simply become yet another way of maintaining that one will never actually arrive, especially if all that is envisioned are changes of degree. However, precisely because of who God is, namely, holy love, the One who is good and generous beyond measure, then all is and cannot be given otherwise than as a gift, rightly understood. Moreover, in receiving such gifts, faith is of course energized by the power of the Holy Spirit and is ever active in love to both God and neighbor in all manner of good works that find their source, once again, in God who is the origin, the foundation, of *every good gift*. Give God the glory! That is an important consequence of a grace that is *free*. The Methodists had learned their lessons well.

Not surprisingly, then, through John Wesley's own ministry, as well as that of the larger Methodist community, the grace of God flowed *freely* to those in the greatest need, even among those who were despised by others and who were housed at such places as Newgate prison awaiting execution. In fact, to cite just one example, Wesley preached at Newgate in 1784 to many prisoners who were about to be hanged. The account of this somber event was recorded in Wesley's journal as follows:

> I preached the condemned criminals' sermon in Newgate. Forty-seven were under sentence of death. While they were coming in, there was something very awful in the clink of their chains. But no sound was heard, either from them or the crowded audience, after the text was named, 'There is joy in heaven over one sinner that repenteth, more than over ninety and nine just persons, that need not repentance.' The power of the Lord was eminently present, and most of the prisoners were in tears. A few days after, twenty of them died at once, five of whom died in peace.[46]

How deep, how wide, is the free mercy of God manifested in Jesus Christ, that *today*, not some ever-retreating-distant future, is the day of salvation! As Charles Wesley, himself, proclaimed:

> Hark, a voice divides the sky!
> Happy are the faithful dead
> In the Lord who sweetly die;
> They from all their toils are freed,
> Them the Spirit hath declared
> Blest, unutterably blest:
> Jesus is their great reward,
> Jesus is their endless rest."[47]

All Can Die Well

Introduced to the Methodists in 1740, the Englishman Silas Told was later judged to be good enough to teach at the Foundery in London. In 1744, he heard John Wesley preach on the text Matthew 25:43 (". . . I was sick and in prison and you did not look after me.'"), and he became convinced to take up a ministry that fleshed out the free love and mercy of God among the prisoners at Newgate prison in London. Sarah Peters joined him in this work, and they both witnessed some of the remarkable effects of their labors as the condemned highwayman, John Lancaster, for example, left this world in 1748 as "a Christian triumphing over death."[48]

13. The Emblems of a Very Generous Theology

One of the consequences of a theology empowered by the engine of *free grace* is the well-developed incarnational movement of such a theology that looks to Christ as the exemplar in which the grace and welcoming love of God is seen to descend to the lowest depths, to be present among the very least of all. And since forgiveness, after all, is *free*, it can be received *now*. To be sure, Wesley never forgot that basic gospel truth once he had learned it back in 1738 when he offered Mr. Clifford redemption today as noted in the last chapter.

Emboldened by such a love freely offered in Christ, Silas Told, himself, so identified with the condemned that he made his way into the death carts for the dreary procession from the portals of Newgate prison to the gallows at Tyburn Hill where the condemned would be hung as a public spectacle. Of this experience, Told remarked: "This was the first time of my visiting the malefactors at Newgate, and of my attending them to the place of execution; and it was not without much shame, because I perceived the greater part of the populace considered me as one of the sufferers."[49] According to McKenzie, "Thus Methodists . . . offered—and converts trumpeted—assurances of the forgiveness of sins and the promise of salvation in terms that no orthodox mid-eighteenth-century Anglican clergyman could easily countenance."[50]

Wesley's own ministry among the condemned was exemplary in highlighting the *free grace* of God as well as in underscoring the welcoming embrace, the encompassing love, of the Almighty that bore all the surprises and joys of an uncanny and distinct holy love. All of these remarkable dynamics can be illustrated in an excerpt drawn from his journal on December 1, 1756, in which Wesley recorded the death of one for whom the *free grace* of God was most welcome, in other words, that the love and mercy of the Holy One were understood to be present in the very darkest of places, in a love-embracing descent, and with respect to those who had been forgotten or outright ignored by so many others:

> The following week his peace increased daily, till on Saturday, the day he was to die, he came out of the condemned room clothed in his shroud and went into the cart. As he went on, the cheerfulness and composure of his countenance were amazing to all the spectators.[51]

Wesley then continued the narrative, taken from the correspondence he had received, whose theology, no doubt, mirrored that of his own: "At the place of execution, after he [the condemned] had spent some time in prayer, he rose up, took a cheerful leave of his friends and said, 'Glory be to God for *free grace."*[52] Indeed, Wesley had affirmed in many ways, from 1738 forward, that so much that matters can happen in such a short period of time. Again, if faith, forgiveness and renewal are gifts of God, freely given, then they can be received *now*. Nothing bars the way for this acceptance and renewal, along with its numerous freedoms, except the stubborn unbelief of sinners with its failure to receive convincing grace, a failure that on some levels remains a mystery. Beyond this, there is the stilted self-righteousness of wayward believers, confused in their theologies, who doubt all of this generosity, and who rush in with numerous requirements yet to be fulfilled, and who therefore fail to appreciate just how wide and deep is the love of God, whose transformative and invigorating holy love can be embraced by the very least of all today especially by those folk, like condemned criminals, who were in extremis.

Wesley's practical theology, then, was gracious, generous and powerful at every turn. It communicated the graces of Jesus Christ in an exemplary manner. It offered faith where there was fear; hope where there was despair; and love where there was none. Its reach was extensive; none were excluded; its depth intensive, whatever the need. To be sure, whatever had been done in the past, no matter how great the sin, the highest reaches of grace were yet possible. Here was a theology, in other words, that glorified God above all and that exalted the neighbor in a thoroughgoing way. It demonstrated not only the glory of the image of God in all people, and that Christ had died for all, but also to what extent the divine love had descended to reach the very least of all. Even the deathbed and the gallows had lost their wretched terrors. Neither was a place of darkness and abject fear anymore. The grace and holy love of God were understood to be greater, ever greater. Again, death was an enemy, to be sure, but it was a conquered enemy. Accordingly, the good news of the gospel was here, even here, precisely in this place. Through the person and work of Jesus Christ, sent by the Father, and witnessed to by the Holy Spirit, death with its darkness in the end had become something new, what it had never been before. It had now become, through Christ's atoning death, the door, the passageway, to a broad, rich and eternal light, marking the goodness, graciousness and generosity of a God of holy love who is not only the center of every good and perfect gift but who is eminently worthy of the most heartfelt adoration and praise now and throughout all eternity. Yes, the Methodists had learned their lessons well.

Epilogue: John Wesley Died Well

"Precious in the sight of the LORD is the death of his saints." (Psalm 116:15 RSV)

As the final year of John Wesley's own life on earth began in January, 1791, the elderly evangelist and practical theologian turned his attention to the things of eternity in a more focused way, and especially in terms of how God had made provision, even here, for knowing what lies ahead. Taking Hebrews 11:1 as his text ("Now faith is the substance of things hoped for, the evidence of things not seen . . ." KJV) Wesley drafted his very last sermon simply entitled "On Faith," and showed how the gracious gift of *faith is*, in a certain way, just like one of the senses, that is, of the seeing eye, or the hearing ear, etc., but that the world it perceives is not the visible one, the world of things and stuff, but the invisible one, the world of God, Spirit and eternity. Wesley explained:

> So little could even the most improved reason discover concerning the invisible and eternal world! The greater cause have we to praise the Father of Lights, who hath opened the eyes of our understanding, to discern those things which could not be seen by eyes of flesh and blood; that He who of old time shined out of darkness, hath shined in our hearts, and enlightened us with the light of the glory of God, in the face of Jesus Christ, 'the author and finisher of our faith;'[1]

Such an edifying gift, graciously given by God, for both knowledge and light, drew back the curtain in terms of what is to come, a revelation *in Christ* that dispelled the darkness along with its vaunted powers. Such a gift could only spark the deepest gratitude as well as establish a fund of peace in the elderly Wesley as is evidenced by his following exclamation: "Upon the whole, what thanks ought we to render to God, who has vouchsafed this 'evidence of things unseen' to the poor inhabitants of earth, who otherwise must have remained in utter darkness concerning them! How invaluable a gift is even this imperfect light, to the benighted sons of men!"[2] Indeed, so great was Wesley's gratitude, his deep and abiding thankfulness for such a thoughtful and providential gift, that the language of this late sermon quickly turned into doxological praise, penned by his brother, Charles, an ebullient heart-felt expression, marked by the strength of great joy:

> The things unknown to feeble sense,
> Unseen by reason's glimmering ray,
> With strong, commanding evidence,
> Their heavenly origin display.
> Faith lends its realizing light:
> The clouds disperse, the shadows fly;
> The Invisible appears in sight,
> And GOD is seen by mortal eye![3]

With the composition of such a sermon, Wesley's own spirit was undoubtedly renewed and strengthened in preparation for all that was to come in this final year. Earlier, Wesley had written to Ann Bolton in 1775, and he affirmed that the believer's transition was indeed gracious: "To die is not to be lost; but our union will be more complete in the world of spirits than it can be while we dwell in tenements of clay."[4] Though his spirit was clearly renewed, his body was by now drained, worn out, exhausted. To illustrate, during the next month, in February, 1791, he preached at Lambeth and at Chelsea though shortly thereafter on the nineteenth of the month, he began to complain of both fever and weakness. Determined to make good use of what powers he yet had, Wesley made his way to Leatherhead on the twenty-third with a certain Mr. Rogers in order to visit a family who was open, receptive, to the truth of the gospel of Jesus Christ. Here Wesley delivered "his last public message beneath their roof."[5]

Having developed a very balanced ministry throughout the years, one that ministered to both body and soul, in other words, one that had both deep personal dimensions appropriate to the wide expanse of a soul created in the image of God, as well as one that had social breadth in terms of the embrace of the poor, the downtrodden and the forgotten, in the face of all of this, the dying Wesley turned his attention once more to the plight of *others*, specifically to those who were suffering under the vicious and sinful practice of slavery. And so on February 24th Wesley composed a letter to William Wilberforce who was a member of Parliament and one determined to abolish the slave trade as well as the practice of slavery itself in all British possessions. Wesley's letter was meant to encourage the British abolitionist in his efforts, and it is therefore worth quoting at length. Wesley wrote:

> Dear Sir, — Unless the divine power has raised you up to be as Athanasius contra mundum, ['Athanasius against the world.'] I see not how you can go through your glorious enterprise in opposing that execrable villainy, which is the scandal of religion, of England, and of human nature. Unless God has raised you up for this very thing, you will be worn out by the opposition of men and devils. But if God be for you, who can be against you? Are all of them together stronger than God? O be not weary of well doing. Go on, in the name of God and in the power of His might, till even American slavery (the vilest that ever saw the sun) shall vanish away before it.[6]

The following day Wesley's decline was clearly evident. He was offered a cup of mulled wine with spices but he quickly threw it up and said, "I must lie down."[7] He rested most of the day, had a rapid pulse, along with a burning fever, and was very sleepy.[8] On Saturday, the 26th, his condition was unchanged, and he hardly spoke at all. The next day, Wesley rallied somewhat, sat in a chair, and recited a verse from "Forsake me not when my strength faileth":

> Till glad I lay this body down
> Thy servant Lord attend,
> And O! my life of mercy crown
> With a triumphant end![9]

In the afternoon the dying leader recited on two occasions the words that he had spoken earlier while at Bristol: "I the chief of sinners am, But Jesus died for me."[10] Not properly understanding what Wesley had said, Elizabeth Ritchie, who was attending to his needs, asked: "Is this the present language of your heart, and do you now feel as you then did?"[11] Wesley quickly replied "Yes," at which point Ms. Ritchie delivered two lines from the last stanza of "And can it be?" in what she likely thought was a much-needed reassuring effort: "Bold I approach th' eternal throne, And claim the crown through Christ my own."

Ritchie's mistake, however, was to fail to realize that Wesley uttered a couplet, not a single line. For one thing, even the holiest of saints, marked by a life of unflagging service to others, would have to exclaim in truthfulness and honesty, as Wesley, himself, had done, "I the chief of sinners am." Indeed, no one less than the Apostle Paul had described himself as the worst of sinners in 1 Timothy 1:15. Accordingly, it is the second line of the couplet that completes the meaning of the first: "But Jesus died for me." Notice the contrast that begins with the little word, "But." It introduces a world of meaning and difference. Observe also that Wesley affirmed in this particular setting, and in a way he had not done earlier in an important interview with August Spangenberg while in Georgia,[12] that Jesus died *for me*. Remarkably enough, the "for me" language reverberates, though in a slightly different form, with what Wesley had written earlier in his Aldersgate narrative: "that Christ had taken away *my* sins, even *mine*, and saved me from the law of sin and death."[13] Put another way, Wesley was revealing to Ms. Ritchie that despite what sins had marked his life, he had received and he continued to receive what Jesus was offering, namely, forgiveness and renewal. Simply put, Christ had died not only for the sins of the whole world, as Wesley had once replied in a very general manner to Spangenberg, but he had also died specifically for John Wesley, and the elderly gentleman clearly knew it!

All Can Live Forevermore!

On Monday the 28th, Wesley once again slept most of the day, and he naturally spoke very little.[14] However, he did gather enough strength to utter a pithy theological statement that had marked so much of his practical theology throughout the years: "There is no way into the holiest but by the blood of Jesus."[15] The following day, March 1st, his powers had returned enough such that he broke out in adoration:

> All glory to God in the sky,
> And peace upon earth be restor'd
> O Jesus, exalted on high,
> Appear our omnipotent Lord!
> Who meanly in Bethlehem born,
> Didst stoop to redeem a lost race;
> Once more to thy people return,
> And reign in thy kingdom of grace,

> Oh! wouldst thou again be made known,
> Again in the Spirit descend;
> And set up in each of thine own,
> A kingdom that never shall end.
> Thou only art able to bless;
> And make the glad nations obey,
> And bid the dire enmity cease,
> And bow the whole world to thy sway.[16]

Wesley called for a pen but was unable to write. Ms. Ritchie then offered, "Let me write for you Sir: tell me what you would say?"[17] "Nothing," Wesley replied, "but that God is with us."[18] Late in the morning, Wesley mustered his strength once more, to the surprise of those present, and began to recite the lines from a hymn by Isaac Watts:

> I'll praise my Maker wile I've breath,
> And when my voice is lost in death,
> Praise shall employ my nobler pow'rs:
> My days of praise shall ne'er be past,
> While life, and thought, and being last,
> Or immortality endures
>
> Happy the man whose hopes rely
> On Israel's God; he made the sky,
> And earth, and fens with all their train;
> His truth forever stands secure,
> He saves th' oppress'd, he feeds the poor,
> And none shall find his promise vain.[19]

Wesley was helped to his bed from which he rose no more. Speaking for all those present who were now on their knees, Elizabeth Ritchie related that "truly our hearts were filled with the divine presence: the room seemed to be filled with God."[20] After those gathered got up from their knees, Mrs. Charles Wesley and Dr. Whitehead among them, Wesley took the hand of Mr. Bradford and said, "Farewell, farewell."[21] Expressing a wish that a sermon he had composed on the love of God should be "scattered abroad and given away to everybody,"[22] Wesley entered into the warmth and joy of doxology once more which now filled the room. He uttered the gracious truth, the comfort of every dying saint, now for the second time, "The best of all is, God is with us."[23]

However, his praising and thankful spirit was not yet done. "Lifting up his dying arm in [a] token of victory,"[24] as observed by Ms. Ritchie, "and raising his feeble voice with a holy triumph not to be expressed,"[25] Wesley repeated now for the third time, each instance like an angel of both comfort and assurance, "The best of all is, God is with us."[26]

Slowly passing in an air of serenity, Wesley repeated throughout the night the first line of the Isaac Watts hymn he had spoken earlier: "I'll praise—I'll praise." As these words, which wafted through the room reveal, though no doubt spoken in nearly hushed tones, Wesley thought not of himself, but of God, not of what he had lacked but of what he had been given, not of what he had done but of *who God is*. Now on the threshold of eternity, Wesley offered to all those present around his deathbed one last gift, because he himself had been given so much, a peaceful and enduring witness that his relation to God through Christ, enlivened by nothing less than the Holy Spirit of love, was marked not by fear of any sort, those days were long gone, but by an uplifting faith and an abiding trust that found their best expressions repeatedly in the resonances of both praise and adoration: "I'll praise—I'll praise." Here was a man who was wonderfully open to all that was yet to come. And there were indeed further gifts to be received. He was ready, in other words, to meet his risen Lord face to face, to be surrounded, indeed to be engulfed, by the light of divine glory, the warmth of embracing love, and the breadth of eternity. In the end, Wesley was graciously anticipating the desire of the ages, a desire soon to be fulfilled:

> Alive in him, my living head,
> And clothed in righteousness divine,
> Bold I approach th'eternal throne,
> And claim the crown, through Christ my own.[27]

Notes

Introduction

1. W. B. Fitzgerald, *The Roots of Methodism* (London: Epworth Press, 1903).

2. Franz Hilderbrandt, and Oliver A. Beckerlegge, *The Works of John Wesley, Volume 7: A Collection of Hymns for the Use of the People Called Methodists* (Nashville: Abingdon Press, 1983), p. 349 (Hymn #215, stanza 1).

3. Rupert E. Davies, *The Works of John Wesley*, vol. 9. *The Methodist Societies: History, Nature, and Design* (Nashville: Abingdon Press, 1989), p. 227.

4. Ibid., p. 70.

5. Ibid., p. 72.

6. Ibid., p. 73.

7. John Wesley, *John Wesley's Sunday Service of the Methodists in North America* (Nashville: The United Methodist Publishing House, 1984), p. 131.

8. For example, see W. Reginald Ward, and Richard P. Heitzenrater, *The Works of John Wesley*, Bicentennial ed., vol. 20: *Journals and Diaries III* (Nashville: Abingdon Press, 1991). See also Albert C. Outler, ed., *The Works of John Wesley*, Vols. 1-4. *The Sermons* (Nashville: Abingdon Press, 1984), 1:312 ("The Witness of Our Own Spirit").

1. God Is Holy Love

1. Franz Hilderbrandt, and Oliver A. Beckerlegge, *The Works of John Wesley, Volume 7: A Collection of Hymns for the Use of the People Called Methodists* (Nashville: Abingdon Press, 1983), p. 126 (Hymn #36, stanza 2).

2. John Wesley, *John Wesley's Sunday Service of the Methodists in North America* (Nashville: The United Methodist Publishing House, 1984), p. 306.

3. Albert C. Outler, ed., *The Works of John Wesley*, Vols. 1-4. *The Sermons* (Nashville: Abingdon Press, 1985), 2:373 ("On the Trinity").

4. Ibid., 2:376.

5. Though the language that Wesley employed here is in harmony with the New Testament witness, the specific phrasing, ". . . that bear record in heaven, the Father, the Word and the Holy Ghost: and these three are one," as found in the KJV, is not however found in the most ancient manuscripts. Accordingly, this phrase is not a part of our preferred translation, the NIV, in terms of its rendering of 1 John 5:7.

6. Outler, Sermons, 2:377 ("On the Trinity"). Michael Servetus rejected the doctrine of the Trinity as articulated by Western theologians, was condemned by Roman Catholic authorities in France, fled to Calvin's Geneva where he was executed as an incorrigible heretic on October 27, 1553. Of this event, Wesley quipped: ""I think them very good words [Trinity and Person]. But I should think it very hard to be burned alive for not using them; especially with a slow fire, made of moist, green wood." See Paul Wesley Chilcote, and Kenneth J. Collins, eds., *The Works of John Wesley: Doctrinal and Controversial Treatises II*, vol. 13 (Nashville: Abingdon Press, 2013), p. 13:398 Bracketed material is mine.

7. Ibid. See also Geoffrey Wainwright, "Why Wesley Was a Trinitarian," *The Drew Gateway* 59 (Spring 1990): 26-43.

8. Outler, *Sermons*, 2:385 ("On the Trinity").

9. Ibid., 2:386.

10. Franz Hildebrandt, and Oliver Beckerlegge, *The Works of John Wesley*, Bicentennial ed., vol. 7: *A Collection of Hymns for the Use of the People Called Methodists* (Nashville: Abingdon Press, 1983), p. 389 (Hymn #248, stanzas 1 and 2). For a helpful exploration of Charles Wesley's hymns on the Trinity see, Barry Edward Bryant, "Trinity and Hymnody: The Doctrine of the Trinity in the Hymns of Charles Wesley," *Wesleyan Theological Journal* 25, no. 2 (Fall 1990): 64-73.

11. This language of "and from the Son," the filioque clause, goes back to the Third Synod in Toledo in 589 when Western Christianity interpolated the ancient Nicene and Constantinopolitan Creed.

12. John Wesley, *Explanatory Notes Upon the New Testament* (Salem, Ohio: Schmul Publishers, no date), 637 (1 John 4:8). Emphasis is mine.

13. The style of this composition, especially in terms of its phrasing, was likely the work of his brother, Charles. See Outler, *Sermons*, 3:559, note # 94.

14. Outler, *Sermons*, 3:560 ("Free Grace").

15. Ibid., 2:39 ("The Law Established Through Faith, Discourse II").

16. Ibid., 1:413 ("The Circumcision of the Heart").

17. Ibid., 2:40 ("The Law Established Through Faith, II"). For a comparative study that considers the similarities and differences between Luther and Wesley on

the moral law see Kiyeong Chang, *The Theologies of the Law in Martin Luther and John Wesley* (Lexington, Kentucky: Emeth Press, 2014).

18. Kenneth J. Collins, and Jason Vickers, eds., *The Sermons of John Wesley: A Collection for the Christian Journey* (Nashville: Abingdon Press, 2013), p. 108.

19. Outler, *Sermons*, 4:62 ("The Unity of the Divine Being").

20. Hildebrandt and Beckerlegge, *Works*, 7:380 (Hymn #238, stanzas 1 and 2).

21. Emil Brunner, *The Christian Doctrine of God* (Philadelphia: The Westminster Press, 1949), p. 158. In this work Brunner develops his systematic principle of divine and human correspondence, with an emphasis on the importance of both "relation" and "I-Thou" truth, which is similar in many respects to Wesley's development of the theme of holy love in his practical theology.

22. Ibid.

23. Outler, *Sermons*, 4:61-71 ("The Unity of the Divine Being").

24. Brunner, *Doctrine of God*, p. 183.

25. Ibid., p. 163-64.

26. Outler, *Sermons*, 2:362 ("On Eternity"). Many early Greek philosophers maintained that matter was not created and therefore eternal, especially Parmenides and the later Atomists such as Democritus and Leucippus. Cf. Frederick Copleston, *A History of Philosophy*, vol 1. *Greece and Rome* (Garden City, New York: Image Books, 1985), p. 47-53, and 72 ff.

27. John Wesley, *Notes Upon the Old Testament*, ed. William M. Arnett, 3 vols. Salem, Ohio: Schmul Publishing Co., 1975), (Exodus 3:14).

28. Outler, *Sermons*, 2:361 ("On Eternity").

29. Ibid.

30. Hildebrandt and Beckerlegge, *Works*, 7:370 (Hymn #231, stanza 1a).

31. Outler, *Sermons*, 4:42 ("On the Omnipresence of God").

32. Ibid. 4:46. For other references to the omnipresence of God Cf. Outler, *Sermons*, 2:569 (The Imperfection of Human Knowledge) and 3:9 (Of Good Angels).

33. Ibid., 4:62 ("The Unity of the Divine Being").

34. Ibid., 4:62.

35. Ibid., 2:539 ("On Divine Providence").

36. Randy L. Maddox, ed., *The Works of John Wesley: Doctrinal and Controversial Treatises I*, vol. 12 (Nashville: Abingdon Press, 2012), p. 468.

37. Hilderbrandt and Beckerlegge, *Works*, 7:368 (Hymn #229, stanzas 3 and 4).

38. Outler, *Sermons*, 1:580-81 (Upon Our Lord's Sermon on the Mount, Discourse the Sixth).

Notes

39. Ibid.

40. Wesley, *NT Notes*, p. 325 (Acts 17:28).

41. Thomas Jackson, ed., *The Works of John Wesley*, 14 vols. (Grand Rapids, Michigan: Baker Book House, 1978), 12:101. ("Letters to John Smith").

42. Gerald R. Cragg, ed., *The Works of John Wesley*, Vol. 11. *The Appeals to Men of Reason and Religion* (New York: Oxford University Press, 1975), p. 47-48. Emphasis is mine.

43. Ibid.

44. Hilderbrandt and Beckerlegge, *Works*, 7: 375 (Hymn #234, stanza 1).

45. Paul Wesley Chilcote, and Kenneth J. Collins, eds., *The Works of John Wesley: Doctrinal and Controversial Treatises II*, vol. 13 (Nashville: Abingdon Press, 2013), p. 548.

46. Ibid.

47. Outler, *Sermons*, 4:69. (The Unity of the Divine Being) Wesley refers to God as a Creator, Sustainer, Preserver, and Governor, although these are not four distinct roles, for the second and third are essentially subsumed under the first. For more references on this subject Cf. Outler, Sermons, 2:538. (On Divine Providence); 3:50 (Of the Church); 2:411-12 (On the Fall of Man); 2:426-27 (God's Love to Fallen Man); 4:71 (The Unity of the Divine Being); and 3:93 (Spiritual Worship).

48. Chilcote and Collins, eds., *The Works of John Wesley*, 13:549.

49. Ibid., 13:550.

50. Hilderbrandt and Beckerlegge, *Works*, 7: 147 (Hymn #54, stanza 1).

51. Outler, *Sermons*, 3:552 ("Free Grace").

52. Chilcote and Collins, eds., *The Works of John Wesley*, 13:284-85.

53. The source of this basic truth likely originated in the theological reflections of professor Dennis Kinlaw, former president of Asbury College, now a university.

54. Hilderbrandt and Beckerlegge, *Works*, 7:81 (Hymn #2, stanzas 1 and 2).

2. Humanity: All People Are Created in the Glorious Image and Likeness of God

1. Paul Wesley Chilcote, and Kenneth J. Collins, eds., *The Works of John Wesley: Doctrinal and Controversial Treatises II*, vol. 13 (Nashville: Abingdon Press, 2013), p. 548.

2. Ibid.

3. Ibid. The word "he" was removed and the word [God] employed.

4. John Wesley, *Notes Upon the Old Testament*, ed. William M. Arnett, 3 vols. (Salem, Ohio: Schmul Publishing Co., 1975), p. 10 (Genesis 1:1).

5. Ibid.

6. Charles Wesley, *Hymns on the Trinity* (Bristol: Pine Publishers, 1767), p. 71 (Hymn #CX).

7. Albert C. Outler, ed., *The Works of John Wesley*, Vols. 1-4. *The Sermons* (Nashville: Abingdon Press, 1984), 1:117-18. "Salvation by Faith" Once humanity is created it then participates in the process of ongoing creation through human sexuality.

8. Wesley, *OT Notes*, p. 16 (Genesis 1:26-28).

9. Ibid.

10. Ibid.

11. Ibid. Emphasis is mine.

12. Thomas Jackson, ed., *The Works of John Wesley*, 14 vols. (Grand Rapids, Michigan: Baker Book House, 1978), 10:70.

13. Franz Hilderbrandt, and Oliver A. Beckerlegge, *The Works of John Wesley, Volume 7: A Collection of Hymns for the Use of the People Called Methodists* (Nashville: Abingdon Press, 1983), p. 102 (Hymn #18, stanza 1).

14. Wesley, *OT Notes*, p. 18.

15. Ibid., p. 18-19.

16. Ibid.

17. Wesley's thinking on human nature is in sharp contrast to the existentialists of the twentieth century, many of whom, such as Jean Paul Sartre, argued that there is not a distinct human nature since "existence precedes essence." See Jean Paul Sartre, *Existentialism Is a Humanism* (New Haven, Connecticut Yale University Press, 2007), p. 38.

18. Outler, *Sermons*, 3:458 ("What is Man? Psalm 8:3-4").

19. Ibid., 3:456.

20. Ibid.

21. Ibid., 3:458.

22. Ibid., 3:456.

23. Hilderbrandt and Beckerlegge, *Works*, 7:597 (Hymn #422, stanza 1).

24. Outler, *Sermons*, 4:21 ("What is Man? Psalm 8:4").

25. Ibid.

Notes

26. Wesley, *OT Notes*, p. 17 (Genesis 1:27).

27. Outler, *Sermons*, 2:438-39 ("The General Deliverance").

28. For a helpful treatment on the topic of the soul by Aristotle see Book II, part 1 of his celebrated *De Anima*. http://classics.mit.edu//Aristotle/soul.html (cited 3/18/2022).

29. Outler, *Sermons*, 2:409 ("On the Fall of Man").

30. Ibid.

31. For two of the better extended anthropological essays see Reinhold Niebuhr, *The Nature and Destiny of Man: A Christian Interpretation* (Louisville, Kentucky: Westminster John Knox Press, 1996) and C. S. Lewis, *The Abolition of Man* (New York: HarperOne, 2009).

32. Outler, *Sermons*, 3:460 ("What is Man? Psalm 8:3-4").

33. Ibid.

34. Ibid., 2:417-18 ("On Predestination").

35. Ibid., 2:440 ("The General Deliverance").

36. Ibid.

37. Ibid.

38. Ibid. Theodore Weber develops the political image in a way that John Wesley never did, that is, as the basis for one group of humans governing others. In another departure from Wesley's thought, Weber rejects an appeal to natural law reasoning in assessing what the will of God would be at the political level. Both of these moves result in a clear departure from Wesley's own reflections in this area. See Theodore R. Weber, *Politics and the Order of Salvation: Transforming Wesleyan Political Ethics* (Nashville: Kingswood Books, 1998).

39. Wesley employs the terms "tempers" and "dispositions" interchangeably. See Kenneth J. Collins, "John Wesley's Topography of the Heart: Dispositions, Tempers and Affections," *Methodist History* 36, no. 3 (April 1998): 162-75.

40. Randy L. Maddox, ed., *The Works of John Wesley: Doctrinal and Controversial Treatises I, vol. 12* (Nashville: Abingdon Press, 2012), p. 354.

41. Maddox, *Works of John Wesley*, 12:354.

42. Hilderbrandt and Beckerlegge, *Works*, 7:488 (Hymn #331, stanza 2).

43. Outler, *Sermons*, 2:441 ("The General Deliverance"). Augustine defined the soul and the image of God largely in terms of reason, that is, as a rational substance that governs the body. For example, he wrote: "if the reasonable soul itself be corrupted; as it was then in me, who knew not that it must be enlightened by another light, that it may be partaker of truth, seeing itself is not that nature of truth." See Saint Augustine Bishop of Hippo, *The Confessions of St. Augustine*, trans. E. B. Pusey (Oak Harbor, WA: Logos Research Systems, Inc., 1996), Book IV, Chapter 15.

44. Ibid. Tom Wolfe, the late and great famous American novelist made the claim that language, itself, is the distinguishing characteristic of humanity as in his following observation: "Speech is not one of man's several unique attributes—speech is the attribute of all attributes! Speech is 95 percent plus of what lifts man above animal!" See Tom Wolfe, *The Kingdom of Speech* (New York: Little, Brown and Company, 2016), p. 37.

45. Franz Hilderbrandt, and Oliver A. Beckerlegge, *The Works of John Wesley*, Vol. 7: *A Collection of Hymns for the Use of the People Called Methodists* (Nashville: Abingdon Press, 1983), p. 389 (Hymn #248, stanzas 1, 2 and 3).

46. Ibid.

3. Humanity: All People Are Fallen

1. Albert C. Outler, ed., *The Works of John Wesley*, Vols. 1-4. *The Sermons* (Nashville: Abingdon Press, 1984), 2:402-403 ("On the Fall of Man"). Bracketed material is mine.

2. John Wesley, *Explanatory Notes Upon the New Testament* (Salem, Ohio: Schmul Publishers), p. 570 Emphasis is mine (Hebrews 3:12).

3. Ibid., p. 260 (John 16:9).

4. Franz Hildebrandt, and Oliver Beckerlegge, *The Works of John Wesley*, Bicentennial ed., vol. 7: *A Collection of Hymns for the Use of the People Called Methodists* (Nashville: Abingdon Press, 1983), 7:225 (Hymn #114, stanza 2).

5. Outler, *Sermons*, 2:480-81 ("The End of Christ's Coming").

6. Ibid., 1:185 ("Justification By Faith").

7. Wesley, *NT Notes*, p. 375 (Romans 5:14).

8. Ibid., Bracketed material is mine.

9. Hilderbrandt and Beckerlegge, *Works*, 7:133 (Hymn #42, stanza 1).

10. Outler, *Sermons*, 1:185 ("Justification By Faith"). Bracketed material is mine.

11. Ibid., 4:297-98 ("The Image of God").

12. Ibid., 4:298.

13. Ibid., 1:185 ("Justification By Faith"). See also "The New Birth" where, once again, Wesley recounts the death of the soul in the sense of its separation from the life of God. Cf. Outler, *Sermons*, 2:189-90.

14. Ibid., 2:361 ("On Eternity").

15. Ibid., 4:298 ("The Image of God"). See Don Marselle Moore, "Immediate Perceptual Knowledge of God: A Study in the Epistemology of John Wesley" (Thesis, Syracuse University, 1993).

Notes

16. Ibid.

17. Ibid. Bracketed material is mine.

18. Ibid.

19. Hilderbrandt and Beckerlegge, *Works*, 7:202 (Hymn #97, stanza 2).

20. Outler, *Sermons*, 2:442 ("The General Deliverance").

21. Ibid.

22. Ibid., 2:399 ("God's Approbation of His Works").

23. Thomas Jackson, ed., *The Works of John Wesley*, 14 vols. (Grand Rapids, Michigan: Baker Book House, 1978), 14:253.

24. Philip Schaff, *The Creeds of Christendom*, vol. III (Grand Rapids, Michigan: Baker Book House, 1983), p. 492-93. I have used the American Revision of 1801 for greater readability. The sense of the text, when compared to the English edition of 1571, is retained.

25. John Telford, ed., *The Letters of John Wesley, A.M.*, 8 vols. (London: The Epworth Press, 1931), 6:239-40.

26. Jackson, *Works*, 10:190.

27. Randy L. Maddox, ed., *The Works of John Wesley: Doctrinal and Controversial Treatises I*, vol. 12 (Nashville: Abingdon Press, 2012), p. 307.

28. Ibid., p. 310.

29. Ibid., p. 439.

30. Ibid., p. 327.

31. Hilderbrandt and Beckerlegge, *Works*, 7:243 (Hymn #132, stanzas 1 and 2).

32. Outler, *Sermons*, 2:184 ("Original Sin").

33. Ibid., 2:170.

34. Ted A. Campbell, ed., *The Works of John Wesley: Letters III 1756-1765*, vol. 27 (Nashville: Abingdon Press, 2015), p. 143 (To Augustus Toplady, December 9, 1758).

35. Outler, *Sermons*, 1:250 ("The Spirit of Bondage and the Spirit of Adoption").

36. Ibid., 2:176 ("Original Sin"). Emphasis is mine.

37. Ibid., 2:177.

38. Ibid., 2:178. ("Original Sin"). Bracketed material is mine. I have also changed the punctuation of this sentence to take into account the coordinating conjunction.

39. Ibid.

40. Ibid., 2:179.

41. Maddox, *Works*, 12:472.

42. Hilderbrandt and Beckerlegge, *Works*, 7:239 (Hymn #128, stanza 2).

43. Outler, *Sermons*, 2:179 ("Original Sin").

44. Ibid.

45. Ibid.

46. Ibid., 2:180.

47. Ibid., 2:181.

48. Ibid., 2:182.

49. Ibid., 2:185.

50. Ibid., 2:183.

51. Ibid., 2:183-84.

52. Ibid.

53. Ibid.

54. Ibid., 1:225 ("The Way to the Kingdom").

55. Ibid., 4:154-55 ("The Deceitfulness of the Human Heart").

56. Ibid., 4:156.

57. Maddox, *Works*, 12:160. On July 31, 1739 Wesley wrote in his journal: "All our tempers and works, in our natural state, being only evil continually." Cf. W. Reginald Ward, and Richard P. Heitzenrater, The Works of John Wesley, Bicentennial ed., vol. 19: *Journals and Diaries II*. (Nashville: Abingdon Press, 1990), p. 84.

58. Wesley, *NT Notes*, p. 377 (Romans 6:6).

59. Outler, *Sermons*, 4:30-31 ("On the Discoveries of Faith"). For example, Wesley observes: "By the same evidence I know that I am now fallen short of the glorious image of God; yea, that I, as well as all mankind, am 'dead in trespasses and sins'. So utterly dead that 'in me dwelleth no good thing'; that I am inclined to all evil, and totally unable to quicken my own soul." Cf. Outler, *Sermons*, 4:30-31 ("On the Discoveries of Faith").

60. Outler; 2:171 (Original Sin).

4. The Holy Spirit Works in All People:
Prevenient Grace

1. John Wesley, *John Wesley's Sunday Service of the Methodists in North America* (Nashville: The United Methodist Publishing House, 1984), p. 307.

2. Lycurgus M. Starkey, *The Work of the Holy Spirit: A Study in Wesleyan Theology* (Nashville: Abingdon Press, 1962), p. 77.

Notes

3. Gerald R. Cragg, ed., *The Works of John Wesley*, Vol. 11. *The Appeals to Men of Reason and Religion* (New York: Oxford University Press, 1975), p. 108.

4. Albert C. Outler, ed., *The Works of John Wesley*, Vols. 1-4. *The Sermons* (Nashville: Abingdon Press, 1984), 2:427 ("God's Love to Fallen Man").

5. Ibid., 3:207 ("On Working Out Our Own Salvation").

6. Ibid.

7. John Wesley, *Sunday Service*, p. 309.

8. Franz Hilderbrandt, and Oliver A. Beckerlegge, *The Works of John Wesley, Volume 7: A Collection of Hymns for the Use of the People Called Methodists* (Nashville: Abingdon Press, 1983), p. 325 (Hymn #195, stanzas 1 and 3).

9. Robert E. Chiles, *Theological Transition in American Methodism, 1790-1935* (Lanham, Maryland: University Press of America, 1984).

10. Paul Wesley Chilcote, and Kenneth J. Collins, eds., *The Works of John Wesley: Doctrinal and Controversial Treatises II vol. 13* (Nashville: Abingdon Press, 2013), p. 287.

11. Outler, *Sermons*, 3: 207 ("On Working Out Our Own Salvation").

12. Ibid., 4:163 ("Heavenly Treasure in Earthen Vessels").

13. Ibid., 2:2 ("The Original, Nature, Properties and Use of the Law").

14. Ibid., 2:9.

15. Ibid., 2:7.

16. Hilderbrandt and Beckerlegge, *Works*, 7:488 (Hymn #331, stanza 2).

17. Rex D. Matthews, "'With the Eyes of Faith': Spiritual Experience and the Knowledge of God in the Theology of John Wesley," in *Wesleyan Theology Today*, ed. Theodore Runyon (Nashville: Kingswood, 1985), p. 406-15.

18. For a view that affirms a basis for natural theology is to be found here, see M. Elton Hendricks, "John Wesley and Natural Theology [Prevenient Grace]," *Wesleyan Theological Journal* 18, no. 2 (Fall 1983): 12.

19. John Wesley, *Notes Upon the Old Testament*, ed. William M. Arnett, 3 vols. Salem, Ohio: Schmul Publishing Co., 1975), p. 363 (John 1:9).

20. Hilderbrandt and Beckerlegge, *Works*, 7:477 (Hymn #293, stanza 4).

21. Ibid., 7:338 (Hymn #207, stanzas 2 and 3).

22. Martin Bobgan, and Deidre Bobgan, *12 Steps to Destruction: Codependecy/Recovery Heresies* (Watertown, Massachusetts: Eastgate Publishers, 1991), p. 9.

23. Ibid., p. 18.

24. For more on the importance of free grace in Wesley's theology see my earlier work, *The Theology of John Wesley: Holy Love and the Shape of Grace* (Nashville: Abingdon Press, 2007), pp. 160-65.

25. Outler, Sermons, 1:117 ("Salvation by Faith").

26. See especially Outler, Sermons, 2:156-157; 3:203-204; and 3:482.

5. Christ Identifies with All People

1. John Wesley, *John Wesley's Sunday Service of the Methodists in North America* (Nashville: The United Methodist Publishing House, 1984), p. 306. Wesley omitted the language of "of her substance," after "the blessed virgin." Later interpreters have suggested a possible move towards monophysitism in Wesley's Christology, though such a judgment is actually eliminated as other considerations are brought to bear as will be argued below. For a view that suggests a possible monophysitism see the following: Randy L. Maddox, *Responsible Grace: John Wesley's Practical Theology* (Nashville: Kingswood Books, 1994), p. 117.

2. Sarah Lancaster, Randy L. Maddox, and Kelly Diehl Yates, eds., *Works of John Wesley: Doctrinal and Controversial Treatises III,* vol. 14 (Nashville: Abingdon Press, 2022), p. 168.

3. For Wesley's estimation of Islam see the following: Kenneth J. Collins, "John Wesley's Engagement with Islam: Exploring the Soteriological Possibilities in Light of a Diversity of Graces and Theological Frameworks," in *The Path of Holiness: Perspectives in Wesleyan Thought in Honor of Herbert B. McGonigle,* ed. Joseph Cunningham and David Rainey (Wilmore, Kentucky: Emeth Press, 2014), p. 172-93.

4. John Wesley, *Explanatory Notes Upon the New Testament* (Salem, Ohio: Schmul Publishers, no date), p. 212 (John 1:1).

5. Ibid.

6. Albert C. Outler, ed., *The Works of John Wesley, Vols. 1-4. The Sermons* (Nashville: Abingdon Press, 1985), 2:360 ("On Eternity").

7. Ibid., 3:90 ("Spiritual Worship").

8. Wesley, *NT Notes*, p. 12 (Matthew 1:23).

9. Jonathan A. Powers, ed., *Our Great Redeemer's Praise* (Franklin, Tennessee: Seedbed, 2022) #184 ("Glory Be to God on High").

10. Ibid., p. 509 (Philippians 2:7).

11. Franz Hilderbrandt, and Oliver A. Beckerlegge, *The Works of John Wesley, Volume 7: A Collection of Hymns for the Use of the People Called Methodists* (Nashville: Abingdon Press, 1983), p. 235 (Hymn # 124, stanza 4).

12. John Deschner, for example, writes: "It is too much to say that Wesley's is a docetic Christology. There is a clear teaching about the human nature, and he intends it to fall within Chalcedonian limits. But the accent lies elsewhere." See the follow-

Notes

ing: John Deschner, Wesley's Christology: An Interpretation (Dallas, Texas: Southern Methodist University Press, 1985), p. 28. Moreover, Randy Maddox declares, "Wesley came right to the border of monophysitism, if not stepping over." See the following: Maddox, *Responsible Grace*, p. 117.

13. Outler, *Sermons*, 4:105 ("On Knowing Christ After the Flesh").

14. Hilderbrandt and Beckerlegge, *Works*, 7:337 (Hymn #206, stanza 3a).

15. Wesley, *NT Notes*, p. 212 (John 1:3).

16. Ibid. (John 1:4)

17. Ibid. (John 1:1).

18. Outler, *Sermons*, 3:94-95 ("Spiritual Worship").

19. Ibid., 3:91 ("Spiritual Worship").

20. Ibid., 3:95 ("Spiritual Worship").

21. Ibid., 1:453 ("The Lord Our Righteousness").

22. Ibid.

23. Hilderbrandt and Beckerlegge, *Works*, 7:379 (Hymn #236, stanza 3).

24. Outler, *Sermons*, 2:523 ("The Signs of the Times").

25. Ibid., 1:121-22 ("Salvation by Faith").

26. Ibid., 2:453 ("The Mystery of Iniquity").

27. Lancaster et al., *Works*, 14:168.

28. Outler, *Sermons*, 1:470 ("Upon Our Lord's Sermon on the Mount, Discourse the First").

29. Ibid., 1:106 (Preface).

30. Ibid., 1:470 ("Upon Our Lord's Sermon on the Mount, Discourse the First").

31. Ibid., 1:553 ("Upon Our Lord's Sermon on the Mount, Discourse the Fifth").

32. Hilderbrandt and Beckerlegge, *Works*, 7:314 (Hymn #186, stanza 6).

33. Outler, *Sermons*, 2:8 ("The Original, Nature, Properties and Use of the Law").

34. Ibid., 2:9 ("The Original, Nature, Properties and Use of the Law").

35. Ibid.

36. Ibid.

37. Ibid.

38. Ibid.

39. Ibid.

40. Ibid., 2:9-10 ("The Original, Nature, Properties and Use of the Law").

41. Ibid., 2:10 ("The Original, Nature, Properties and Use of the Law").

42. Ibid.

43. Ibid.

44. Ibid.

45. Deschner, *Christology*, p. 107.

46. Wesley, *NT Notes*, p. 585 (Hebrews 10:31).

47. Hilderbrandt and Beckerlegge, *Works*, 7:80 (Hymn #1, stanza 3).

48. Outler, *Sermons*, 1:470 ("Upon Our Lord's Sermon on the Mount, Discourse the First").

49. John Lawson, *The Wesley Hymns as a Guide to Scriptural Teaching* (Grand Rapids: Francis Asbury Press, 1987), p. 64.

50. Randy L. Maddox, ed., *The Works of John Wesley: Doctrinal and Controversial Treatises I*, vol. 12 (Nashville: Abingdon Press, 2012), p. 157-58.

6. Christ Died for All People

1. Albert C. Outler, ed., *The Works of John Wesley*, Vols. 1-4. *The Sermons* (Nashville: Abingdon Press, 1984), 1:456 ("The Lord Our Righteousness").

2. John Wesley, *John Wesley's Sunday Service of the Methodists in North America* (Nashville: The United Methodist Publishing House, 1984), p. 313.

3. Harald Lindstrom, *Wesley and Sanctification: A Study in the Doctrine of Salvation* (Grand Rapids: Francis Asbury Press of Zondervan Publishing House, 1982), p. 61.

4. Franz Hilderbrandt, and Oliver A. Beckerlegge, *The Works of John Wesley, Volume 7: A Collection of Hymns for the Use of the People Called Methodists* (Nashville: Abingdon Press, 1983), p. 234 (Hymn 123, stanza 8).

5. Rupert E. Davies, *The Works of John Wesley*, Bicentennial ed., vol. 9: *The Methodist Societies, I: History, Nature and Design* (Nashville: Abingdon Press, 1989), p. 69. (*A Plain Account of the People Called Methodists*).

6. Sarah Lancaster, Randy L. Maddox, and Kelly Diehl Yates, eds., *Works of John Wesley: Doctrinal and Controversial Treatises III vol. 14* (Nashville: Abingdon Press, 2022), p. 438. (To William Law, 1756).

7. Paul Wesley Chilcote, and Kenneth J. Collins, eds., *The Works of John Wesley: Doctrinal and Controversial Treatises II*, vol. 13 (Nashville: Abingdon Press, 2013) p. 569.

8. Ibid.

9. Ibid.

Notes

10. John Telford, ed., *The Letters of John Wesley, A.M.,* 8 vols. *(London: The Epworth Press, 1931),* 6:298 (To Mary Bishop, 1778).

11. John Lawson, *The Wesley Hymns as a Guide to Scriptural Teaching* (Grand Rapids: Francis Asbury Press, 1987), p. 64.

12. Lancaster, *Doctrinal and Controversial III*, 14:439 (To William Law, 1756).

13. John Wesley, *Explanatory Notes upon the Old Testament,* vol. 3 (Bristol: William Pine, 1765), p. 2090 (Isaiah 53:4).

14. Thomas Jackson, ed., *The Works of John Wesley,* 14 vols. (Grand Rapids, Michigan: Baker Book House, 1978), 9:412.

15. Hilderbrandt and Beckerlegge, *Works*, 7:114 (Hymn #27, stanza 3).

16. Wesley, *NT Notes*, p. 613 (1 Peter 2:24).

17. G. Osborn, ed., *The Poetical Works of John and Charles Wesley,* vol. IV, p. 371.

18. Ibid., p. 219 (John 3:16).

19. Maddox, *Doctrinal and Controversial I*, 12:420.

20. Wesley, *NT Notes*, p. 219 (John 3:17).

21. Ibid.

22. Outler, *Sermons*, 2:428 ("God's Love to Fallen").

23. Hilderbrandt and Beckerlegge, *Works*, 7:347 (Hymn #212, stanza 4).

24. Outler, *Sermons*, 2:425-26.

25. Ibid.

26. Ibid., 2:428.

27. Ibid.

28. Hilderbrandt and Beckerlegge, *Works*, 7:114 (Hymn #27, stanza 1).

29. Outler, *Sermons*, 2:38 ("The Law Established by Faith, Discourse II").

30. Ibid., 2:10 ("The Original, Nature, Properties and Use of the Law").

31. Wesley, *NT Notes*, p. 442 (1 Cor. 15:26).

32. Ibid., p. 568 (Hebrews 2:15).

33. Ibid.

34. Ibid.

35. Ibid.

36. Jonathan A. Powers, ed., *Our Great Redeemer's Praise* (Franklin, Tennessee: Seedbed, 2022), #40 ("Ye Servants of God").

7. The Church Is For All People

1. John Wesley, *John Wesley's Sunday Service of the Methodists in North America* (Nashville: The United Methodist Publishing House, 1984), p. 310.

2. Albert C. Outler, ed., *The Works of John Wesley*, Vols. 1-4. T*he Sermons* (Nashville: Abingdon Press, 1984), 3:52 ("Of the Church").

3. Ibid.

4. Ibid.

5. Ibid., 3:50.

6. John Wesley, *Explanatory Notes Upon the New Testament* (Salem, Ohio: Schmul Publishers, no date), p. 287 (Acts 5:10),

7. Franz Hilderbrandt, and Oliver A. Beckerlegge, *The Works of John Wesley, Volume 7: A Collection of Hymns for the Use of the People Called Methodists* (Nashville: Abingdon Press, 1983), p. 97-98 (Hymn #15, stanzas 1 and 2).

8. Thomas Jackson, ed., *The Works of John Wesley*, 14 vols. (Grand Rapids, Michigan: Baker Book House, 1978), 8:317.

9. Frank Baker, ed., *The Works of John Wesley*, vol. 26. *The Letters* (New York: Oxford University Press, 1982), p. 483.

10. Jackson, *Works*, 1:189.

11. Outler, *Sermons*, 2:197 ("The New Birth").

12. W. Reginald Ward, and Richard P. Heitzenrater, *The Works of John Wesley*, Bicentennial ed., vol. 18: *Journals and Diaries I* (Nashville: Abingdon Press, 1988), pp. 242-43.

13. Rupert E. Davies, *The Works of John Wesley*, Vol. 9. *The Methodist Societies: History, Nature, and Design* (Nashville: Abingdon Press, 1989), p. 225.

14. Hilderbrandt, and Beckerlegge, *Hymns*, 7:646 (Hymn # 464, stanzas 1 and 2).

15. John Wesley, *Sunday Service*, p. 125.

16. Brian Cummings, *The Book of Common Prayer* (Oxford: Oxford University Press, 2011), p. 389.

17. John Wesley, *Sunday Service*, p. 313.

18. Ibid., p. 312. Emphasis is mine.

19. Hilderbrandt, and Beckerlegge, *Hymns*, 7:682 (Hymn # 493, stanzas 5 and 6).

20. Ward and Heitzenrater, *Journals and Diaries*, 19:158;

21. Ibid.

Notes

22. Ibid., 19:159.

23. Ibid., 19:158

24. Hilderbrandt and Beckerlegge, *Works*, 7:324 (Hymn #194, stanzas 1 and 2).

25. Wesley, *Sunday Service*, p. 131.

26. Outler, *Sermons*, 3:436 ("The Duty of Constant Communion").

27. Hilderbrandt and Beckerlegge, *Works*, 7:81 (Hymn #2, stanzas 1 and 2).

28. Davies, *Methodist Societies*, 9:538.

29. Ted A. Campbell, *John Wesley and Christian Antiquity: Religious Vision and Cultural Changes* (Nashville: Kingswood Books, 1991), p. 12-13.

30. Sarah Lancaster, Randy L. Maddox, and Kelly Diehl Yates, eds., *Works of John Wesley: Doctrinal and Controversial Treatises III vol. 14* (Nashville: Abingdon Press, 2022), pp. 410-11.

31. Frank Baker details the Methodist difference in what became a community of extraordinary care through its independent societies, itinerant ministry, and deliberative assemblies, among other things. See Frank Baker, *John Wesley and the Church of England* (Nashville: Abingdon Press, 1970), p. 162.

32. Hilderbrandt, and Beckerlegge, *Hymns*, 7:193 (Hymn # 91, stanzas 1, 2 and 3).

33. Jackson, *Works*, 8:299.

34. Ibid., 8:300.

35. Outler, *Sermons*, 2:302 ("The Reformation of Manners"). Emphasis is mine.

36. Hilderbrandt and Beckerlegge, *Hymns*, 7:659 (Hymn # 475, stanzas 1 and 2).

37. Gerald R. Cragg, ed., *The Works of John Wesley*, vol. 11. *The Appeals to Men of Reason and Religion* (New York: Oxford University Press, 1975), pp. 246-247.

38. Ibid., p. 246.

39. Ibid.

40. Peter Ackroyd, *Revolution: The History of England from the Battle of the Boyne to the Battle of Waterloo* (New York: Thomas Dunne Books, 2017), p. 20.

41. For some of the social, political and religious dimensions of English society at the time see J.C.D. Clark, *English Society* 1660-1832: Religion, Ideology and Politics During the Ancien Regime (Cambridge, England: Cambridge University Press, 2000), especially the chapter on "National Identity: The Matrix of Church and State," pp. 232-317.

42. Ted A. Campbell, ed., *The Works of John Wesley: Letters III 1756-1765,* vol. 27 (Nashville: Abingdon Press, 2015), p. 100.

43. Ward and Heitzenrater, *Journals and Diaries III*, 20:445.

44. Ibid.

45. Richard P. Heitzenrater, "The Poor and the People Called Methodists," in *The Poor and the People Called Methodists*, ed. Richard P. Heitzenrater (Nashville: Kingswood Books, 2002), p. 17.

46. See George E. Hendricks, and M. Elton Hendricks, "Mr. Wesley, since You Wanted to Help the Poor, Why Did You Ignore the English Poor Law of Your Day?," *The Asbury Journal* 70, no. 2 (2015): 55-77.

47. See the following article in which it is shown how Wesley embraced both the temporal and spiritual needs of the poor, greatly valued the later, as he took up the rounds of ministry. Kenneth J. Collins, "The Soteriological Orientation of John Wesley's Ministry to the Poor," *The Asbury Theological Journal* 50, no. 1 (Spring 1995): 75-92.

48. Ward and Heitzenrater, *Journals and Diaries*, 19:46.

49. Ibid.

50. Hilderbrandt, and Beckerlegge, *Hymns*, 7:99 (Hymn # 16, stanzas 3 and 6).

51. Davies, *The Methodist Societies*, p. 9.

52. Outler, *Sermons*, 1:533 ("Upon Our Lord's Sermon on the Mount, Discourse IV").

53. Hilderbrandt and Beckerlegge, *Works*, 7:683-84 (Hymn #495, stanzas 2, 3 and 4).

54. Davies, *The Methodist Societies*, p. 70.

55. Ibid., p. 73.

56. Henry Rack, *The Works of John Wesley: The Methodist Societies the Minutes of Conference*, vol. 10 (Nashville: Abingdon Press, 2011), p. 126.

57. Outler, *Sermons*, 4:90 ("On the Inefficacy of Christianity").

58. Ward and Heitzenrater, *Journals and Diaries*, 21:424.

59. For two helpful studies on the role that the class meeting played in the life of Methodism, see Kevin M. Watson, *The Class Meeting: Reclaiming a Forgotten (and Essential) Small Group Experience* (Wilmore, Kentucky: Seedbed Publishing, 2014), and D. Michael Henderson, *John Wesley's Class Meeting: A Model for Making Disciples* (Nappanee, Indiana: Evangel Publishing House, 1997).

60. Davies, *The Methodist Societies*, p. 9.

61. Along these lines Manfred Marquardt points out: "His [John Wesley's] limitations are evident: an overestimation, though not entirely uncritical, of governmental authority; a mistrust of all democratic strivings: and his inadequate insight into the laws of economics and commerce." See Manfred Marquardt, *John Wesley's Social Ethics: Praxis and Principles* (Nashville: Abingdon Press, 1992), p. 48.

62. Hilderbrandt, and Beckerlegge, *Hymns*, 7:662 (Hymn # 477, stanza 1a).

Notes

63. Davies, *Methodist Societies*, 9:77.

64. Ibid. 9:78.

65. Ibid.

66. Ibid.

67. Hilderbrandt, and Beckerlegge, *Hymns*, 7:287 (Hymn # 165, stanza 2).

8. God Has Forgiven All People of Everything

1. Rupert E. Davies, *The Works of John Wesley*, vol. 9. *The Methodist Societies: History, Nature, and Design* (Nashville: Abingdon Press, 1989), p. 227.

2. Albert C. Outler, ed., *The Works of John Wesley*, Vols. 1-4. *The Sermons* (Nashville: Abingdon Press, 1984), 2:187 ("The New Birth") Italics have been added.

3. Ibid., 3:544 ("Free Grace").

4. Ibid., 3:553 ("Free Grace").

5. Ibid., 3:560, 561 ("Free Grace").

6. Ibid., 1:119 ("Salvation by Faith").

7. Ibid.

8. John Wesley, *Explanatory Notes Upon the New Testament* (Salem, Ohio: Schmul Publishers, no date), p. 601 (James 2:19).

9. Outler, *Sermons*, 1:119 ("Salvation by Faith").

10. Ibid., 1:121 ("Salvation by Faith").

11. Ibid., 1:120 ("Salvation by Faith").

12. Ibid ("Salvation by Faith") Emphasis is mine.

13. Ibid., 1:121 ("Salvation by Faith").

14. Davies, *Methodist Societies*, p. 51.

15. Outler, *Sermons*, 1:187 ("Justification by Faith") Emphasis is mine.

16. Gerald R. Cragg, *The Works of John Wesley*, Bicentennial ed., vol. 11: *The Appeals to Men of Reason and Religion and Certain Related Open Letters* (Nashville: Abingdon Press, 1975), p. 176.

17. Ibid.

18. Outler, *Sermons*, 1:431-32 ("The Great Privilege of Those Who are Born of God").

19. Randy L. Maddox, ed., *The Works of John Wesley: Doctrinal and Controversial Treatises I*, vol. 12 (Nashville: Abingdon Press, 2012), p. 101.

20. Ibid.

21. Wesley, *NT Notes*, p. 44 (Matthew 12:31).

22. John Wesley, *John Wesley's Sunday Service of the Methodists in North America* (Nashville: The United Methodist Publishing House, 1984), p. 309.

23. Franz Hilderbrandt, and Oliver A. Beckerlegge, *The Works of John Wesley, Volume 7: A Collection of Hymns for the Use of the People Called Methodists* (Nashville: Abingdon Press, 1983), p. 288 (Hymn #166).

24. Cragg, *Appeals*, 11:443.

25. W. Reginald Ward, and Richard P. Heitzenrater, *The Works of John Wesley*, Bicentennial ed., vol. 18: *Journals and Diaries I* (Nashville: Abingdon Press, 1988), p. 46.

26. Outler, *Sermons*, 1:190 ("Justification by Faith").

27. Ibid., 2:28 ("Justification by Faith").

28. Hilderbrandt and Beckerlegge, *Works*, 7:291 (Hymn #168, stanza 3).

29. Ward and Heitzenrater, *Works*, 18:272.

30. Cragg, *Appeals*, 11:48.

31. Observe the spiritual autobiography offered by Wesley in a narrative insert, literarily speaking, found in his journal. See the following: Ward and Heitzenrater, *Works*, 18:242-50.

32. Outler, *Sermons*, 2:162 ("The Scripture Way of Salvation").

33. Wesley, *NT Notes*, p. 487 (Galatians 6:12) Emphasis is mine.

34. Outler, *Sermons*, 3:561 ("Free Grace").

35. Ward and Heitzenrater, *Works*, 18:228.

36. Ibid.

37. Ward and Heitzenrater, *Works*, 18:234.

38. Ibid.

39. Hilderbrandt and Beckerlegge, *Works*, 7:142 (Hymn #50, stanza 2).

40. Outler, *Sermons*, 2:169 ("The Scripture Way of Salvation").

41. Hilderbrandt and Beckerlegge, *Works*, 7:117 (Hymn #29, stanza 5).

42. Ward and Heitzenrater, *Works*, 19:132.

43. Ibid., 19:162.

Notes

44. John Telford, ed., *The Letters of John Wesley, A.M.*, 8 vols. (London: The Epworth Press, 1931), 7:202.

45. Ibid.

46. Ibid.

47. Outler, *Sermons*, 3:206, 208 ("On Working Out Our Own Salvation").

48. Ibid., 1:301-305 ("The Witness of Our Own Spirit").

49. Paul Wesley Chilcote, and Kenneth J. Collins, eds., *The Works of John Wesley: Doctrinal and Controversial Treatises II, vol. 13* (Nashville: Abingdon Press, 2013), p. 360. The work in question is Romaine's Seasonable Antidote Against Popery.

50. Outler, *Sermons*, 2:44 ("The Nature of Enthusiasm").

51. Frank Baker, ed., *The Works of John Wesley*, vol. 26. *The Letters* (New York: Oxford University Press, 1982), p. 254-55.

52. Telford, *Letters*, 5:358.

53. Hilderbrandt and Beckerlegge, *Works*, 7:195 (Hymn #93, stanza 1).

54. Baker, *Letters*, 26:575.

55. Randy L. Maddox, *The Works of John Wesley: Letters V 1774-1781*, vol. 29 (Nashville: Abingdon Press, 2023), p. 17.

56. Outler, *Sermons*, 2:283 ("The Good Steward").

57. Ibid., 2:284.

58. Ibid., 2:285.

59. Ibid.

60. Ibid., 2:286.

61. Ibid.

62. Ibid.

63. Ibid.

64. Hilderbrandt and Beckerlegge, *Works*, 7:470-71 (Hymn #316, stanza 1).

65. Outler, *Sermons*, 1:662 ("Upon Our Lord's Sermon on the Mount, Discourse the Tenth") Emphasis is mine.

66. Ibid., 2:266-280 ("The Use of Money").

67. Ibid., 2:273-74.

68. Ibid., 1:628-29 (Upon Our Lord's Sermon on the Mount, VIII).

69. Ward and Heitzenrater, *Works*, 19:173.

70. Richard P. Heitzenrater, ed., *The Poor and the People Called Methodists* (Nashville: Kingswood Books, 2002), p. 26.

71. Ibid.

72. Ward and Heitzenrater, *Works*, 19:12.

73. Hilderbrandt and Beckerlegge, *Works*, 7:684 (Hymn #495, stanza 4).

74. Heitzenrater, *The Poor*, p. 228.

75. Ibid.

76. Outler, *Sermons*, p. 390-91 ("On Visiting the Sick"). Emphasis is mine.

77. Ibid., 3:393 ("On Visiting the Sick"). Emphasis is mine.

78. Ibid., 1:519 ("Upon Our Lord's Sermon on the Mount, Discourse the Third"). "You could not gain that increase in lowliness, in patience, in tenderness of spirit, in sympathy with the afflicted," Wesley notes, "which you might have gained if you had assisted them in person." Cf. Outler, *Sermons*, 3:389, 393.

79. Ibid., 1:695 ("Upon Our Lord's Sermon on the Mount, Discourse the Thirteenth"). Emphasis is mine.

80. Hilderbrandt and Beckerlegge, *Works*, 7:668 (Hymn # 481).

9. All People Can and Must Be Born Again

1. Albert C. Outler, ed., *The Works of John Wesley*, Vols. 1-4. *The Sermons* (Nashville: Abingdon Press, 1985), 2: 158 ("The Scripture Way of Salvation").

2. Ibid., 2:187 ("The New Birth"). Emphasis is mine.

3. Rupert E. Davies, *The Works of John Wesley*, Bicentennial ed., vol. 9: *The Methodist Societies, I: History, Nature and Design* (Nashville: Abingdon Press, 1989), pp. 226-27.

4. Outler, *Sermons*, 2:185 ("Original Sin").

5. Ibid., 2:190 ("The New Birth").

6. Ibid., 2:185 ("Original Sin").

7. Ibid., 2:190 ("The New Birth").

8. Franz Hildebrandt, and Oliver Beckerlegge, *The Works of John Wesley*, Bicentennial ed., vol. 7: *A Collection of Hymns for the Use of the People Called Methodists* (Nashville: Abingdon Press, 1983), p. 243 (Hymn # 132, stanza 1).

9. Outler, *Sermons*, 1:279 ("The Witness of the Spirit, I").

10. Ibid., 2:193-94 ("The New Birth").

Notes

11. Ibid.

12. Ibid., 2:194 ("The New Birth")

13. Ibid., 4:173-74 ("On Living Without God").

14. Ibid., 2:198 ("The New Birth").

15. Ibid.

16. Ibid.

17. Horace Bushnell, *Christian Nurture* (New York: Charles Scribner's and Sons, 1923), p. 4.

18. William James, *The Varieties of Religious Experience* (New York: E-Bookarama, 2022), p. 191.

19. Hilderbrandt and Beckerlegge, *Works*, 7:271 (Hymn #152, stanza 2).

20. Outler, *Sermons*, 2:200-01 ("The New Birth").

21. Ibid., 1:279 ("The Witness of the Spirit, I").

22. Ibid.

23. Hilderbrandt and Beckerlegge, *Works*, 7:181 (Hymn #81, stanza 8).

24. Outler, *Sermons*, 4:144 ("The Wedding Garment").

25. Ibid.

26. Ibid., 2:195 ("The New Birth").

27. Ibid.

28. Ibid.

29. Gerald R. Cragg, ed., *The Works of John Wesley*, vol. 11. *The Appeals to Men of Reason and Religion* (New York: Oxford University Press, 1975), pp. 47-48.

30. Hilderbrandt and Beckerlegge, *Works*, 7:271 (Hymn #152, stanza 1).

31. Outler, *Sermons*, 2:163-64 ("The Scripture Way of Salvation").

32. Ibid., 1:383 ("The Means of Grace"). Bracketed material is mine.

33. Ibid., 3:545 ("Free Grace").

34. Ibid., 1:419 ("The Marks of the New Birth").

35. Thomas Jackson, ed., *The Works of John Wesley*, 14 vols. (Grand Rapids, Michigan: Baker Book House, 1978), 11:180 Emphasis is mine.

36. Hilderbrandt and Beckerlegge, *Works*, 7:495 (Hymn #336, stanza 4).

37. Outler, *Sermons*, 4:26 ("What is Man?") Emphasis is mine.

38. Ibid., 1:420 ("The Marks of the New Birth").

39. Hilderbrandt and Beckerlegge, *Works*, 7:510 (Hymn #346, stanza 10).

40. Frank Baker, ed., *The Works of John Wesley*, vol. 25. *The Letters* (New York: Oxford University Press, 1982), p. 598.

41. Ibid.

42. Ibid.

43. Outler, *Sermons*, 2:107 ("Christian Perfection").

44. Jackson, *Works*, 10:368.

45. Hildebrandt and Beckerlegge, *Works*, p. 270 (Hymn #151, stanza 9).

46. John Wesley, *Explanatory Notes Upon the New Testament* (Salem, Ohio: Schmul Publishers), p. 454 (2 Cor. 3:17).

47. Outler, *Sermons*, 2:193-94 ("The New Birth").

48. Ibid., Bracketed material is mine.

49. Ibid.

50. Ibid., 1:443 ("The Great Privilege of Those Who are Born of God").

51. Ibid., 3:202 ("On Working Out Our Own Salvation").

52. Ibid., 1:427 ("The Marks of the New Birth").

53. Ibid., 1:301-305 ("The Witness of Our Own Spirit").

54. Hildebrandt and Beckerlegge, Works, 7:535 (Hymn #365, stanza 4).

55. Paul Wesley Chilcote, and Kenneth J. Collins, eds., *The Works of John Wesley: Doctrinal and Controversial Treatises II*, vol. 13 (Nashville: Abingdon Press, 2013), p. 243.

56. Ibid., 13:245.

57. John Wesley, *Explanatory Notes Upon the New Testament* (Salem, Ohio: Schmul Publishers, no date), 637. (1 John 4:8).

58. Chilcote and Collins, *Works*, 13:285.

59. Outler, *Sermons*, 3:560 ("Free Grace").

60. Chilcote and Collins, *Works*, 13:232.

61. Outler, *Sermons*, 3:555 ("Free Grace").

62. Ibid., 3:560.

63. Wesley does make a concession to his Calvinist critics by pointing out: "I allow, God may possibly, at some times, work irresistibly in some souls. I believe he does. But can you infer from hence, that he always works thus in all that are saved? Alas! my brother, what kind of conclusion is this?" Here it seems as if Wesley is referring to a *psychological* understanding (how the reception of saving grace appears) rath-

er than to a *soteriological* understanding (how grace is actually received which is never in a coercive or deterministic manner). See Chilcote and Collins, *Works*, 13:314-15.

64. Chilcote and Collins, *Works*, 13:290.

65. Ibid., 13:535-36.

66. Hilderbrandt and Beckerlegge, *Works*, 7:331. (Hymn #200, stanzas 2 and 3).

10. Entire Sanctification: What It Is and Is Not

1. Albert C. Outler, ed., *The Works of John Wesley*, Vols. 1-4. *The Sermons* (Nashville: Abingdon Press, 1986), 3:266 ("The More Excellent Way") Emphasis is mine.

2. Ibid., 3:501 ("On Faith").

3. Ibid.

4. Randy L. Maddox, ed., *The Works of John Wesley: Letters IV: 1766-1773*, vol. 28 (Nashville, Tennessee: Abingdon Press, 2023), p. 294.

5. Ibid., 28:309.

6. Henry Rack, *The Works of John Wesley: The Methodist Societies the Minutes of Conference,* vol. 10 (Nashville: Abingdon Press, 2011), p. 154.

7. Outler, *Sermons*, 3:206-09 ("On Working Out Our Own Salvation").

8. Randy L. Maddox, ed., *The Works of John Wesley: Doctrinal and Controversial Treatises I,* vol. 12 (Nashville: Abingdon Press, 2012), p. 158.

9. Ibid.

10. Outler, *Sermons*, 1:321 ("On Sin in Believers").

11. For Wesley's own use of the vocabulary of "second blessing," see the following: Ted A. Campbell, ed., *The Works of John Wesley: Letters III 1756-1765*, vol. 27 (Nashville: Abingdon Press, 2015), pp. 76-77; 241-42; and Telford, Letters, 6:116.

12. Outler, *Sermons*, 1:350 ("The Repentance of Believers").

13. Ibid., 1:351.

14. Ibid.

15. Paul Wesley Chilcote, and Kenneth J. Collins, eds., *The Works of John Wesley: Doctrinal and Controversial Treatises II,* vol. 13 (Nashville: Abingdon Press, 2013), 13:140.

16. Outler, *Sermons*, 1:346 ("The Repentance of Believers").

17. Chilcote and Collins, *Works*, 13:157.

18. Outler, *Sermons*, 2:100 ("Christian Perfection").

19. Ibid., 2:569 ("The Imperfection of Human Knowledge").

20. Ibid., 2:101-02 ("Christian Perfection").

21. Ibid., 2:102.

22. Ibid.

23. For examples of such usage, see Outler, *Sermons*, 1:139 ("The Almost Christian") and Outler, *Sermons*, 2:121 ("Christian Perfection").

24. Outler, *Sermons*, 2:103 ("Christian Perfection").

25. Ibid.

26. Ibid., 2:104.

27. Paul Wesley Chilcote, and Kenneth J. Collins, eds., *The Works of John Wesley: Doctrinal and Controversial Treatises II,* vol. 13 (Nashville: Abingdon Press, 2013), 13:146.

28. Outler, *Sermons*, 3:74 ("On Perfection")

29. Chilcote and Collins, *Works*, 13:155.

30. Ibid., 13:190.

31. Outler, *Sermons*, 1:413 ("The Circumcision of the Heart").

32. Rupert E. Davies, *The Works of John Wesley,* Bicentennial ed., vol. 9: *The Methodist Societies, I: History, Nature and Design* (Nashville: Abingdon Press, 1989), 9:54.

33. Chilcote and Collins, *Works*, 13:190.

34. Ibid.

35. Maddox, *Works*, 28:371 (Emphasis is mine).

36. Chilcote and Collins, *Works*, 13:187-88.

37. Chilcote and Collins, *Works*, 13:167.

38. Ibid., 13:153. These sixteen descriptions of entire sanctification or Christian perfection are not exhaustive but are meant to be suggestive of John Wesley's basic teaching.

39. Outler, *Sermons*, 2:105 ("Christian Perfection").

40. Ibid., 1:327 ("On Sin in Believers").

41. Ibid.

42. Ibid., 1:328.

43. Jonathan A. Powers, ed., *Our Great Redeemer's Praise* (Franklin, Tennessee: Seedbed, 2022), Hymn #88, stanza 2.

11. All the Children of God Can Receive Entire Sanctification

1. Albert C. Outler, ed., *The Works of John Wesley*, Vols. 1-4. *The Sermons* (Nashville: Abingdon Press, 1984), 2:167 ("The Scripture Way of Salvation").

2. Ibid., 2:167-68.

3. Ibid., 2:168.

4. Ibid.

5. A favorite passage of the Apocrypha that Roman Catholics cite in this area is 2 Maccabees 12:44-45, which is not a part of the Protestant Bible whose Old Testament content is exactly that of the Jewish Bible, the Masoretic text, though the content is arranged differently both in terms of the order of the books and how they are numbered.

6. John Telford, ed., *The Letters of John Wesley, A.M.*, 8 vols. (London: The Epworth Press, 1931), 8:238.

7. Outler, *Sermons*, 2:163-64 ("The Scripture Way of Salvation"). Emphasis is mine.

8. Ted A. Campbell, ed., *The Works of John Wesley: Letters III 1756-1765*, vol. 27 (Nashville: Abingdon Press, 2015), p. 394.

9. Outler, *Sermons*, 2:169 ("The Scripture Way of Salvation").

10. Ibid.

11. Ibid., 3:544-45 ("Free Grace").

12. Randy L. Maddox, ed., *The Works of John Wesley: Letters IV: 1766-1773*, vol. 28 (Nashville, Tennessee: Abingdon Press, 2023), p. 61.

13. Ibid.

14. Paul Wesley Chilcote, and Kenneth J. Collins, eds., *The Works of John Wesley: Doctrinal and Controversial Treatises II*, vol. 13 (Nashville: Abingdon Press, 2013), p. 175.

15. Franz Hilderbrandt, and Oliver A. Beckerlegge, *The Works of John Wesley, Volume 7: A Collection of Hymns for the Use of the People Called Methodists* (Nashville: Abingdon Press, 1983), p. 657 (Hymn #473, stanza 6).

16. Outler, *Sermons*, 2:168-69 ("The Scripture Way of Salvation").

17. Henry Rack, *The Works of John Wesley: The Methodist Societies the Minutes of Conference*, vol. 10 (Nashville: Abingdon Press, 2011), p. 195.

18. Gerald R. Cragg, ed., *The Works of John Wesley,* vol. 11. *The Appeals to Men of Reason and Religion* (New York: Oxford University Press, 1975), p. 369.

19. Rack, *Works,* 10:154.

20. Maddox, *Works,* 28:61. Emphasis is mine.

21. Ibid.

22. Outler, *Sermons,* 2:169 ("The Scripture Way of Salvation").

23. Ibid., 2:167 ("The Scripture Way of Salvation").

24. Ibid., 2:163-64.

25. Hilderbrandt and Beckerlegge, *Works,* 7:506 (Hymn #344, stanza 1).

26. Thomas Jackson, ed., *The Works of John Wesley,* 14 vols. (Grand Rapids, Michigan: Baker Book House, 1978), 8:325.

27. Outler, *Sermons,* 2:584 ("The Scripture Way of Salvation").

28. John Telford, ed., *The Letters of John Wesley, A.M.,* 8 vols. (London: The Epworth Press, 1931), 6:267 Emphasis is mine.

29. Outler, *Sermons,* 1:342 ("The Repentance of Believers").

30. Maddox, *Works,* 28:24.

31. Hilderbrandt and Beckerlegge, *Works,* 7:510 (Hymn #346, stanza 5 and 6).

32. Chilcote and Collins, 13:174. Emphasis is mine.

33. Hilderbrandt and Beckerlegge, *Works,* 7:495 (Hymn #336, stanza 7).

34. Maddox, *Works,* 28:80.

35. Rupert E. Davies, *The Works of John Wesley,* vol. 9. *The Methodist Societies: History, Nature, and Design* (Nashville: Abingdon Press, 1989), 9:100.

36. Jackson, *Wesley's Works,* 11:422. Emphasis is mine and bracketed material is mine.

12. Death and the Greater Powers of Grace

1. Thomas Jackson, ed., *The Works of John Wesley,* 14 vols. (Grand Rapids, Michigan: Baker Book House, 1978), 11:521-23.

2. I had a hospice chaplain who was in my Wesley theology course approach me after class and reveal quite frankly that some Christians in her experience did not die well. This, however, is not the fault of grace but of the reception of such grace—and for all sorts of reasons.

Notes

3. For several accounts of death bed scenes drawn from the *Arminian Magazine* see the following: Joseph D. McPherson, *Our People Die Well: Glorious Accounts of Early Methodists at Death's Door* (Bloomington, Indiana: Author House 2008).

4. Luke Wiseman. *Charles Wesley: Evangelist and Poet* (London: Epworth Press, 1932), p. 184.

5. Randy L. Maddox, ed., *The Works of John Wesley: Letters IV: 1766-1773*, vol. 28 (Nashville, Tennessee: Abingdon Press, 2023), p. 156.

6. Richard J. Bell, "Our People Die Well: Deathbed Scenes in John Wesley's Arminian Magazine," *Mortality* 10, no. 3 (August 2005): 210-223.

7. W. Reginald Ward, and Richard P. Heitzenrater, *The Works of John Wesley*, Bicentennial ed., vol. 23: *Journals and Diaries VI* (Nashville: Abington Press, 1995), p. 51.

8. Maddox, *Letters IV*, 28:279.

9. John Wesley, *Notes Upon the Old Testament*, ed. William M. Arnett, 3 vols. (Salem, Ohio: Schmul Publishing Co., 1975), Genesis 2:17. Emphasis is mine.

10. Albert C. Outler, ed., *The Works of John Wesley*, Vols. 1-4. *The Sermons* (Nashville: Abingdon Press, 1984), 4:25 ("What is Man?").

11. Ibid., 4:23.

12. Ibid., 2:361 ("On Eternity").

13. Ibid.

14. Ibid., 1:676 ("Upon Our Lord's Sermon on the Mount, Discourse the Twelfth").

15. Outler, *Sermons*, 3:35 ("On Hell").

16. Ibid.

17. Wesley, *NT Notes*, p. 534 (2 Thess. 1:8).

18. Since the soul for Wesley is immortal, then this means that the damned will continue to exist. That existence, that being, is in some sense good, a thought that Wesley hardly developed.

19. Outler, *Sermons*, 3:34 ("On Hell").

20. Wesley, *NT Notes*, p. 568 (Heb. 2:14-15).

21. Ibid.

22. Ibid.

23. Franz Hilderbrandt, and Oliver A. Beckerlegge, *The Works of John Wesley, Volume 7: A Collection of Hymns for the Use of the People Called Methodists* (Nashville: Abingdon Press, 1983), p. 505 (Hymn #343, stanza 505).

24. Ibid., p. 375 (Rom. 5:14).

25. Ibid., p. 445. (I Cor. 15:54).

26. W. Reginald Ward, and Richard P. Heitzenrater, *The Works of John Wesley*, Bicentennial ed., vol. 18: *Journals and Diaries VI* (Nashville: Abington Press, 1988), p. 143. For more on the fear of death and its connection with real, vital Christianity Cf. Kenneth J. Collins, "Real Christianity as Integrating Theme in Wesley's Soteriology: The Critique of a Modern Myth," *The Asbury Theological Journal* 51, no. 2 (Fall 1996): 15-45.

27. Ibid.

28. Gerald R. Cragg, ed., *The Works of John Wesley*, vol. 11. *The Appeals to Men of Reason and Religion* (New York: Oxford University Press, 1975), p. 136. Emphasis is mine.

29. Wesley, *NT Notes*, p. 381. (Romans 8:1-2).

30. Ibid.

31. Outler, *Sermons*, 1:122-123 ("Salvation By Faith").

32. Ibid., 1:223. ("The Way to the Kingdon"). For an older treatment which seeks to appropriate the art and manners of an earlier age with respect to "holy dying," Cf. Robert Cecil, "Holy Dying: Evangelical Attitudes to Death," *History Today* 32 (August 1982): 30-34.

33. Maddox, *Letters*, 28:578.

34. Paul Wesley Chilcote, and Kenneth J. Collins, eds., *The Works of John Wesley: Doctrinal and Controversial Treatises II*, vol. 13 (Nashville: Abingdon Press, 2013), p. 565.

35. Hilderbrandt and Beckerlegge, *Works*, 7:547 (Hymn #374, stanza 3).

36. Jeremy Taylor, *The Rule and Exercises of Holy Living and Holy Dying*, Reprint ed. (Whitefish, Montana: Kessinger Publishing, 1710), p. 275.

37. Ibid., p. 276.

38. Ibid.

39. Maddox, *Letters IV*, 28:515 Emphasis is mine.

40. Randy L. Maddox, ed., *The Works of John Wesley: Letters IV 1766-1773*, vol. 28 (Nashville: Abingdon Press, 2023), p. 515.

41. Taylor, *The Rule and Exercises*, p. 277 Emphasis is mine.

42. Ibid., p. 145. See also Kenneth J. Collins, and Christine L. Johnson, "From the Garden to the Gallows: The Significance of Free Grace in the Theology of John Wesley," *The Wesleyan Theological Journal* 48, no. 2 (2013): 7-29.

43. Ward and Heitzenrater, *Journals and Diaries I*, 18:223.

44. Ibid., p. 228.

45. Ibid.

46. Ward and Heitzenrater, *Journals and Diaries II*, 19:21.

47. Outler, *Sermons*, 1:117 ("Salvation By Faith"). Observe that the language of free grace here is expressed in the first paragraph of the sermon.

48. Hilderbrandt and Beckerlegge, *Hymns*, 7:287 (Hymn #165).

13. The Emblems of a Very Generous Theology

1. Hilderbrandt and Beckerlegge, *Hymns*, 7:610 (Hymn #433, stanza 1).

2. Ted A. Campbell, ed., *The Works of John Wesley: Letters III 1756-1765*, vol. 27 (Nashville: Abingdon Press, 2015), p. 87.

3. Albert C. Outler, ed., *The Works of John Wesley*, Vols. 1-4. *The Sermons* (Nashville: Abingdon Press, 1984), 1:197 ("Salvation By Faith").

4. Ibid., 1:517 ("Sermon on the Mount, III").

5. Thomas Jackson, ed., *The Works of John Wesley*, 14 vols. (Grand Rapids, Michigan: Baker Book House, 1978), 11:245.

6. Outler, *Sermons*, 1:585 ("Sermon on the Mount, VI").

7. Ibid., 1:626 ("Sermon on the Mount, VIII").

8. Ibid., 1:309 ("The Witness of Our Own Spirit").

9. Frank Baker, ed., *The Works of John Wesley*, vol. 25. *Letters I* (New York: Oxford University Press, 1982), 576.

10. W. Reginald Ward, and Richard P. Heitzenrater, *The Works of John Wesley*, Bicentennial ed., vol. 19: *Journals and Diaries V* (Nashville: Abingdon Press, 1990), p. 101.

11. Ibid., 19:335.

12. Outler, *Sermons*, 1:203 ("The Righteousness of Faith").

13. Ward and Heitzenrater, *Journals and Diaries IV*, 21:355.

14. Outler, *Sermons*, 2:342 ("On the Death of George Whitefield").

15. Rupert E. Davies, *The Works of John Wesley*, vol. 9. *The Methodist Societies: History, Nature, and Design* (Nashville: Abingdon Press, 1989), p. 179.

16. Ward and Heitzenrater, *Journals and Diaries I*, 18:239.

17. Ibid., 21:310.

18. Ibid., 19:322.

19. Outler, *Sermons*, 2:169 ("The Scripture Way of Salvation").

20. Jackson, *Works,* 11:421.

21. Paul Wesley Chilcote, and Kenneth J. Collins, eds., *The Works of John Wesley: Doctrinal and Controversial Treatises II,* vol. 13 (Nashville: Abingdon Press, 2013), p. 191.

22. Ibid., 13:169.

23. Jackson, *Works,* 10:308.

24. Ibid., 10:309.

25. Outler, *Sermons,* 3:49 ("Of the Church").

26. Frank Baker, ed., *The Works of John Wesley,* vol. 25. *The Letters* (New York: Oxford University Press, 1982), p. 541.

27. Ward and Heitzenrater, *Journals and Diaries I,* 18:248.

28. Ibid., 18:272.

29. Outler, *Sermons,* 1:186 ("Justification by Faith").

30. Sarah Lancaster, Randy L. Maddox, and Kelly Diehl Yates, eds., *Works of John Wesley: Doctrinal and Controversial Treatises III,* vol. 14 (Nashville: Abingdon Press, 2022), p. 282.

31. Outler, *Sermons,* 1:643 ("Sermon on the Mount, IX").

32. Randy L. Maddox, ed., *The Works of John Wesley: Letters IV: 1766-1773,* vol. 28 (Nashville, Tennessee: Abingdon Press, 2023), p. 309.

33. Ted A. Campbell, ed., *The Works of John Wesley: Letters III 1756-1765,* vol. 27 (Nashville: Abingdon Press, 2015), p. 394.

34. Outler, *Sermons,* 2:208 ("The Wilderness State").

35. Ibid., 2:343 ("On the Death of George Whitefield").

36. Jackson, *Works,* 12:332.

37. Ward and Heitzenrater, *Journals and Diaries II,* 19:253.

38. Ibid., 19:254.

39. Outler, *Sermons,* 2:411 ("On the Fall of Man").

40. This is a point missed by Michael Gibson in his recent account. He writes: "Prison visiting and providing solace for the condemned was by no means the monopoly of the Methodists in the eighteenth century." What Gibson neglects in his otherwise helpful historical account are the theological differences of such ministries. Anglican ordinaries in the eighteenth-century were hardly known for celebrating the wonders of free grace and for claiming that the condemned could be free and delivered today. See William Gibson, *The Church of England 1688-1832: Unity and Accord* (Philadelphia: Routledge 2012), p. 219. See also McKenzie (p. 36) for a helpful

Notes

corrective which is cited below, though the careful nuances of Wesley's own practical theology are the best correctives of all.

41. Andrea McKenzie, *Tyburn's Martyrs: Execution in England 1675-1775* (London: Hambledon Continuum, 2007), p. 182. For more on the topic of sanctification and death see Christine L. Johnson, *Triumphant Death: Grace, Holiness and Death in the Theology of John Wesley* (Eugene, Oregon: Cascade Books, 2025).

42. Ibid., p. 183.

43. Ibid., p. 186-87.

44. Ward and Heitzenrater, *Journals and Diaries II*, 19:12.

45. Outler, *Sermons*, 2:163-64 ("The Scripture Way of Salvation"). Emphasis is mine.

46. Ward and Heitzenrater, *Journals and Diaries VI*, 23:340.

47. Franz Hilderbrandt, and Oliver A. Beckerlegge, *The Works of John Wesley, Volume 7: A Collection of Hymns for the Use of the People Called Methodists* (Nashville: Abingdon Press, 1983), p. 142 (Hymn #50, stanza 1).

48. McKenzie, *Tyburn's Martyrs*, p. 184-85.

49. Silas Told, *The Life of Mr. Silas Told* (London: G. Whitfield, 1796), p. 73.

50. McKenzie, *Tyburn's Martyrs*, p. 182.

51. Ward and Heitzenrater, *Journals and Diaries IV*, 21:82.

52. Ibid. Emphasis is mine.

Epilogue: John Wesley Died Well

1. Albert C. Outler, ed., *The Works of John Wesley*, Vols. 1-4. *The Sermons* (Nashville: Abingdon Press, 1984), 4:199 ("On Faith").

2. Ibid.

3. Ibid., 4:200 ("On Faith").

4. Randy L. Maddox, *The Works of John Wesley: Letters V 1774-1781*, vol. 29 (Nashville: Abingdon Press, 2023), p. 135.

5. Elizabeth Ritchie, *An Authentic Narrative of the Passing of the Rev. John Wesley* (City Road, London: Eighteenth Century Collections Online, 1791), p. 1.

6. John Telford, ed., *The Letters of John Wesley, A.M.*, 8 vols. (London: The Epworth Press, 1931), 8:265.

7. Ritchie, *Authentic*, p. 1.

8. Ibid.

9. Ibid.

10. Ibid., p. 2. Wesley repeated these exact words the same day in the midst of the conversation with Elizabeth Ritchie.

11. Ibid.

12. Reginald W. Ward, and Richard P. Heitzenrater, eds., *The Works of John Wesley*, vol. 18. *Journals and Diaries I* (Nashville: Abingdon Press, 1988), p 146.

13. Ibid., 18:250.

14. Ritchie, *Authentic*, p. 2.

15. Ibid.

16. Ibid.

17. Ibid.

18. Ibid.

19. Ibid.

20. Ibid.

21. Ibid., p. 3.

22. Ibid.

23. Ibid.

24. Ibid

25. Ibid.

26. Ibid.

27. Franz Hildebrandt, and Oliver Beckerlegge, *The Works of John Wesley*, Bicentennial ed., vol. 7: *A Collection of Hymns for the Use of the People Called Methodists* (Nashville: Abingdon Press, 1983), p. 323 (Hymn #193; stanza 5b).

www.ingramcontent.com/pod-product-compliance
Lightning Source LLC
LaVergne TN
LVHW031925170925
821167LV00005B/17